RED MAFIYA

ALSO BY ROBERT I. FRIEDMAN

Zealots for Zion: Inside Israel's
West Bank Settlement Movement

RED MAFIYA

HOW THE RUSSIAN MOB HAS INVADED AMERICA

BY ROBERT I. FRIEDMAN

LITTLE, BROWN AND COMPANY
BOSTON NEW YORK LONDON

First Edition

ISBN 0-316-29474-8
Library of Congress Control Number 99-69061

10   9   8   7   6   5   4   3   2   1

Q-FG

Book design by H. Roberts Design

Printed in the United States of America

To Christine

CONTENTS

Acknowledgments / *ix*

Introduction: The Superpower of Crime / *xi*

PART ONE THE INVASION / *1*

1 The Hit Man / *3*

2 The Little Don / *23*

3 Brighton Beach Goodfellas / *41*

4 Operation Red Daisy / *69*

5 Red Tide / *97*

6 Invasion of America / *119*

7 Tarzan / *141*

PART TWO COLONIZATION AND CONQUEST / *171*

8 Power Play / *173*

9 The Money Plane / *203*

10 The World's Most Dangerous Gangster / *237*

11 Global Conquest / *263*

Postscript: God Bless America / *285*

Index / *289*

ACKNOWLEDGMENTS

I would like to thank the following organizations for their support: the Dick Goldensohn Fund, the Fund for Investigative Journalism, and the Committee to Protect Journalists.

I would also like to thank Michael Caruso, Tim Moss, Jim Rosenthal, and my agents Kris Dahl at International Creative Management and Eric Simonoff at Janklow & Nesbit Associates.

INTRODUCTION

THE SUPERPOWER
OF CRIME

I had just returned from a vacation in June 1998 when I found out how dangerous it is to investigate the Russian mob. Mike McCall, a top agent on the FBI's Russian Organized Crime Squad in Manhattan, called me with chilling news. "I hate to be the bearer of bad tidings," he said gently, "but the FBI has reliable information that a major Russian organized crime figure has taken out a contract on your life."

Belgian journalist Alain Lallemand, an expert on Russian organized crime who has suffered through hair-raising attempts on his life, once told me that the Russian mob would leave journalists alone as long they didn't come between the mobsters and their money. In a series of revelatory articles about the growing threat of the Russian mob in such publications as *New York*, *Details*, and *Vanity Fair*, I had apparently crossed this dangerous line.

Stunned, I finally managed to ask McCall what I was supposed to do in response. "We are working on this just as hard as we can," he answered, "but right now we can't preclude the possibility of something happening to you, okay?" But how could I protect myself—and my wife? McCall bluntly replied that it wasn't the FBI's responsibility to offer that kind of advice. After some pleading, he at last offered a tip: "If you have the opportunity to lie low," he said simply, "take it."

At the time, I was getting ready to fly to Miami to interview a Russian crime lord nicknamed Tarzan, a man who had sold Russian military helicopters to Colombian drug barons and was in the process of brokering a deal to sell them a submarine, complete with a retired Russian captain and a crew of seventeen, when he was arrested by the Drug Enforcement Agency. McCall told me to forget about the trip to Miami, which has the second largest concentration of Russian mobsters in the United States; a hit man could easily trace me to my South Beach hotel. For that matter, he said, I should also forget about doing any more interviews in Brighton Beach, Brooklyn—ground zero for the Russian mob in America. In fact, he advised, I should consider forgetting doing any more reporting at all on the subject.

The next day, a magazine that had just published one of my exposés of the Russian criminals generously supplied me with some getaway money and a bulletproof vest. Before I could flee town, however, I noticed a thickly bearded, muscular Russian loitering around my apartment building whom I was certain I had once seen in the company of a notorious Russian don nicknamed Fat Felix. I didn't waste any more time. I quickly collected my wife and drove up to a rented hideaway in Vermont.

One week spent pacing the floors of our retreat left me restless and upset, and I resolved not to be intimidated into silence or to spend another day underground. Despite the risk, I returned to my home. As far as the FBI was concerned, however, I was on my own; they refused to tell me anything further about the death order, feebly explaining that the bureau couldn't jeopardize its "sources and methods." One sympathetic DEA agent suggested that I buy myself a .357 revolver; as he explained, although it flares when it's fired and there is quite a jolt, it's more reliable than an automatic, which can jam if not constantly cleaned.

I later learned (though not through the FBI) that the author of the anonymous death threat against me was Semion Mogilevich, the Budapest-based leader of the Red *Mafiya*, the most brilliant and savage Russian mob organization in the world. It was after I had written a long exposé of his criminal career in *The Village Voice* that he put out a contract on my life, a threat that was picked up during a telephone intercept by the Central Intelligence Agency, according to the *New York Times*. A European law enforcement official told the *Times* that the contract was for $100,000. At least one key witness in the murder plot was killed before he could testify against Mogilevich, the *Sunday Times* of London reported.

I first began exploring the shadowy world of Russian organized crime in the late 1980s. I had spent much of my career documenting the primordial struggle between Palestinians and Jews over a tiny, bloodstained strip of land on the Mediterranean that both sides passionately love and call home. On occasion, I'd tackle such diverse stories as AIDS, prostitution, and political corruption in India. While working on an Italian Mafia story, I was introduced by a Genovese organized crime family source in New York to several of his Russian criminal colleagues, a meeting that opened a door for me into this little known, nearly impenetrable ethnic underworld. I found them to be devilishly crooked wunderkinder, who in a few years' time, I suspected, could establish a New World Criminal Order. Over the following years, I ventured into the Russians' gaudy strip clubs in Miami Beach; paid surprise visits to their well-kept suburban homes in Denver; interviewed hit men and godfathers in an array of federal lockups; and traveled halfway around the world trying to make sense of their tangled criminal webs, which have ensnared everyone from titans of finance and the heads of government to entire state security services.

In the sheltered, seaside community of Brighton Beach, I had become a polite, but persistent pest. One Brighton Beach mobster tried to bribe me; another tied me up in a frivolous, though costly, libel suit; other Russian wiseguys tried to scare me off with angry, abusive invective. Several gangsters simply accused me of being biased against Russian émigrés — a ridiculous accusation, as all four of my grandparents were Jews who fled czarist Russia for America to escape religious persecution.

Ironically, the first wave of Russian mobsters used the same excuse to gain entry to America. During the détente days of the early 1970s, when Soviet leader Leonid Brezhnev had agreed to allow the limited emigration of Soviet Jews, thousands of hard-core criminals, many of them released from Soviet Gulags by the KGB, took advantage of their nominal Jewish status to swarm into the United States. The majority settled in Brighton Beach, where they quickly resumed their cruel criminal vocation.

The Russian mob may act like Cossacks, but I never seriously considered running away an option. Yet then I received a second, particularly violent death threat: "Friedman! You are a dirty fucking American prostitute and liar! I WILL FUCK YOU! And make you suck my Russian DICK!" The obscenity-laced note was placed inside a Hallmark Valentine Day's card that teased: "It was easy finding a Valentine for someone like you." The author of the threat hadn't bothered to hide his identity. It was signed Vyacheslav Kirillovich Ivankov.

The FBI has described Ivankov as the most powerful Russian mobster in the United States. Before coming to the U.S. in 1992, he spent many years in the Gulag for a number of gruesome crimes, including torturing his extortion victims, and he had personally ordered the killing of so many journalists, police, and civilians in Russia that a ruling council of mob bosses banished him to America. He arrived with several hundred no-neck thugs led by a former KGB colonel. Using his considerable intelligence and muscle, Ivankov quickly seized control of the Russian Jewish mob, which by then had grown from a neighborhood extortion racket in Brighton Beach to a brutal, innovative, multibillion-dollar-a-year criminal enterprise.

Despite his conviction in 1996 of extorting two Russian Wall Street investors, and his subsequent sentencing to a prison term in a federal penitentiary until 2005, Ivankov, according to the FBI, had continued to issue commands from his upstate New York cell, ordering the execution of his enemies and underworld rivals. When he mailed me the handwritten death threat, the fifty-nine-year-old gangster was so brazen that he included his cell block unit and prison ID number.

This time, I phoned the FBI. McCall rushed to my

cramped New York apartment, where he gingerly picked up the caustic message with rubber gloves, placing it into a clear plastic folder. The bureau later considered making Ivankov's mordant valentine part of a multicount federal indictment against the godfather. "Our idea is to put him away for life," an FBI agent told me, explaining that, the longer Ivankov was in jail, the less sway he'd have over his criminal comrades. I was asked whether I'd be willing to publicly testify against the Russian. "If it makes you feel any better, I'm on his hit list, too," admitted one top FBI official in Washington. In fact, as one of the two agents who put Ivankov in prison, so was Mike McCall. But of course, they both had badges—and guns. Still, I agreed to testify, fully aware of the fact that the witnesses who had stood up against Ivankov in the Wall Street extortion case were now living secretly in the Federal Witness Protection Program.

However perilous the situation into which I was placing myself, I was aware that in Europe and the former Soviet bloc, the dangers faced by journalists are far, far worse. "Journalists pursuing investigative stories on corruption and organized crime have found themselves at great risk," stated a 1997 report from the New York–based Committee to Protect Journalists, "especially in Russia and Ukraine, where beatings have become routine. These physical assaults have had the expected chilling effect on investigative journalism, frightening some reporters into self-censorship or even quitting the profession, while many have resorted to using pseudonyms."

In all, thirteen journalists from the Russian Federation have been killed by the mob since the fall of communism, according to the committee. In one of the worst incidents of intimidation, Anna Zarkova, a forty-year-old award-winning crime reporter, had sulfuric acid hurled in her face in downtown Sofia in May 1998. From her hospital bed, now blind in one eye, the mother of two appealed to her colleagues not to be cowed into silence. "If they don't splash acid in your face as a journalist," she said, "tomorrow they will kill you in the street as a citizen. That's how crime escalates in this country."

Russian mobsters, in the United States, simply don't play by the unwritten rules of the acceptable uses of gangland violence. Rarely has the Italian Mafia, for instance, inflicted harm on a member of the American media, prosecutors, or judges, fully aware of the retaliation that would likely result. The Russians, however, have no such prohibition. Murder, for them, is a blood sport. "We Italians will kill you," a John Gotti associate once warned a potential snitch over a government wire. "But the Russians are crazy—they'll kill your whole family." Some eighty Russian mob–related murders still languish unsolved on the books in Brooklyn alone. "The Russians are ruthless and crazy," a retired New York City cop told me. "It's a bad combination. They'll shoot you just to see if their gun works."

It is no small irony that the FBI has become my guardian angel, for if not for its own sluggishness in addressing the problem, the Russian mob in the United States would never have become as powerful as it is today. Though FBI boss Louis Freeh has said that Russian criminals pose an "immense" strategic threat to America, the bureau didn't even set up a Russian organized crime squad in New York until May 1994, long after the Russian mob in America was well entrenched. It should perhaps come as no surprise that the FBI, which likewise failed to go after La Cosa Nostra for thirty-five years, is now playing a desperate game of catch-up.

Blending financial sophistication with bone-crunching

violence, the Russian mob has become the FBI's most formidable criminal adversary, creating an international criminal colossus that has surpassed the Colombian cartels, the Japanese Yakuzas, the Chinese triads, and the Italian Mafia in wealth and weaponry. "Remember when Khrushchev banged his shoe on a table at the U.N. and said he would bury the West?" a baby-faced Russian gangster once asked me in a Brighton Beach cabaret. "He couldn't do it then, but we will do it now!"

With activities in countries ranging from Malaysia to Great Britain, Russian mobsters now operate in more than fifty nations. They smuggle heroin from Southeast Asia, traffic in weapons all over the globe, and seem to have a special knack for large-scale extortion. The Russian mob has plundered the fabulously rich gold and diamond mines in war-torn Sierra Leone, built dazzling casinos in Costa Rica with John Gotti Jr., and, through its control of more than 80 percent of Russia's banks, siphoned billions of dollars of Western government loans and aid, thereby exacerbating a global financial crisis that toppled Wall Street's historic bull market in August 1998.

Tutored in the mercenary ways of a brutal totalitarian state riddled with corruption, the Russians have developed a business acumen that puts them in a class by themselves. Many of today's foremost Russian mobsters have Ph.D.'s in mathematics, engineering, or physics, helping them to acquire an expertise in advanced encryption and computer technology. "Hell," a senior Treasury Department official remarked, "it took them about a week to figure out how to counterfeit the $100 Super Note," which was unveiled in 1997 with much fanfare as "tamper-proof."

More ominously, U.S. intelligence officials worry that Russian gangsters will acquire weapons of mass destruction such as fissionable material or deadly, easily concealed pathogens such as the smallpox virus—all too readily available from poorly guarded military bases or scientific labs— and sell these deadly wares to any number of terrorist groups or renegade states.

In North America alone, there are now thirty Russian crime syndicates operating in at least seventeen U.S. cities, most notably New York, Miami, San Francisco, Los Angeles, and Denver. The Russians have already pulled off the largest jewelry heist and insurance and Medicare frauds in American history, with a net haul exceeding $1 billion. They have invaded North America's financial markets, orchestrating complex stock scams, allegedly laundering billions of dollars through the Bank of New York, and coolly infiltrating the business and real estate worlds. The Russian mob has even penetrated the National Hockey League, where many players have either been its victims or become *Mafiya* facilitators, helping the mob sink its roots further into American soil. There is even fear that NHL games may be fixed. "The Russians didn't come here to enjoy the American dream," New York State tax agent Roger Berger says glumly. "They came here to steal it."

Russian mobsters in the United States aren't just Italian wiseguy wannabes. Merging with the even more powerful *Mafiya* groups that have flourished in post-perestroika Russia, they have something La Cosa Nostra can only dream about: their own country. Just as Meyer Lansky ran Cuba for a short time until Castro seized power in 1959, the Russian mob virtually controls their nuclear-tipped former superpower, which provides them with vast financial assets and a truly global reach. Russian President Boris Yeltsin wasn't exaggerating when he described Russia as "the biggest Mafia state in the world" and "the superpower of crime."

In 1993, a high-ranking Russian immigration official in Moscow told U.S. investigators that there were five million dangerous criminals in the former U.S.S.R. who would be allowed to immigrate to the West. It's nearly impossible for the State Department to weed out these undesirables because the former states of the Eastern bloc seldom make available the would-be émigré's criminal record.

"It's wonderful that the Iron Curtain is gone, but it was a shield for the West," Boris Urov, the former chief investigator of major crimes for the Russian attorney general, has declared. "Now we've opened the gates, and this is very dangerous for the world. America is getting Russian criminals. Nobody will have the resources to stop them. You people in the West don't know our *Mafiya* yet. You will, you will!"

*   *   *

For nearly a year, the FBI promised to prosecute Ivankov for his death threat — or at least punish him by taking away some of his basic privileges. When they refused to act, I went to the Committee to Protect Journalists, which contacted the *New York Times*. On March 5, 1999, Pulitzer Prize–winning reporter Blaine Harden wrote a front-page Metro section story about the death threats. "I was a good soldier for a long time," I told Harden, "but then I felt like a billy goat on a stake. I have been exposed too long and the people making these threats have gone unpunished too long."

Within days after Harden called the FBI for comment, Ivankov was transferred in the middle of the night from his comfy cell at Ray Brook Correctional Institution, a medium-security federal prison near Lake Placid, New York, to the maximum-security prison at Lewisburg, Pennsylvania. The *Times* reported that Lewisburg would impose considerably tighter security restrictions on him because of the threat. "I want him to know I am behind this punishment," I told the *Times*. "And I want him to know that he cannot threaten the American press the same way the *Mafiya* does in Russia."

PART ONE
THE INVASION

THE HIT MAN

On a spring day when warm sunshine flooded the narrow, potholed streets, I took a taxi to Metropolitan Correctional Center (MCC), an imposing collection of tomblike cinder block towers in lower Manhattan, to interview Monya Elson—one of the most dangerous Russian mobsters the feds ever netted. I passed through several layers of security before I was shepherded by an armed guard up an elevator and deposited in a small, antiseptic cubicle with booming acoustics where lawyers meet their clients. I had a tape recorder and four hours of Memorex. At least half a dozen armed guards stood outside the door, which was closed but had an observation window.

Elson, an edgy man with a dark mien, was brought into the room, his hands and feet chained. He is considered a maximum-security risk, and for good reason: a natural-born extortionist and killing machine, Elson is perhaps the most prolific hit man in Russian mob history, making Sammy "the Bull" Gravano, with nineteen acknowledged hits, a mere piker. Elson boasts one hundred confirmed kills, a figure the authorities don't dispute. With his dour-faced wife, Marina, Elson would allegedly go out on murderous rampages, rumbling around Brooklyn in the back of a van. After flinging open its doors, they would gleefully execute their shakedown victims, à la Bonnie and Clyde.

"It was a sex thing," claims a Genovese goodfella who worked closely with Elson. "They got off on the withering bodies."

Elson emigrated from the Soviet Union in 1978, claiming Jewish refugee status, and settled in Brighton Beach, Brooklyn. His mission: to become the most legendary gangster of all time. "Nobody remembers the first man who walked on the moon," Elson explains. "Everybody remembers Al Capone."

Elson wore a drab brown prison uniform; his close-cropped hair, formerly thick and black, had thinned and turned salt-and-pepper like his mustache. His once handsomely roguish face was puffy and pale. Cyrillic letters were tattooed onto each finger, identifying him as a made man in the Russian mob.

When the last prison guard left the room, Elson, his hands unshackled, scooped me up in a bone-jarring Russian bear hug, kissing me on both cheeks. He was enormously strong. Elson granted me an interview, in part, because my maternal grandfather was from Kishinev, Elson's hometown. "Oh, we have the same blood!" he said. "But it went in a different direction. I come from a different culture. I am a criminal. And for you this is bad: you were raised to believe in the law. What is good for you is not good for me. I am proud of what I am."

Elson suddenly started pulling off his shirt and pants.

"Look here! Look here!" he shouted excitedly, showing off his battle trophies. Pointing to a crater from a dumdum bullet near his heart, he boasted, "It's still inside. And look at this: I was shot all over. It wasn't a joke. The pain in my arm from a shooting goes through me like electricity on wet and humid days. It really hurts."

Elson was most proud of a large tattoo that covered his right shoulder. It depicted an anguished-looking skeleton immersed in a vat of acid, desperately reaching up to grasp two angels hovering above. "In this world, a young man seeks a name," said Elson, laying out his bleak criminal philosophy. "When he has found a name, he seeks money. When he has found money, he seeks power. But when he has power, he doesn't wish to lose it." Elson has spent his career clawing over the corpses of his enemies, trying to reach the top rung of Russian organized crime — a metaphorical place he calls the "warm spot."

MCC hadn't dampened Elson's egomania. He wanted to know what every wiseguy I interviewed had to say about him.

"You spoke to somebody about me?" Elson asked, playing with an empty plastic ashtray.

"Of course."

"Don't say to whom. But what did they say? Tell me description. Don't tell me who because I'll lose my patience."

"They say you're a hit man, professional, one of the best," I replied.

"Brave. Tough."

"Also cruel."

"Unforgiving," Elson added. "But fair or not? I never touched an innocent person. Or they said that I did? People say I don't have feelings, that I don't give a fuck. It's not true. It's not true. First of all, if you don't have feelings you'd have to be a Hitler, or you'd have to be a Stalin. But when you lead the kind of criminal life where somebody wants to kill you, that somebody wants to take your warm spot. You cannot let them. I don't kill people for fun. That's not true . . ."

Elson suddenly became sullen, irritable; his mouth twisted into a tight sneer. "This place is like a mental institution," he moaned with disgust. Prison was eating into his soul, although he denied that he was having a hard time dealing with it. "I've been fighting since I was eleven years old. I'm a fighter. I'm not a punk."

Elson was born to a Jewish family two years before Stalin's death, on May 23, 1951. Kishinev, the five-centuries-old city on the banks of the river Dnestr, was a town without pity for Jews. A pogrom on April 3, 1903, incited by the czar's minister of the interior Vyacheslav von Plehve, killed more than fifty Jewish residents; scores of Jewish women were raped by pillaging Cossack horsemen. The pogrom was memorialized in an epic poem by Bialik, in which he lamented the plight of the Diaspora Jew as "the senseless living and the senseless dying" in a world that would always remain hostile to them. Bialik underscored the Jewish people's deep yearnings for an independent homeland—or a ticket to safety in the West.

From the time that he was a boy, Elson instinctively recognized that there was only one way out of the Jewish ghetto: to excel at crime. He grew up in a rough neighborhood, which grew even rougher when, the year before he died, Stalin released thousands of inmates from the Gulag into the district. These hooligans became Elson's heroes. "We had guys who were like the kings of the neighborhood. Tough guys. They were fighters. They weren't afraid of the police. And in every conversation they spoke about jail.

How to survive the Gulag. How to be independent of the law Russia imposed on you. When you grow up and you hear only bad things about the government, and the words were coming from cruel people who had passed through the harshest system in the world—the Gulag, the Stalin regime, and World War II—this environment, of course, has some influence on you. Because every kid, as I understand it, in any country, wants to be tough, wants to be famous, wants to be strong somehow." The songs Elson relished as a youth were not communist odes to the motherland, but rather, criminal folk songs with lyrics like: "This street gave me the nickname thief and gradually put me behind bars."

Given the gross inequities of communism, where corruption wasn't just widespread but the business of the state, it was almost inevitable that the Soviet Union would be plagued by an almost institutionalized culture of thievery. As Pulitzer Prize winner David Remnick, a former *Washington Post* correspondent in Moscow, has portrayed the situation, "It was as if the entire Soviet Union were ruled by a gigantic Mob family known as the C.P.S.U. [Communist Party of the Soviet Union]." Beneath the thin veneer of official communism lay a vast underground economy of off-the-book factories, food co-ops, and construction companies that were the basis of the burgeoning black market in everything from medicines to foodstuffs. Store and restaurant managers, directors of state enterprises, officials of local, regional, and even national party institutions, and operators of collective and state farms all trafficked in illegal business. Corruption was so pervasive in the Black Sea port of Odessa, historically a major seat of organized crime in Russia, that the first secretary of the city's party committee was sentenced to death in the early 1970s for black-marketeering.

By the end of the Brezhnev period, the underground sector of the economy accounted for as much as 50 percent of the personal income of Soviet workers. But it was the apparatchiks and black marketeers who profited the most, living like feudal lords in ornate hilltop palaces and summer villas, relaxing in private sanatoriums, shopping in special stores filled with Japanese consumer goods, and traveling abroad—the most coveted privilege in the restrictive Soviet Union. But the black marketeers weren't only ambitious Russians with an entrepreneurial bent; they often included nationally renowned members of the intelligentsia, sports stars, chess champions, and the cream of the art and entertainment worlds. These individuals would journey overseas under the patronage of a friendly politician, bringing back choice wares like Citroën cars, motorboats, and designer fashions for resale. Many became multimillionaires.

Unsurprisingly, the State, while officially denying the existence of crime, tolerated the criminal underworld, the thugs and extortionists who played a prime role in feeding the country's repressed appetite for consumer goods. "Organized crime in the Soviet Union bears the stamp of the Soviet political system," wrote Konstantin Simis, a lawyer who had worked in the Soviet Ministry of Justice, in his exposé, *USSR: The Corrupt Society.* "It was characteristic of the system that the ruling district elite acted in the name of the Party as racketeers and extortionists, and that the criminal underworld per se paid through the nose to the district apparat for stolen goods and services."

Left out of this lucrative equation were most average Russians. Although the majority also learned to deal in illegal black market contraband to one degree or another— there was simply no other way to survive—the greedy nomenklatura, the elite membership of the Soviet governing system, and criminal demimonde hoarded the greater share of the nation's already scarce resources for themselves. Victims of the raw fear that was a legacy of the terrors of the Stalin regime as well as of communism's own ongoing murderous abuses, most of the "proletariat" literally despised the State. "Everyone in my neighborhood was bitter toward Lenin, Stalin, and later Khrushchev," Elson remembered.

In towns like Kishinev, this tremendous cynicism and distrust of authority went beyond simply an acceptance of criminality. Most people not only did business with mobsters on a daily basis, but held powerful criminals—as opposed to the loathed apparatchiks—in the highest regard. These criminals often enjoyed a reputation among the populace for their Robin Hood–like honesty; they even meted out justice in local tribunals called People's Courts, where common folk, eschewing State authorities, flocked to solve their personal disputes.

The People's Courts, which existed in towns and communities throughout the country, were largely administered by a special breed of colorful lawbreaker called *vor v zakonye*—or "thieves-in-law"—a fraternal order of elite criminals that dates back to the time of the czars. They first arose during the reign of Peter the Great (1682–1725), incubated in the vast archipelago of Russia's prison camps. There, hard-core felons banded together in tight networks that soon spread throughout the Gulags. Members were sworn to abide by a rigid code of behavior that included never working in a legitimate job, not paying taxes, refusing to fight in the army, and *never, for any reason*, cooperating with the police or State, unless it was to trick them. A giant eagle with razor-sharp talons emblazoned on their chests announced their status as *vors*; tattoos on their kneecaps meant they would not bow to anyone. They even developed a secret language that proved to be virtually indecipherable to authorities, and set up a communal criminal fund, or *obshchak*, to bribe officials, finance business ventures, and help inmates and their families.

The *vor* brotherhood grew in strength to the point that they began to play an unusual role in the nation's history. They taught Lenin's gangs to rob banks to fund the communist revolution. Later, enemies of the new State used them to sow dissension, fear, and chaos. During the Second World War, Stalin devised a plot to annihilate the thriving *vor* subculture by recruiting them to defend the motherland. Those who fought with the Red Army, defying the age-old prohibition of helping the State, were rewarded by being arrested after the war and thrown into the same prison camps with the *vors* who had refused to join the epic conflict. The "collaborators" were branded *suki*, or bitches. At night, when the Arctic concentration camps grew miserably cold, knives were unsheathed, and the two sides hacked each other to pieces; barracks were bombed and set on fire.

The "*Vor* Wars," or "Bitches' Wars," lasted from 1945 to 1953. When they were over, only the *vors* who refused to battle the Nazis had survived. By then, they wielded ultimate authority in prison, even over wardens, importing liquor, narcotics, and women. They slept near open windows, away from the communal toilet, where, according to their beliefs, only homosexuals and weaklings were fit to reside. *Vors* became made men in Soviet prisons only after they were recommended by at least two other *vors*. Even today, this nearly mythic criminal cult is one of the most dynamic forces in the Russian underworld.

Elson thrived among men like these. "I loved Kishinev," Elson fondly recalls. "The big guys and the tough guys used to teach me to steal from childhood. They let me go with them on burglaries. I was so skinny and small, they used to send me through the windows, and I used to open the door for them. We used to compare ourselves to the wolves of the forest, because the wolves eat only the weak animals."

By the age of nine, Elson was a full-fledged member of a fierce street gang. "We used to go from neighborhood to neighborhood to fight. The only reason we did it was to show we were strong and weren't afraid. When I was eleven, someone pulled a stiletto on me. I couldn't refuse to fight, because if I refused, I would be a hated person." His opponent made a swift, jutting move, slicing his blade through Elson's chin and into his tongue. "It was painful and I wanted to cry, but the gang leader who ordered me to fight was looking at me. I didn't cry."

Elson's parents had little patience for their son's criminal activities. "Oh, my parents beat the shit out of me," he said. Elson's father, Abraham, was a master tailor who fled Poland on the heels of the Nazi invasion. The Russians suspected that he was a German spy and exiled him to Siberia for the duration of the war. Elson's mother had been previously married, but her first husband died in the war, and their two children perished of starvation. "My mother and father used to tell me: 'Monya, don't go with those bad guys, because this reflects on you. You will have a bad reputation.' But in school, I wasn't very good. I liked to fight. I liked to steal. The older guys would extort money from me, then I'd extort money from the younger kids.

"But even as a child, I thought, 'If I was born and raised in a different area, would I be the same, or different?' But later, I understood that being a criminal was my destiny. I don't know. I don't believe in God."

Inevitably Elson began to have serious run-ins with Soviet law—a crucial step in becoming a full-fledged member of the underworld. If you didn't break during a police beating, you were considered a stand-up guy. If you cracked, and became a snitch, you'd be labeled a *musor*, a Russian word that literally meant "garbage," but that has taken on the pejorative meaning of either "cop" or "rat," the worst epithet in the Russian criminal lexicon. "Before the detectives interrogated you, they'd try to beat a confession out of you," Elson said. "They put dirt in special socks and beat your kidneys. Afterward, you urinate blood." Elson insists that he never squealed.

Before long, Elson graduated to one of the highest callings in the Eastern bloc's criminal pecking order—a pickpocket. Skilled pickpockets received immense respect from other criminals, and were often accorded leadership status in their gangs. Polish Jewish thieves who came to Russia during World War II were considered the best pickpockets, Elson says. They could slip a wallet out of a jacket, snatch the rubles, and return it in a split second, the victim remaining unaware.

Bent on proving his mettle, Elson moved to Moscow and joined a gang that specialized in extortion. "I don't want to brag, but I was great at this," Elson recounted. "I did it thousands of times." If the victim balked, "I could talk nice, or put a gun to his ear." Monya's motto: "Don't show pity or regret when you [kill someone]. Don't even think about it."

Although by the time he was twenty-six, Elson was married, had two young daughters, and was flourishing in his gang life, political events conspired to create an even greater opportunity for him. These were the early years of détente, and the American Jewish establishment and their congressional allies, who had long been trying to bring Soviet Jews westward, saw a way to leverage their cause. Leonid Brezhnev saw détente as a way to shore up an ailing economy. In September 1972, in a speech before the

National Conference on Soviet Jewry, Washington State Democratic Senator Henry "Scoop" Jackson proposed linking U.S. trade benefits to emigration rights in the Soviet Union. He later co-sponsored the Jackson-Vanik Amendment, which withheld most-favored-nation status from socialist countries that restricted Jewish emigration. The effort, which was bitterly opposed by Nixon and Kissinger as a threat to détente, was one of the factors that pressured Russia to allow tens of thousands of Jews to leave the country. In the two-year period between 1972 and 1973 alone, more than 66,000 Russian Jews emigrated, compared to just 2,808 in 1969.

But with what must have been considerable amusement, the Soviets made certain that this vast exodus was not made up solely of innocent, persecuted Jews. Much as Fidel Castro would do several years later during the Mariél boatlift, the KGB took this opportunity to empty its jails of thousands of hard-core criminals, dumping vast numbers of undesirables like Monya Elson on an unsuspecting America, as well as on Israel and other Western nations.

Persecution certainly played no role in Elson's application for Jewish refugee status. He was typical of his era—a dcracinated Soviet Jew with a touch of self-loathing. "They called me a 'fucking kike' everywhere," said Elson, and "if someone called me a Zhid, I fought back." But otherwise, "I was thinking, What kind of Jew am I? I don't know any Jewish holidays—I never heard of them. But I sang Russian songs. I ate Russian food. I spoke Russian language. I sucked inside Russian culture." The only thing he liked about being Jewish per se, he admits, was that some of the Soviet Union's top crooks were also Jews.

However, if stealing from the workers in the workers' paradise was pure pleasure, Elson reasoned, then stealing from the workers in the vastly richer capitalist paradise would be nirvana. Fortunately, his Soviet passport was stamped "Jew," and in 1977 he obtained a precious exit permit, and moved his family to a transit camp outside Vienna, run by the Jewish Agency.

Elson was given an Israeli visa; it was the only way the Soviets would let a Jew leave the U.S.S.R. But like many Jewish refugees, he wanted to go to the United States instead, and well-funded American Jewish organizations who supported the concept of free immigration helped large numbers of them to gain entry to America, infuriating Israel's Zionist establishment, which believed that Israel should be the destination for all the Jewish people. Soon, he was moved from Vienna to a transit camp near Rome operated by the Hebrew Immigration Aid Society for émigrés headed to Western nations. It was in these camps, where criminals from the far reaches of the Soviet empire converged, languishing for up to months at a time, that the global menace of Russian organized crime was fomented. They proved to be both excellent recruiting stations and networking centers, where gangsters on their way to Brighton Beach met gangsters bound for Antwerp, Brussels, or London. Once the mobsters reached their destinations, they could phone up their new friends for criminal advice, intelligence, and additional contacts. Scattered around the world, Russian criminals passed on what they "learned about the local law enforcement system, the monetary system, how the banks work," said a frustrated Drug Enforcement Agency official in New York. "And they just started beating the hell out of us. The Italians will come to New York, and that's it. The most they can do is phone somebody back in Italy. But they don't know anybody in London or Belgium."

"It's the Red Octopus," said Louis Cardenelli, a DEA

supervisor in Manhattan. "We helped foster this global organized crime monster."

Elson waited in the Rome transit camp for three months. During his idle hours, he pickpocketed unwary Italians, using the plunder to buy designer blue jeans for his wife and daughters. Meanwhile, hoodlum comrades from Moscow who had already visited the United States paid calls on Elson to regale him with the criminal splendors of Brighton Beach. "When I asked Elson why he came to America," one of his defense lawyers in Brooklyn bluntly acknowledged, "he said, 'To shake people down.'"

When he arrived in New York in 1978 on a flight paid for by the U.S. government, Elson was like a nine-year-old kid who had won a lifetime pass to Disneyland. "I was free!" he said. "I could rob! I could steal! I could do whatever I wanted!"

In the 1970s, more than forty thousand Russian Jews settled in Brighton Beach, the formerly stolid working-class Jewish neighborhood that inspired Neil Simon's gentle play *Brighton Beach Memoirs*. It was under the shadow of the elevated subway tracks on Brighton Beach Avenue, bustling with Russian meat markets, vegetable pushcarts, and bakeries, that the Russian gangsters resumed their careers as professional killers, thieves, and scoundrels. By the time of Elson's arrival, Brighton Beach had already become the seat of the dreaded *Organizatsiya*, the Russian Jewish mob.

Elson quickly discovered that Brighton Beach was two communities. Affluent Russians resided in the well-kept Art Deco apartment buildings that lined the Atlantic Ocean, while on the many side streets, littered with crack dens and decaying clapboard homes, poor Russian families lived sometimes ten to a squalid room. The neighborhood had decayed so badly that even the local McDonald's had shut down. Bordered on one side by the ocean and on another by an enormous middle-class housing project referred to by the émigrés as the "Great Wall of China," the Russians built a closed world, inhospitable to outsiders, that was self-consciously modeled on the city many once called home—Odessa—a tawdry Black Sea port that was once considered the Marseilles of the Soviet Union. Beefy men in fur caps walked down the boardwalk on frigid winter mornings, ice caught in their beards and hair, stopping at vendors to buy pirogi, pastry shells filled with spicy pork, topped with a dollop of sour cream. Movie houses showed first-run Russian-language films; cafés crackled with the voices of gruff conversations in Russian and Ukrainian.

The streets also crackled with gunfire. "Little Odessa" was the new Klondike, a town full of dangerous desperadoes, where the powerful crooks preyed upon the small. During this anarchic epoch of Russian organized crime in America, a "big man" gathered around him other strong men to form a gang. These groups were amoebalike; there was little loyalty, and entrepreneurial wiseguys constantly shifted allegiances in search of a score, vying with one another over Medicare and Medicaid scams, counterfeiting schemes, and drug deals. A professional hit cost as little as $2,000, and it was often cheaper to hire a hit man than it was to pay off a loan.

The gangsters devoted most of their energy to preying on the community they helped to create. Nearly every Russian in Brighton Beach had a family member who was either connected to the mob or paying off an extortionist.

Gang leaders would headquarter their operations in one of the multitude of Russian restaurants and cabarets. The most notorious one, on Brighton Beach Avenue in the heart of Brooklyn's émigré community, was named, appropriately enough, the Odessa. It was owned by Marat Balagula, a bookish-looking hood, who bought it in 1980 and quickly turned it into mob central. He replaced the flaking paint and frayed industrial carpeting with chrome and parquet, and hired a stunning African-American singer fluent in Russian. Downstairs, he opened a seafood cafeteria.

The Odessa attracted huge crowds of locals, who gorged themselves on inexpensive, family-style meals that included gluttonous portions of chopped liver, caviar, slabs of sable, beef Stroganoff, and skewers of lamb, all washed down with the bottle of Smirnoff vodka that was placed on each table. As a four-piece band that looked more Vegas than Moscow played Sinatra standards and Russian pop tunes, buxom bottle blondes in black leather miniskirts danced with barrel-chested men among the cabaret's Art Deco columns. A corner of the room was sometimes reserved for members of Hadassah, a woman's Zionist group, who came to express solidarity with the Russians.

The club had odd brushes with celebrity. After an arch portrait of the Odessa appeared in *The New Yorker*'s "Talk of the Town," it briefly became a popular nightspot for thirty-something yuppies who wanted to savor beans in a Caucasian walnut sauce and the titillating aura of organized crime. And pop singer Taylor Dayne got her first break at the Odessa when she answered an ad in *The Village Voice* seeking musicians. Dayne, then a plump fifteen-year-old high school girl from Long Island, was friendly with Balagula, and her picture still hangs on the nightclub's wall. When director Paul Mazursky wanted to film the cabaret scene in *Moscow on the Hudson* with Robin Williams in the Odessa, Balagula declined, afraid of drawing too much attention to the club. The scene was shot at the National restaurant, a rival Brighton Beach mob hangout then owned by Alexander "Cabbagehead" Skolnick, a Danny DeVito look-alike with a violent streak.

Late at night, after the last diner left the Odessa, the American version of the People's Court often convened upstairs in the disco. But unlike back in the Soviet Union, in Brighton Beach the tradition of influential criminals adjudicating local disputes "became corrupt," explained a prominent Russian émigré. "There is never a time when the judges don't take a piece of the action." The judges were often Balagula and two of his thugs, who meted out sentences while seated around a table in the cabaret. The lights were dimmed, and no food or water was provided. "It is very, very dark, like a *Godfather* movie," said an émigré who was summoned to several proceedings. "The first thing I said was 'Why don't you turn on the lights?' Silence. Total silence."

It was just such a setting that greeted the small-time jewel thief Vyacheslav Lyubarsky, who was ordered to appear in "court" to settle a $40,000 gambling dispute. The judges quickly ruled against him, and when Lyubarsky balked, he was suspended, naked, from a light fixture. Then one of the judges, Emile Puzyretsky, whacked out on coke and vodka, threatened to disembowel him. Puzyretsky, who had spent twelve years in the Soviet Gulag for murder and was decorated with Technicolor tattoos of a skeleton, bats, a snow leopard, and an angel, had become one of Little Odessa's most feared enforcers. "He uses his knife on every occasion," notes his FBI file.

As a newcomer to Brighton Beach, Elson found himself in a strange and unfamiliar land, and he had to learn a different set of survival skills. "One thing that disappointed me about America is that people don't carry money," he said with a frown. "Everything is credit card." He adapted in the manner he knew best: "I started working credit card scams, even though I didn't know how to speak English."

Elson soon teamed up with forty-eight-year-old Yuri

Brokhin, an intellectual of modest accomplishments who had immigrated to the United States with his wife in 1972. Since then he had managed to foster a reputation for himself as a prominent Russian Jewish dissident. He wrote two books, as well as articles for *Dissent, Jewish Digest*, and the *New York Times Magazine*, most of which were fierce anticommunist polemics.

"I heard about Brokhin in Moscow," Elson said. "He was well known. His nickname was 'Student.' I used to call him 'Brain.'"

Together, the pair embarked on a lucrative crime spree, stealing hundreds of thousands of dollars' worth of jewelry, often using a simple, no-risk scam. Corruption in Manhattan's diamond district on 47th Street was so rampant at the time that the authorities had all but given up policing it. All Brokhin and Elson had to do was to identify crooked storeowners, visit their shops, and demand the goods. "We tried to rob thieves," Elson says. They knew that their "victims" were so deep into their own crimes that they'd never call the police, but would simply pass the losses on to their insurance companies. Soon, storeowners throughout the diamond district were seeking out the Russian robbers to stage fake burglaries so that they, too, could scam their insurers.

The duo employed a different gambit to rob honest jewelers. They'd dress up as ultra-Orthodox Jews, replete with paste-on beards, side curls, long black coats, and black hats. Entering a jewelry store run by an Orthodox Jew, they would ask to see a variety of expensive diamond stones from the display case. Brokhin would babble away in Yiddish, distracting the salesman, while Elson switched the diamonds with zirconium. They'd continue to haggle, and after failing to make a deal, would slip away with the jewels tucked snugly inside the pockets of their coats. The con is called the "fast-finger." "We made a lot of money with that," Elson boasts.

Once, after pulling the scam on a trip to Chicago, the two men were arrested in their Orthodox Jewish attire as they boarded a plane at Midway Airport. It happened to be Yom Kippur, the holiest day of the Jewish calendar, when observant Jews are strictly forbidden to travel. An airport security guard who was Jewish became suspicious, thinking the men looked more like Cuban terrorists than rabbis. Pictures of them in Hasidic garb appeared the next day in Chicago newspapers. Brokhin's wife rushed to Chicago with $175,000 in cash for bail; somehow, they both got off without a jail sentence. Their records were also expunged. "It's a lot of money to get off the hook" and beat a felony rap, said Elson enigmatically.

Although they were pulling in good money, it was still a small-time operation and Elson was burning with ambition. He increasingly turned to vicious acts of drug-influenced extortion to make a name for himself. Failing to move up the criminal food chain, he decided to join the most powerful gang in Brighton Beach, headed by the rapacious Evsei Agron. Elson, however, was disappointed in his new boss's management style. "Agron wanted to be the sun, but he didn't want the sun's rays to fall on somebody else," Elson grumbled. "I wanted to kill him. But you see, it was not so easy."

The tempestuous gangster from Kishinev realized that his future—if he had one at all—showed little promise in the Darwinian world of Brighton Beach. Frustrated, Elson trekked to the jungles of South America in 1984 to set up a cocaine smuggling operation. "I went to Peru, I went to Bolivia, I passed through a lot of South America," Elson recounted. Although he didn't yet speak Spanish, he ventured deep into the tropical rain forest to purchase cocaine.

"I wasn't interested in one key, two keys, three keys. I was making huge deals," crowed Elson, who operated out of Europe and Israel. Still, the criminal big time eluded him and he was incarcerated in Israel for trafficking in cocaine.

Years later, however, Elson would return to Brighton Beach with a vengeance, creating one of the most powerful Russian mob families in the world, while initiating a gangland war that left a trail of bodies from the street corners of New York to the back alleys of Moscow.

THE LITTLE DON

The man who deprived Monya Elson of his warm spot, seemed, at first glance, too unprepossessing a figure to become Brighton Beach's first don. A short, grandfatherly man, Evsei Agron attracted little attention as he passed through Immigration at Kennedy Airport on October 8, 1975. He was one of the 5,200 Soviet Jewish émigrés to enter the United States that year, many of them gangsters sent from Russia by the KGB. He had listed his occupation as "jeweler," and perhaps he had even once been one. But he had also served seven years for murder in a Soviet prison camp, from which he emerged as a *vor*. After leaving Russia in 1971, he ran a large prostitution and gambling ring in Hamburg, West Germany. And even though he had supposedly been cast out of the *vor* brotherhood for welshing on a gambling debt, the order's ferocious reputation gave him sufficient cachet to quickly seize

power when he arrived in Brighton Beach. Little else is
known about Agron's early years. His records from the
Soviet Union were sealed, and few of his victims from the
Old Country who are still alive are willing to share their
reminiscences.

From a modest office at the El Caribe Country Club, a
catering hall and restaurant, the Leningrad-born Agron ran
a vicious extortion ring that terrorized the Russian émigré
community. "They were scared shitless of him," FBI agent
William Moschella has recalled. By 1980, his gang was
bringing in tens of thousands of dollars a week. Agron's victims ran the gamut from Russian doctors and lawyers to
shopkeepers and grocery store owners on Brighton Beach
Avenue. "What if they refused to pay?" chuckled a gang
member in mock amusement. "We'd beat them in their
store right in front of everybody. But they paid. They knew
what was coming if they didn't pay. They knew they'd get
murdered, if they don't pay."

Agron once threatened to kill a Russian émigré's daughter on her wedding day if he didn't pay $15,000. Going to
the police would have simply guaranteed a late-night visit
from one of Agron's henchmen, like the Nayfeld brothers,
or the forty-five-year-old Technicolor killer Emile Puzyretsky. "Puzyretsky had a great contempt for life. He killed his
enemies with force, fury, and no mercy," a Russian Militia
colonel recalled.

One of the most terrifying sounds in Brighton Beach
was Puzyretsky's voice on the other end of the phone. "You
have to pay!" Puzyretsky screamed at a recalcitrant shakedown victim in one tape-recorded conversation. "Otherwise you're not going to live! And if you survive, you're not
going to be able to work anymore!"

"Willy, please don't terrorize me anymore," pleaded
the distraught Russian émigré, who was being ordered to

hand over $50,000. "We aren't livin' in a jungle. We live in U.S.A."

"You fuckin' rat . . . I'll make you a heart attack. This is the last time you'll be able to see. If you don't give the money . . . just wait and see what's goin' to happen to you."

Puzyretsky was paid—with interest.

The Nayfeld brothers were just as savage. The steroid-enhanced thugs emigrated from Gomel, Russia, in the early 1970s. The black-bearded Benjamin, a former member of the Soviet Olympic weightlifting team, was a bear of a man with a twenty-two-inch neck. He once killed a Jewish youth in a Brighton Beach parking lot in front of dozens of witnesses by picking him up like a ragdoll with one hand and plunging a knife into his heart with the other. The teenager had allegedly insulted Benjamin's girlfriend and reached for a weapon. After the murder, eighteen witnesses vouched for Benjamin's version of events, insisting the stabbing was a justifiable homicide, and the case was dropped.

By all accounts, Boris Nayfeld was even more fearsome than his brother. To this day, superstitious Russian émigrés insist that his eyes are sheer white orbs, a sign that he has no soul and is possessed by the devil.

Olga, the owner of two hair salons in Manhattan's Greenwich Village, recalls the day in the mid-1980s when Boris and Agron swaggered into her brother's Brooklyn restaurant and ordered him to sell his one-third stake at a rock-bottom price. "The restaurant was not doing well," she says. "He wanted to sell, but at a fair price." When he refused, "Boris clubbed my brother over the head with his gun."

Olga and her family lived in the same Brighton Beach apartment complex as Nayfeld and his non-Jewish wife. "Boris's kids were always playing with *my* kids in *my*

house," said Olga, still enraged over the decade-old incident. One night, she tailed Boris's Mercedes. At an inter-
section, she hit her brights, and flew out of the car to pick a
fight: "How dare you, you shit! To do this in the house
where you live, you bastard!"

"We're only trying to help your brother," replied an
unfazed Nayfeld, who with Agron stole the restaurant anyway.

Resistance like Olga's was rare. For the most part, the
community endured the horrible violence inflicted on them
by a large and growing criminal class. They had left a brutal
society where the state and the government were as
crooked as the crooks. Their blatant distrust of authority
carried over to the United States. The American government, which had generously given them refuge and financial assistance, was still the enemy. There was a great
tolerance for white-collar crime. The new émigrés routinely
cheated on their taxes, stole food stamps and welfare
benefits, and shopped in sable coats while their late-model
Mercedes were parked in the mall. Medicare, Medicaid,
and other forms of insurance scams were ubiquitous. Stealing from the government was as much a part of their culture as was paying off the mob. Their own xenophobia was
one of their greatest enemies. It allowed the mobsters in
their midst to act with impunity.

However viciously cruel his subordinates, it was Agron
who was despised above all in Brighton Beach. His own brand
of cruelty involved carrying around an electric cattle prod,
with which he enjoyed personally torturing his victims.
Unlike some Russian *vors*, Agron held fear above honor. "If
Agron had been an honorable godfather, he wouldn't have
had to use brute force to extort shopkeepers," says Ivan, a
former resident of Brighton Beach and a Gulag vet. "Instead,
he would have been showered with gifts, both as a sign of

homage and as payment for protection from ruthless street predators like Monya Elson. The owners of the stores would have said, 'Oh, please take from me.'"

The widespread antipathy toward Agron finally found its release one night in 1980. While strolling down the Coney Island boardwalk, Agron was shot in the stomach and lost part of his lower intestine.

"We hired a retired cop to stand guard over him at Coney Island Hospital," recalled a Genovese wiseguy who had begun a close alliance with Agron. "I have a friend in police intelligence. He went to talk to Evsei, who had tubes in his nose and arms."

"Do you know who shot you?" asked the detective.

"Yes," Agron nodded.

The detective reached into his suit and took out a ball-point pen and pad. "Who? We'll take care of it," he said soothingly.

Wagging his finger, Agron rasped, "I'll take care of it myself."

There was no shortage of theories about who shot Agron: Perhaps it was connected to Agron's local gambling debts, said the smart money on the Brighton Beach board-walk. Perhaps the hit was contracted by someone Agron had chiseled in Germany, the Genovese source surmised. Perhaps a member of his own gang thought it was time to replace the imperious don, shopkeepers along Brighton Beach Avenue prayed.

Agron shrugged off the attempt on his life. He remained supremely self-confident. His boys were making major scores in everything from truck hijackings to Medicare fraud. He even purchased a Russian-language newspaper in Brighton Beach so the burgeoning émigré community could read all the news that was fit to print according to the little don.

The paper was torched.

Still, Agron retained an iron grip over the most powerful Russian crime group in Brighton Beach, with outposts in at least a half dozen North American cities. Agron's criminal authority was bolstered by two highly potent allies: the Genovese crime family and Ronald Greenwald, a politically savvy, well-connected Orthodox Jewish rabbi. These connections, Agron concluded, made him invincible. More than that, without Greenwald's careful nurturing of Agron's criminal career, and the Italian Mafia's muscle, the Russian mob in America might never have been anything more than a minor annoyance, a two-bit gang of émigré hoodlums.

The nexus between the Russian mob and the Italians was a man named Murray Wilson, whose consummate money laundering skills had earned him a reputation at the FBI as a modern-day Meyer Lansky. Wilson, a Genovese associate, engineered some of the Russian mob's first big criminal scores, and eventually he would help a second generation of Russian racketeers become a financially sophisticated global peril.

Wilson was raised in a bare-knuckles neighborhood in the Bronx, where Jewish gangs like Murder Inc. once roamed. He preferred hanging out with street corner wiseguys to pursuing a "legit" career, like his able cousin, Marvin Josephson, the founder of International Creative Management, the largest theatrical and literary talent agency in the world. Barely managing to eke out a diploma from Taft High School, Wilson nonetheless effortlessly mastered the intricacies of offshore accounts, letters of credit, and complicated international stock market transactions. In the process, Wilson, who has an import-export firm and is a restaurateur, became the focus of at least eight criminal probes.

Wilson's patron in the Genovese family was underboss Venero "Benny Eggs" Mangano. Benny Eggs began his career as a soldier with Lucky Luciano and rose to oversee the Genovese family's multibillion-dollar-a-year racketeering enterprise. He once boasted over an FBI wire that he surrounded himself with Jewish associates as fronts to help generate and hide illicit funds because they were shrewder at such financial dealings than the Italians. According to Benny Eggs, when a Jew had an annual income of two or three million dollars he would declare a healthy $300,000 of it on his taxes, enough to avoid raising any suspicions with federal authorities. An Italian wiseguy, on the other hand, might declare only ten grand. It was the IRS, he warned, that had nailed Al Capone.

Fortunately for La Cosa Nostra, Wilson, a pugnacious, right-wing Jewish militant who was active in resettling Russian Jewish émigrés in Brooklyn, quickly deduced that many of the new arrivals were not long-suffering, downtrodden Jewish dissidents, but professional thieves and hit men—a potential bonanza for the Genovese crime family. The Italians were not only getting the services of highly skilled Russian crews, but were extending their control to a new neighborhood. They already had affiliations, for example, with the Greek mob in Queens and the coke-pushing Dominican gangs in Washington Heights.

Wilson introduced Agron to the Genovese chieftains, forming the nucleus of the dark alliance. "A day didn't go by when a truck hijacking or a jewelry heist didn't go down," a Genovese goodfella who committed many street crimes with the Russians admitted. "It was a time of high adrenaline." Although Agron was very much the junior partner, enamored of the Italians for their well-entrenched national power base, their vast army of soldiers and political connections, the Genovese bosses valued Agron's crew for its tireless work ethic, ruthlessness, and most especially, its global connections.

Nevertheless, there were major cultural differences between the ethnic crime groups that sometimes caused friction: with a few exceptions, the Italian gangsters lived quiet lives in modest houses, trying not to call attention to themselves. On the other hand, "the Russians have a tremendous zest for life and like to live large," says James DiPietro, a criminal attorney in Brooklyn who has represented both Russian and Italian underworld figures. "They keep saying we are Russians and we are proud of being Russians. Russians are the best! One Halloween at Rasputin"—a Russian mob haunt in Brooklyn—"they came in Ronald Reagan masks, in limos; they love to flaunt their affluence."

And unlike the Russians, the Italian mobsters more or less adhere to established rules of conduct. "The Italians don't kill civilians—not even the family members of rats. The Russians have no such codes," says DiPietro.

Rabbi Ronald Greenwald did as much for Agron's career as did the Italian gangsters, and then helped groom a new generation of Russian wiseguys to enter corrupt Third World countries and loot their natural resources, a charge the rabbi denies. But well-placed sources say that some of the little don's biggest scams were hatched in the rabbi's downtown Manhattan commodities firm. Greenwald says he first met Agron in West Berlin while he was innocently sitting in a hotel lobby wearing a yarmulke. The rabbi says Agron started a conversation with him about Judaism. He claims he didn't know that Agron was a vicious extortionist who tortured victims with a cattle prod and ran an infamous prostitution and gambling empire. Greenwald allegedly helped Agron get a U.S. visa, according to several former business associates of both men. The rabbi denies that he helped Agron enter the United States, but admits that the mobster would sometimes visit his Manhattan office. In fact his office was a magnet for a host of Russian and Italian gangsters, as well as a powerful U.S. congressman and a convicted KGB spy.

Greenwald was born on the Lower East Side in 1934. "I was the only kid in school who played hardball without a glove," Greenwald told me. "That's how tough I am!" He went to Jewish day schools and then to rabbinical college in Cleveland. Though he is an ordained Orthodox rabbi, he never took the pulpit. "I felt I should be out in the work world."

At one time or another Greenwald has been a bank director, president of a small business college, gas station owner, chaplain for the New York state police, a liaison between a segment of New York's Orthodox Jewish community and the state Republican party—and a high-risk entrepreneur with ties to the Genovese crime family and the Russian mob.

But it was as a political operative for Richard Nixon that Greenwald first made a name for himself. The then-president had received 17 percent of the Jewish vote in 1968, and he wanted to double it in 1972. New York, with its huge Jewish population, was a crucial state. And Greenwald, as one 1971 *New York Times* story put it, was "key to [Nixon's] New York effort."

Greenwald was recruited by CREEP—the Committee to Reelect the President—to mine for Orthodox Jewish votes. He toured synagogues, warning that McGovern would betray Israel and wipe away Jewish gains by giving away too much to blacks. His efforts paid off: Nixon received nearly 36 percent of the Jewish vote in 1972.

The rabbi was repeatedly in the throes of some political

scandal or other. After Nixon was reelected, for example, he was rewarded with a plum post at the Department of Health, Education, and Welfare as a consultant on Jewish poverty programs, including a job-training program for Brooklyn's Hasidic community. Greenwald was soon being investigated by a young federal prosecutor named Rudolph Giuliani for allegedly placing jobs program trainees in a garage in Williamsburg of which he was part-owner, as well as for creating no-show jobs. (The investigation was dropped, and Greenwald has denied wrongdoing.)

A few years later, he was in front of Giuliani again, this time pleading for Marc Rich and Pinky Green—the billionaire fugitive financiers and commodities brokers who fled the United States in 1983 one step ahead of a sixty-five-count federal indictment for fraud and income tax evasion. Greenwald, who was their business representative in the United States, tried to cut a deal that would bring them home to face civil, but not criminal, charges. Hasidic community leader Rabbi Bernard Weinberger, who along with a group of Orthodox rabbis sat in on the meetings, said that Greenwald told Giuliani that the fugitives were great humanitarians because they gave vast sums of money to Jewish charities. Giuliani was unmoved.

Thanks to his friendships with Greenwald and the Italians, Agron was soon participating in schemes that dwarfed the type of street crime that had been the Russians' mainstay. In 1983, federal agents investigating a Mafia skim of the casino at the Dunes Hotel in Las Vegas stumbled onto a multimillion-dollar fraud perpetuated jointly by Agron and Wilson and planned with Greenwald in Greenwald's office. ("Ridiculous," Greenwald says.) The Dunes was owned by Morris Shenker, Jimmy Hoffa's attorney and a longtime target of FBI probes. During the

1950s and 1960s, Shenker, himself a Russian-born Jew, had invested hundreds of millions of dollars of the Teamsters union Central States Pension Fund, which he and Hoffa controlled, into the Dunes and other famous Las Vegas hotels, giving the Mafia a hidden share of the gambling Mecca. According to the FBI, some of that money was being siphoned off in the scam set up by Wilson and the others. He arranged for Agron and a dozen members of his crew to fly into Las Vegas on all-expense-paid junkets. The gangsters were each given lines of credit of up to $50,000, but instead of gambling the money, they simply turned their chips over to Wilson. The chips were later cashed in; the markers never repaid. In this way, over a period of several months, the Russians helped defraud the Dunes of more than $1 million. The government believed that Shenker had masterminded the scheme. He eventually plundered the Dunes into Chapter 11. Indicted for personal bankruptcy fraud in 1989, Shenker died before the government could mount its case. When Russian-speaking FBI agents traveled to Brighton Beach to question the erstwhile junketeers, "the Russians wouldn't talk to us," said the agent who ran the investigation. "They said, 'What can you do to us after the KGB and the Gulag?' The only thing they were afraid of is that we would deport them, and we won't do that."*

---

*On June 30, 1989, Murray Wilson was convicted by a federal jury in Las Vegas of conspiring to defraud the Dunes of more than a million dollars. The feds offered Wilson his freedom if he would flip on Shenker, who they believed ordered the scam. He declined, preferring to take his chances with the judge at sentencing. It was a bad bet: he was sentenced to three years. The assistant U.S. attorney lacerated Wilson, calling him "a conniving, calculating thief" and "a habitually violent man" who is "known to have a major influence over the Russian Jewish Mafia, the group that is tied to the Genovese LCN [La Cosa Nostra] family. The group specializes in robberies, thefts, and burglaries. Evsei Agron, a close associate of Wilson, is one of the individuals that Wilson admitted recommending to the Dunes. Agron [runs] the Russian Jewish Mafia."

By the mid-1980s not only had Agron achieved a certain measure of criminal notoriety and power, but he was also beginning to add more sophisticated schemes to his criminal repertoire, a development that did not go unnoticed among the Italian Mafia's bosses. The Italians were particularly impressed with the Russians' growing adeptness at bilking financial markets, which was aided by members of a younger generation of Russians who were now returning from graduate schools with MBAs and getting jobs on Wall Street. Gambino crime family head Paul Castellano, for instance, was overheard on an FBI wire praising a Russian fraud that involved manipulating the stock in Bojangles, a fast food chain.

But as potent a force as Agron had become, he was still prey to the cutthroat struggles for dominance that continued among the lawless Russian gangs, and on a cold evening in January 1984, as he walked up a gentle slope from the garage in the basement of his home on 100 Ocean Parkway in Brooklyn, Agron was shot again—this time, twice in the face and neck at point-blank range. The don was rushed for a second time to Coney Island Hospital. Though Dr. Larissa Blinkin was unable to remove the slugs, she did save his life, but not without leaving the mobster's face paralyzed on one side, twisted in a permanent sneer. Once again, when the police asked him if he knew the assailant, he said he'd take care of it himself.

As he had during the earlier attack, Agron believed he knew who had authorized the hit. He had recently been feuding with an upstart Russian gang led by Boris Goldberg, an Israeli army veteran from the U.S.S.R., and Ukrainian-born David "Napoleon" Shuster, a criminal mastermind who was reputedly the best pickpocket in Brighton Beach. The Goldberg gang maintained a formidable arsenal in a safe house on West 23rd Street in Man-

35

hattan's Chelsea neighborhood. The armory included an assortment of pistols and silencers, and cartons of hand grenades and plastic explosives, as well as numerous remote control detonators.

Goldberg owned a kiddy-ride company off Kings Highway in Brooklyn called Rainbow Amusements. As a cover to score narcotics, "he used to do a lot of travel to the Far East to look at new rides," says Joel Campanella, a former New York City cop who is now a U.S. Customs official. The gang sold coke out of its Chelsea stronghold to midlevel street dealers, and, according to police statements made by a gang member, to film stars and the managers of rock bands.

It was also the scene of nonstop drug and sex orgies. Goldberg, a bland-looking man with black-framed, coke-bottle glasses, had a growing cocaine dependency that made him so paranoid that once, after hearing a siren, he flushed two kilos of coke down the toilet, then pulled a sweaty wad of cash from his pocket and ordered an underling to run out and procure two more kilos so he could continue his sybaritic party.

When Goldberg wasn't holed up in his hideout, he was often cuddling with his girlfriend Tonia Biggs, the daughter of *Penthouse* publisher Bob Guccione. Biggs was an editor of *Forum*, an adult magazine also published by her father. "She lived in Beverly Hills [and] was about thirty years old, blond, big chest, but a little sagging," Goldberg gang member Charlie Rivera, a razor-thin man who is half Sicilian on his mother's side, told law enforcement agents. "She also had a penthouse [in New York], and he sold coke out of both places. Boris would bring coke out from New York and he would sell some out there." Biggs later conceded that she let Goldberg use her home for coke parties, but she denied helping him peddle it.

Meanwhile, the Goldberg gang, hopped up on drugs, insanely violent and indiscriminate, was responsible for a staggering string of robberies, shootings, insurance frauds, auto thefts, and narcotics sales. They hurled grenades at the storefronts of recalcitrant extortion victims in California, and performed contract murders as far away as Texas. They assassinated competing drug dealers, the wife of a gang member suspected of cheating on him, and an elderly man, who was chased across a busy boulevard in Queens and shot twice in the head for refusing to vacate his rent-stabilized apartment. On another occasion, gang members were paid to kill two teenagers who had robbed and beaten a man with a hammer known on Brooklyn streets as Jacmo. Jacmo, who owned an antique Mercedes-Benz dealership, was also a major drug dealer with a long rap sheet. Jacmo dispensed the contract at Coney Island Hospital. A day later, one of the teens was lured from his apartment to meet a "friend" who was supposedly waiting downstairs in a parked car. When he peered inside the window, he was shot in the face with a .38 caliber revolver loaded with copper-jacketed bullets.

It was inevitable that, given their shared interests in the spoils of Brighton Beach, Goldberg and Agron would run afoul of each other. One issue that proved to be a constant source of friction was the collection of extortion money from Brighton Beach businesses. Sit-downs to discuss their turf disputes had never been able to resolve the problems. Once, the Nayfeld brothers even broke Shuster's nose. Goldberg finally became so frustrated that he put out a standing $25,000 contract on Agron's head.

In May 1984, Agron commanded Goldberg to attend a meeting at the El Caribe Country Club. Goldberg, his lieutenant Rivera, and several other gang members showed up to find fifty taciturn, heavily armed Russians waiting for them around a large oak table. Agron demanded to know if Goldberg was responsible for having had him shot. In the dim room, Agron's face seemed to dissolve into the shadows, but there was enough light to see that he was cradling a shotgun as he sat in a white wicker chair across from Rivera. The diminutive don leaned forward and spat, "Why you shoot me in the fucking face?"

Goldberg and Rivera were silent, each waiting for the other to respond. "We didn't do it," Rivera said finally, although he was, in fact, the one who had disfigured Agron in the botched hit ordered by Goldberg.

Although Agron had not seen the shooter's face, he had caught a glimpse of the man's boots as he lay crumpled on the ground.

"Let me see your fuckin' boots," Agron growled.

"I don't own a pair," Rivera replied, his eyes darting to his feet.

Eying him suspiciously, Agron looked around the room and then demanded that Goldberg's crew all put their feet up on the table. He intended to inspect each of their footwear.

When nobody moved, he shouted, "What's da matter? You don't want to?"

One by one, Goldberg's men raised their feet onto the table. The don was enraged: he didn't recognize anyone's shoes.

Goldberg settled back in his chair uneasily. Speaking in Russian, he swore he was innocent. But if Agron wanted trouble, he warned, he had brought sufficient firepower. Agron sent a scout outside, who returned and reported that the parking lot was swarming with gunmen. It was a Mexican standoff.

Goldberg convinced Agron that he was not involved in the attempt on his life, and the meeting ended without bloodshed. But if Goldberg was the most likely suspect in the attempt on Agron's life, he was hardly the only rival who wanted the don dead.

On May 4, 1985, Agron's brawny chauffeur Boris Nayfeld was sitting outside his boss's apartment building in a black Lincoln Town Car, waiting to make the weekly drive across the East River into Manhattan. Every Saturday morning, Agron went to the Russian and Turkish Baths on Manhattan's old Lower East Side. The ornate nineteenth-century bathhouse had been a favorite hangout of Meyer Lansky, Bugsy Siegel, and Lucky Luciano during Prohibition, when the establishment kept a special cubbyhole behind the towel counter where the gangsters could deposit their tommy guns. It was a perfect place for Agron to have sit-downs with his pals, all of them sweating in the heat of the 200-degree steam room while burly attendants struck their backs with bundles of oak branches.

On that morning, the fifty-three-year-old Agron was still upstairs in his sixth-floor apartment, shaving in his lavish bathroom. Its imported marble and gold-leaf fixtures—a recently completed renovation that had cost $150,000—were elegant even by Russian mob standards. Agron patted his disfigured face with expensive cologne, slipped on his baggy, blue pin-striped suit, and grabbed his brown fedora. While most Russian mobsters swaggered around in sharkskin suits and enough gold jewelry to stand out like lighthouses on a moonless night, Agron's associates joked that he dressed more like a longtime resident of a senior citizens' home. Just before he left, he told his common-law wife, a striking blond cabaret singer, that he would meet her for dinner that night at a Brighton Beach restaurant.

At exactly 8:35 A.M. Agron pressed the elevator button outside his apartment door. Suddenly, a man wearing

a jogging suit and sunglasses stepped from behind a corner in the hallway and shot him at point-blank range, hitting him twice in the right temple. He fell to the floor,
blood pooling around him on the black and white marble
tiles.

BRIGHTON BEACH
GOODFELLAS

A few days after Agron was found in a pool of his own blood, his driver, Boris Nayfeld, strolled into what had been Agron's modest office at the El Caribe Country Club in Brighton Beach. He was there to begin his new job as the driver and bodyguard of the man who benefited the most from the execution of Evsei Agron: Marat Balagula, the new godfather of the Russian mob.

Virtually everyone in law enforcement who has had anything to do with investigating the Russian mob believes Balagula ordered the hit, but he has always denied it. "Evsei used to come to the Odessa [restaurant] and pick fights," Balagula claims. "Sometimes ten or twenty people would get into a brawl. Maybe Evsei was killed by someone he fought with before."

Balagula had been serving as Agron's consigliere for several years, and while he was always careful to pay Agron the respect due a "great man," he had his own ideas. All along, he had been forging a rival criminal syndicate of his own, and as Balagula's star began to rise, explains a former insider, Agron "wanted a piece of the action. Because of his status, Agron expected something." What Agron got, of course, was two bullets in the head.

Within a few months of seizing power, Balagula demonstrated that he was the very model of a modern don. Unlike Agron, who had been a thuggish neighborhood extortionist, Balagula was a brilliant, coldly efficient crime boss who was soon not only conspicuously enjoying the lushest version of the American dream but bestowing his largesse on members of the small Russian émigré community.

"Marat was the king of Brighton Beach," recalled a former employee. "He had a Robin Hood complex. People would come over from Russia and he'd give them jobs. He liked professional men. Guys came over and couldn't practice medicine or use their engineering degrees. He sought them out. He was fascinated with intellectuals. He co-opted them. He put them into the gasoline business, he put them into car washes or taxi companies. He'd reinvest his own money in their business if they were having trouble. He had a heart." Such generosity was, of course, also good for building loyalty. It seemed that everyone in Brighton Beach owed him a favor, and he wasn't hesitant about collecting on them.

Though Brighton Beach residents had good reason to be tight-lipped about Balagula, tales of his enormous wealth began circulating in cafés and over dinner tables: he tried to purchase an island off the coast of South Africa to set up a bank for money laundering; he circled Manhattan on luxury yachts, holding all-night drug and sex orgies; he rode in a custom stretch limo, white and immaculate, with a black-liveried chauffeur and stocked with ice-cold bottles of vodka. "Marat throws around diamonds the way we throw around dollar bills," Joe Galizia, a soldier in the Genovese family, enviously told an associate in a conversation taped by police.

"Everybody in Brighton Beach talked about Balagula in hushed tones," says Ray Jermyn, former chief of the Rackets Bureau for the Suffok County DA in New York. "These were people who knew him from the Old Country. They were really, genuinely scared of this guy."

Marat Balagula was born in 1943 in Orenburg, a small Russian town, at the height of World War II. His mother, Zinaida, fled with the children from their home in Odessa as the German Wehrmacht swept across the Russian steppes. Marat's father, Jakov, was a lieutenant in the Red Army; Balagula claims that he was with one of the armored corps that stormed Berlin during the last desperate hours of the war.

In the harshness of the Stalin era, the Balagulas led a comfortable, middle-class life. Jakov worked in a factory manufacturing locks, as did his wife. Young Marat, an average high school student, was drafted into the Soviet army at the age of nineteen and served as a bursar for three years, after which the party assigned him to manage a small food co-op in Odessa. Determined to get ahead, Marat attended night school, receiving a diploma as a teacher of mathematics and then a business degree in economics and mathematics. Like many ambitious Russians with a capitalist predilection, he promptly plunged into the country's flourishing black market. He quickly learned to attend to the demanding appetites of the apparatchiks, making certain the choicest meats and produce was diverted to them.

He was only twenty-two years old when he was

rewarded with a prestigious job as a bursar on the *Ivan Frankel*, a Soviet cruise ship that catered to foreign tourists. According to American law enforcement sources and Brighton Beach colleagues, party bosses slipped Balagula currency, gold, valuable Russian artifacts, and stolen art-work to sell to the tourists or to fence in Europe. "It was a good job," Balagula recalls. "I got good money. My salary was in dollars and rubles. I traveled to Australia, France, England, and Italy. The KGB gave me visas, no problem. I brought back lots of stuff: stereos, cameras. I was not middle-class. I was upper-middle-class. I had a nice apart-ment in Odessa, a dacha on the Black Sea."

He met his wife, Alexandra, at a friend's wedding party in 1965 and married her the following year. Because she didn't like his traveling, in 1971, after five years at sea, he got himself appointed manager of the largest food co-op in the Ukraine, a huge promotion that allowed him to rise to even greater heights as a black marketeer. On his thirtieth birthday, the flourishing Balagula threw himself a gala party at his dacha in the sunny Crimea. Many of the region's elite were in attendance—including Mikhail Gorbachev, then a young regional party boss, who posed for a photo with Marat and his wife. Balagula later bragged to his Brighton Beach mob associates that Gorbachev was on his pad, a claim that seems doubtful: even then, Gorbachev was a stern reformer. It would have been impossible, however, for a Soviet party boss to avoid dealing with black marke-teers in some way, since they played such an integral role in the economic life of the country.

The fact that Balagula was Jewish apparently never hin-dered his career, even though government-sponsored anti-Semitism surged after Israel's victory over five Arab armies in the June 1967 Six Day War. "I never felt anti-Semitism," Balagula says, though he admits he was only nominally a

Jew: he never attended Odessa's lone synagogue and was ignorant of Jewish history and religion. "Jews had some of the best positions in the country. They were the big artists, musicians — they had big money."

When he decided to journey to America, therefore, it was not because he suffered as a Jew, though he concedes, "I used that as an excuse when I applied for my visa." Although he was leading the charmed life of a high-flying black marketeer, he decided to leave it behind when "I saw with my own eyes how people lived in the West," says Balagula. "This pushed me to move." A business associate explains: "Marat said he read about capitalism and knew he could do well over here."

On January 13, 1977, Balagula, his wife, and their two young daughters, together with his elderly parents and younger brother, Leon, moved to Washington Heights in upper Manhattan, where a small enclave of German Jews who had fled from Hitler lived precariously among drug dealers and boom-box din. Balagula attended English classes arranged by a Manhattan-based organization that settles Soviet Jews, which then found him a job in the garment district. He worked for six months as a textile cutter for $3.50 an hour, claims Alexandra, his wife. "It was hard for us, with no language, no money," she says.

Balagula's fortunes improved markedly when he relocated his family to Brighton Beach and he started to work for the infamous *vor* Evsei Agron. "Everybody knew his name," Alexandra cheerfully recalled. "He was so much in the [Russian] newspapers."

Agron, it turned out, was no match for the ambitious Balagula. While Agron's technical expertise didn't go beyond seeking sadistic new uses for his electric cattle prod, Balagula wanted to lead the *Organizatsiya* into the upscale world of white-collar crime, and with the experience he had gained in the Soviet Union, he developed a business acumen that put him in a class by himself. Surrounded by a cadre of Russian economists and math prodigies at the Odessa restaurant, he acquired a knowledge of global markets that enabled him to make millions in the arcane world of commodities trading. He also energetically cultivated the Italian mobsters he met as Agron's consigliere. After Agron was executed, Balagula organized his followers in a hierarchy, much like the Italian Mafia, and before long, he succeeded in transforming the *Organizatsiya* into a multibillion-dollar-a-year criminal enterprise that stretched across the tatters of communist Eastern Europe, Africa, and Southeast Asia. Ultimately, however, it was Balagula's spectacular success in the gasoline bootlegging business—a scheme that would reportedly earn him hundreds of millions of dollars and an honored position with the Italian Mafia—that would usher in the first Golden Age of Russian organized crime in America.

Balagula's bootlegging career began modestly enough. Within just a year after arriving in New York, he managed to gain control over fourteen gas stations. He then formed two fuel dealerships, and bought gas from a corporation owned by the Nayfeld brothers. This transaction was the foundation for an ingenious way to avoid paying billions of dollars of gasoline taxes.

Gasoline bootleggers, mostly Turkish and Greek immigrants, had been operating in New York since the early 1960s. They simply collected taxes at the pump and instead of turning the money over to the government, pocketed the cash and disappeared before the IRS caught on. "They'd make their $600,000 and go back and buy an island and you'd never hear from them again," says Sam

Racer, a Russian-born attorney who has represented Balagula. "It was a nice scam until it got into the hands of the
Russians. They bought Rollses and Ferraris and walked
around Atlantic City with stacks of hundred-dollar bills,
and suddenly the IRS realized they were getting fucked for
hundreds of millions of dollars."

What the Russians had discovered was a way to expand
the scam into the biggest tax heist in U.S. history. Prior to
1982, thousands of individual gas stations in New York
State were responsible for collecting state and federal
taxes—amounting to as much as 28 cents a gallon—and
then passing them on to the relevant authorities. Because
of rampant cheating, however, state lawmakers decided
that year to shift the responsibility to New York's four
hundred gasoline distributors, who had to assess the fuel
before it was moved to the stations. But clever Russians
like Balagula found in fact that the new tax law presented
opportunities for even larger scores. They would first set
up a welter of phony distributorships. One of these companies would then purchase a large shipment of gasoline
and, on paper at least, move it to another distributor
through a so-called daisy chain. The transactions were carried out quickly and generated a blizzard of paper. One of
the dummy enterprises was designated as the "burn company," the one that was required to pay the taxes to the
IRS. Instead, the burn company sold the gas at cut-rate
prices to independent retailers with a phony invoice
stamped "All taxes paid." The bootleggers pocketed the
money, and the burn company—no more than a post office
box and a corporate principal, usually a Russian émigré living in a rooming house on Brighton Beach Avenue—disappeared. By the time the IRS came looking for the taxes
due, the revenue agents were buried under an intricate
paper trail that led nowhere.

Balagula proved a master at this scheme, and he, along with many other Russian groups, began amassing enormous sums from it. Through their control of gasoline distributorships in the New York metropolitan area and elsewhere, the Russian mobsters evaded as much as $8 billion a year in state and federal taxes by 1985.

Balagula's fraudulent fuel syndicate received a major boost from the involvement of Power Test, a midsize, $160-million-a-year gasoline company on Long Island that was itself being driven into bankruptcy by independent stations selling cheap or bootleg gas. (Indeed, by 1980 half of all unbranded gas sold on Long Island was bootlegged, destroying the livelihood of many honest businessmen who couldn't afford to compete against cut-rate prices.) Rather than see his company fail, Power Test CEO Leo Liebowitz decided to join the bootleggers. According to court testimony and interviews, he instructed two Power Test executives, John Byrne, a district sales manager and former New York City police sergeant, and Robert Eisenberg, the company's in-house counsel, to buy bootleg gas. Byrne and Eisenberg then set up bootlegging companies with Balagula that would sell "cheap" gas exclusively to Power Test.

The plan worked—so successfully, in fact, that Power Test soon had enough cash to begin negotiating with Texaco to purchase Getty Oil, one of the fabled Seven Sisters. (Because of antitrust problems, Texaco was being forced to sell the East Coast marketing operation of Getty, which it had acquired in 1984.) According to a Power Test insider, Liebowitz had joined the bootleggers not merely to save his company but also because of his aspirations to become a major player in the oil business. "Leo started talking to Texaco in the winter of 1983," recalls the insider. "If he was going into receivership, he couldn't talk to Texaco. He had to keep the company solvent. So he did deals with gasoline bootleggers. He did lots of those deals."

In 1985, Power Test concluded the deal for Getty, and Liebowitz—triumphant atop the $1.3 billion company that adopted the lustrous Getty name—was lauded in *Forbes* as one of the most brilliant businessmen in America. "The sky's the limit," Liebowitz told *Newsday*. "We are the largest independent in the United States and we are just getting started!"

Six years later Getty became the first major oil corporation in recent history to be convicted of gasoline bootlegging. John Byrne and Robert Eisenberg escaped prosecution by becoming government witnesses. Two senior company executives were convicted and sentenced to jail terms, and Getty was fined $400,000. Liebowitz, to the surprise of many, was never indicted. Getty's role in the scheme was uncovered by the Long Island Motor Fuel Task Force, a group of federal, state, and local prosecutors and investigators formed to combat gasoline bootlegging. "Gasoline excise tax evasion is no longer a local problem. It's a national problem," said James Rodio, a tax attorney with the U.S. Justice Department and a member of the task force. "Cheating of this magnitude has to stop," U.S. District Court Judge Leonard Wexler chided during sentencing.

By this time, however, the money from bootlegging had spread far beyond the gasoline industry. It was being used, New York and federal officials feared, to corrupt politicians, labor unions, and law enforcement itself. Consider the revelations of Lawrence Iorizzo, a six-foot, 450-pound, self-confessed bigamist who became a government informant after he was indicted for stealing $1.1 million in gas taxes in 1984. A New York gasoline company executive who is credited with inventing the daisy chain, Iorizzo ran an enormously successful bootlegging empire in the early to mid-1980s with the help of Michael Franzese, the vicious "Yuppie Don" of the Colombo crime family and a consortium of Russian and Eastern European gangsters. In sworn testimony before the oversight subcommittee of the House Ways and Means Committee, Iorizzo charged that one of his former partners, Martin Carey, had skimmed millions of dollars of tax money from his Long Island gas stations and illegally channeled it into the campaign treasury of his older brother, Hugh, then the governor of New York. Martin Carey escaped prosecution because he had been granted immunity by testifying in another case.

Incredibly, Iorizzo's charges of political corruption were never investigated. In 1987, when Jeremiah McKenna, the counsel to New York's Crime and Correction Committee, called for a hearing to probe Iorizzo's allegations, he was forced to resign by New York governor Mario Cuomo, who had been Carey's running mate as lieutenant governor in 1978. Cuomo complained that McKenna, a respected Republican investigator, was spreading false and malicious stories. Iorizzo had previously testified to Congress that he had made political contributions to Governor Cuomo's 1984 campaign from some of these bootleg funds, asserting that he had done so at the "directions of people above me."*

Though Iorizzo's allegations about political corruption were ignored by prosecutors, his court testimony did help break up the powerful Russian-Italian bootlegging combine

---

*NBC-TV national news later reported that it was Franzese who had ordered Iorizzo and the heads of the Russian consortium to send checks for $5,000 drawn on their shell company accounts to Cuomo's campaign. In all, $25,000 was diverted to Cuomo in this way. Confronted with this revelation, Cuomo replied that it was impossible to do due diligence on each and every political donation.

led by Franzese, which paved the way for Balagula to gain uncontested control of the operation. By 1985, Balagula was well on his way to becoming the undisputed king of American bootleggers: his domain was a self-contained, vertically integrated behemoth that included oceangoing tankers, seven terminals, a fleet of gasoline trucks, truck stops (including even their greasy spoon diners), and more than one hundred gas stations, all operated by fiercely loyal Soviet Jewish émigrés. Balagula even negotiated to take over oil-refining terminals in Eastern bloc countries, which would process fuel waste products known as derivatives, then sell shiploads of the toxic by-products in North America. Balagula's headquarters in New Rochelle, New York—which ironically stood next to an FBI building—looked like a scene in a Stanley Kubrick black comedy. Russian secretaries wearing identical zebra-print dresses and fur hats worked at computer terminals while video cameras scanned the office. "The obsession with security," says one of Balagula's associates, "came from the paranoid Russian personality that one develops growing up in a police state."

Flush with cash, Balagula began to run his empire like a profligate oil sheik. Joe Ezra, a former attorney for Balagula, once accompanied the Russian godfather and his retinue on an epicurean "business trip" to Europe, to broker oil deals with Marc Rich, the billionaire fugitive commodities trader. The group paid visits to Cartier shops in every airport along the way, spending thousands of dollars on "shit like little leather-bound address books that cost $300 each," Ezra remembered. Often, they would stop in a city and take over entire whorehouses and go on food binges. "They'd go to meals in Germany with ten people, and when they finished, somebody would say, 'I'm still hungry,' and [Marat] would order a second meal for everybody." Most of the food would be thrown away. "If a bill was $1,500, the tip would be $1,500. If a guy would come over and sing a song, Marat would give him a hundred-dollar bill. I remember saying to myself, 'These people need intensive psychiatric help.'"

Balagula was also a compulsive gambler, and the joke in Brighton Beach was that you would know how he did at the craps tables over the weekend by the price of gas at the pump on Monday. "Marat says he's got a photographic memory, but he don't," grumbled a powerful Genovese crime family figure who went to Atlantic City with Balagula after the Russian boasted that he could count cards. "We lost $20,000. I told Marat, 'How the fuck do you remember anything?'"

Befitting his new status, Balagula bought a $1.2 million home on Long Island, to which he relocated his family from Brighton Beach. His reputation as Little Odessa's godfather, however, was met with consternation by his new neighbors and caused his younger daughter a bit of grief in school. "I love my dad very much. My father's my world to me," Aksana, a sullen, curly haired, nineteen-year-old optometry student told me in a 1992 interview. "There was a lot of harassment, a lot of fights," she recalled. Once, after a classmate called her father a gangster, "I just got very upset and I threw a book at his head. They [the school] made me see a psychologist."

As Balagula's wealth grew, so did the violence in Brighton Beach. At least fifteen unsolved homicides were attributed to his turf wars with rival Russian mobsters. "Marat ordered many murders. I know!" insisted an Italian mob boss. Many of the gangland-style slayings were brazen, broad-daylight shootings carried out in Brighton Beach restaurants in front of numerous witnesses. "These guys are worse than the [Italian] wiseguys," says Ray Jermyn. "They have no hesitation at all to whack somebody. They are cowboys."

Balagula may have employed enough wild, Uzi-wielding Russians to reign supreme in Brighton Beach, but he didn't dare fight with the Italians. When a Mafia associate told John Gotti in 1986 about the Russian-dominated gasoline bootlegging scam, the "Dapper Don" was heard to reply over a government bug, "I gotta do it right now! Right now I gotta do it!" He wasn't alone in coveting a share of this business: heads of four of the five New York Italian Mafia families imposed a 2-cents-per-gallon "family tax" on the Russian bootleggers, and the levy became their second largest source of revenue after drugs, worth an estimated $100 million a year. Genovese soldiers guarded the family's take at Balagula's terminals in Westchester, while Christopher "Christie Tick" Furnari, then the sixty-eight-year-old underboss of the Lucchese crime family and one of the most powerful mobsters in the country, got Brooklyn, Queens, and Staten Island.

Balagula's closest aides had argued to keep the Italians out of the bootlegging operation. Marat had "capable guys," said a key associate. "They weren't afraid of fights." But Balagula believed he could never win a war with the Italians, so he invited them in, confident he could outsmart them into accepting less than they had agreed upon. Marat "didn't realize how insidious they were," says the associate. "He fell for their charm. He had watched too many American movies.

"The LCN didn't want to know the ins and outs of the gas business," but simply wanted their cut, the source asserts. "The LCN reminded Balagula of the apparatchiks in the Soviet Union. He thought as long as he gave them something they'd be valuable allies" with their political connections and muscle. "Then all of a sudden he was at risk of being killed if he couldn't pay to the penny."

Whatever it cost him in lost revenue, Marat was grateful to have the Italians on his side. According to a mob source, their new relationship enabled him to forge a protective alliance with the Genovese and Lucchese families against the Colombo family's Yuppie Don, Michael Franzese. One of Franzese's crew, Frankie "the Bug" Sciortino, had been going around with a Gotti soldier "shaking down a bunch of Russian bootleggers," says Jermyn. "They would just go into places in Brooklyn and make them pay $25,000 a clip for protection, or else they'd use a ball peen hammer on them. The Russians are scared to death of the Italians. They scored over half a million dollars by shaking these guys down."

At around the same time, Franzese himself "tried to hustle Marat," says a well-placed Genovese underworld figure. "I showed up at a restaurant, and two of Franzese's guys was sitting with Marat. I said, 'Who are these guys?'"

"They are not with me," Balagula said.

"The next time I saw Michael [Franzese] and mentioned Marat, his face went white," the Genovese gangster says with a laugh. "Christie Tick had put out the word that Marat was under his protection."

When in 1986 the Brooklyn office of Balagula's company Platenum Energy was riddled with Uzi submachine gunfire, killing one of Balagula's bodyguards with eight shots in the chest and two in the head, it was the Italians who came to Balagula's aid. According to law enforcement sources, the shooters were two Russians, Michael Vax and Vladimir Reznikov, who were disgruntled because Balagula had sold them invalid state gasoline distributorship licenses. (Balagula told me the shooting was an attempted robbery.)

A short time after the Platenum Energy incident, Reznikov, an infamous Brighton Beach hit man, stuck a gun in Balagula's face outside the Odessa restaurant and demanded $600,000 and a partnership in his bootlegging empire. Balagula was so frightened by the assault that he suffered a heart attack but refused to go to the hospital. Instead, he persuaded his doctors to set up a makeshift intensive care unit in the bedroom of his fortresslike mansion, whose sandstone spires bristled with gunmen. "When we went to Marat's house, I remember seeing Marat in bed hooked up to all kinds of machines," Anthony "Gas Pipe" Casso, a Lucchese mob boss turncoat, recalled.*

On June 13, 1986, Reznikov was lured to the Odessa to parley with Balagula, who was actually in California convalescing. When Balagula didn't appear, Reznikov strolled back across Brighton Beach Avenue and climbed into his new brown Nissan. Suddenly, Lucchese soldier Joe Testa emerged from behind a car and pumped six bullets from a .380 automatic handgun into Reznikov's arm, leg, and hip. As the grievously wounded Russian grabbed for his own weapon, Testa fired a fatal shot to his head. "After that," Casso said, "Marat did not have any more problems from any other Russians."

However greatly the Russians may have feared the Italian Mafia, they had little regard for American law enforcement, manipulating the FBI as easily as they had the apparats in the Soviet Union. "As soon as they knew they were in trouble and law enforcement was breathing down their necks," says Ray Jermyn, "they ran to the counterintelligence guys [the FBI and CIA] and tried to sell what

---

*Casso, speaking behind a black veil, testified to a Senate panel probing the Russian mob in 1996.

they considered to be secrets and stuff." In the years before glasnost, the strategy often worked, for the FBI routinely placed advertisements in New York's Russian-language newspapers, offering cash rewards for information about KGB spies. When a Russian gangster became an intelligence asset, the feds would often shelve pending investigations targeting him. "We never stopped doing stuff because we were requested to," Jermyn says. "But a lot of times the agents would change their focus and slow down. . . . You put it on the back burner, and then it kind of goes away."

Jermyn pleaded with the FBI to lend him Russian-speaking agents to monitor the voluminous, court-authorized wiretaps of Russian bootleggers. "We were always asking for agents to give us assistance to do translations," he recalls. "They wouldn't help. They said they were too busy, they are working at the [Soviet] embassy" in New York.

"Then I got a phone call from a woman who said she was a deputy counsel in the CIA. I thought somebody was pulling my leg. She gave a callback number, and, sure enough, she worked for the Central Intelligence Agency. She was trying to bring to our attention that there was this guy who was a driver for Marat who had been a Russian submarine captain. She said that he had performed many valuable services for the agency and that he was still cooperating. And that's when the bureau really first started to make inquiries [about our investigation]." When the court-authorized wiretaps revealed that Balagula and his comrades were major players in the bootlegging business, the bureau suddenly "gave us an agent full-time who had a Russian background and who had counterintelligence training," Jermyn explained.

The intelligence community's interest in Balagula was undoubtedly heightened by his many friendships with KGB spies, corrupt Third World despots, and international ter-

rorists. Exploiting his connections within the Russian criminal diaspora, Balagula had begun forming criminal networks with outposts in Russia, Europe, and Asia. In a
typical transaction that exploited this international reach,
his henchmen would buy automatic weapons in Florida,
move them up the East Coast to New York, and ship them
to the U.S.S.R., where firearms of this sort were extremely
difficult to come by.

But these were relatively small ventures for Balagula.
From Brighton Beach, he and his cronies virtually ran the
small, diamond-rich West African nation of Sierra Leone,
whose president, Joseph Momoh, allowed the Russian mobsters to set up a global smuggling and money laundering
operation there. Diamonds smuggled out of Sierra Leone
were transported to Thailand, where they were swapped for
heroin, which was then distributed in Europe by Balagula's
close friend Efim Laskin, who had been deported by the
United States as an undesirable in 1986, and who had been
arrested for illegally importing weapons and explosives to
the Red Brigades in Milan.* The Russians even brought Genovese crime family members to Sierra Leone, where, among
other activities, they plundered diamond mines with the
help of corrupt tribal chieftains. The Italian gangsters, who
helped bankroll Momoh's 1985 presidential campaign,
became so prevalent in Freetown that when he was sworn
in, a contingent of Genovese goodfellas stood proudly on the
dais next to Balagula under a fierce tropical sun.

---

*In 1990, Laskin accepted a large advance on a heroin deal from two Italian
organized crime drug traffickers, Renato Pantanella and Francesco Guarnacchia, says a secret FBI report. He reneged on the deal. In May 1991,
Laskin was attacked in the parking garage outside his Munich apartment.
One attacker shoved a gun to his head, and squeezed the trigger. It jammed.
The assailant then took out a knife and stabbed him. As Laskin struggled,
another assassin stepped out of the shadows and stabbed him eleven more
times. "He gutted him like a pig," said a source.

Balagula's main contact in Sierra Leone was Shabtai Kalmanovitch, a charming, tanned Russian-Israeli entrepreneur. The two hatched numerous deals together, including one to import gasoline to Sierra Leone, which was brokered through the Spanish office of Marc Rich by Rabbi Ronald Greenwald, and another to import whiskey; the pair even had a contract to print Sierra Leone's paper currency at a plant in Great Britain. Kalmanovitch also handled President Momoh's personal security. In 1986, his Israeli-trained palace guard crushed an attempted coup; according to one account, Kalmanovitch pulled Momoh out of his bed just before rebels sprayed it with machine gunfire. As a reward, Kalmanovitch was granted major fishing and mining concessions and was allowed to run the nation's largest bus company. He was also an operative for Mossad, Israel's intelligence agency. Kalmanovitch's Freetown office was a prized listening post in a city with a large, prosperous Afro-Lebanese Shi'ite Muslim community in close contact with Lebanon's then warring Shi'ite militias. It was only later that Mossad discovered that Kalmanovitch was not as valuable an asset as it had supposed: in 1988 he was arrested in Tel Aviv and charged with being a KGB spy. Yitzhak Rabin, then defense minister, said he was "almost certain" that the Soviets had passed on information obtained from Kalmanovitch to Syria and other Arab countries hostile to Israel. Wolf Blitzer, at the time a correspondent for the *Jerusalem Post*, reported speculation that sensitive material stolen by Israeli spy Jonathan Pollard was passed on to the KGB by Kalmanovitch.*

---

*In 1999, U.S. government sources leaked to *Newsday* and *The New Yorker* that in exchange for Soviet Jewish immigrants, Pollard gave the Soviets, among other things, a computer file that allowed them to identify American foreign agents in the field.

BRIGHTON BEACH GOODFELLAS

It was the peripatetic Rabbi Greenwald who introduced Kalmanovitch and Balagula to moneymaking opportunities in Africa. In May 1980, the rabbi had been asked by Lucas Mangope, the president of Bophuthatswana, one of the so-called independent black homelands inside South Africa during apartheid, to be its economic adviser with the rank of ambassador in New York and Washington.

"But because there is a strong black opinion here and a strong liberal opinion that the black homelands are just an extension of apartheid," Greenwald said, "I told Mangope that there was only so much I could do for him in the U.S. and he would be more successful dealing with Israel. Israel is closer, Israel doesn't have political restrictions with South Africa like America has. I suggested they hire Shabtai," who was a close friend and business associate.

Within several years after being introduced to Mangope, Kalmanovitch was a millionaire. Through a newly formed company called Liat, he landed lucrative contracts to build a soccer stadium, and imported Israeli specialists to train the Bantustan's police and security service. In February 1987, when rebel armies revolted and placed Mangope in the soccer stadium Kalmanovitch had built, the Russian took his considerable wealth and relocated to Sierra Leone, using Greenwald's contacts in the government.

Eventually, the Russian and Italian gangsters were to lose more than $3 million in deals with Kalmanovitch. The Russian mobsters became so furious with Kalmanovitch that they threatened to kill him, said the Genovese source, who mediated peace talks between Kalmanovitch and Balagula. "The Russian mobsters wanted their money," he said. "Marat said, 'Don't kill him, you can attract more flies with honey than vinegar.' "

In order to pay back his business losses, Kalmanovitch entered into an intricate scheme with Russian and Italian gangsters to defraud Merrill Lynch, according to several of the participants. These sources say that the Russian mobsters bribed a Merrill Lynch employee to steal unused company checks worth more than $27 million by illegally accessing the company's computer. The employee also stole valid signature stamps. The checks and stamps were then sent by courier to Kalmanovitch.

According to Interpol reports and sources involved in the scheme, on April 27, 1987, Kalmanovitch, Greenwald, and an associate left Kalmanovitch's lavish home in Cannes and drove to Monte Carlo where the associate opened up a business account at Republic National Bank for a paper company called Clouns International. He then desposited a number of fraudulently endorsed checks worth some $2.7 million. When the checks cleared three days later, Greenwald and the associate returned to the bank, where Greenwald was given $400,000 in cash from the Merrill Lynch funds. Greenwald carried the money in a large black bag via Germany to Switzerland, where he allegedly turned the cash over to Balagula's representatives in a Zurich hotel men's room. According to the scheme's participants, Greenwald was paid $50,000, an allegation the rabbi flatly denies.

On May 22 of that year, Scotland Yard arrested Kalmanovitch at the Sheraton Park Tower Hotel in London at 3:00 A.M. It found three rubber stamps used to endorse the checks in Kalmanovitch's room. Earlier that day, Kalmanovitch had had lunch with Uri Lubrani, the head of Israeli intelligence in south Lebanon, according to a source who attended the meeting.

While Kalmanovitch was being led away in handcuffs, Greenwald, who was also staying at the Sheraton, threw his bags together and, without paying his bill, caught a Concorde flight back to America, according to the FBI and an associate of Greenwald. Greenwald returned home just in time for the Friday night Sabbath meal.

Kalmanovitch was extradited to America to stand trial on fraud charges. (The FBI questioned Greenwald three times, but didn't arrest him.) Greenwald rounded up a select group of prominent Americans and Israelis to provide character references, including New York Republican congressman Benjamin Gilman, who wrote that "Mr. Kalmanovitch enjoys a wide reputation for his integrity and business acumen." He obtained bail and flew to Israel, where he was immediately arrested for being a Soviet spy.

In 1986, at the height of his power, Marat made a reckless error. Robert Fasano, a small-time hood who traveled around Brooklyn in an ostentatious white Excalibur, phoned Balagula with an interesting proposition. Fasano had obtained the numbers of two dozen Merrill Lynch credit cards with six-figure authorization codes. Fasano also had sheets of white plastic and a machine that could emboss the stolen numbers on dummy cards. All he needed to use the material was some cooperative merchants who would agree to accept the phony cards to charge merchandise. The merchants would get a cut, though the goods, of course, would never leave the stores. At a meeting with Fasano, Balagula agreed to introduce him to Russian merchants in New York and Philadelphia. He then instructed two of his henchmen to accompany Fasano to the stores.

The scam worked as planned, and the men took in more than $750,000, stopping only long enough in their shopping spree to feast at Russian restaurants. But Fasano was arrested by the Secret Service not long afterward, and agreed to wear a wire in meetings with Balagula. In those discussions Balagula not only implicated himself in the "white plastic" fraud, but also commiserated with Fasano about their sexual problems; both men, it seems, had trouble achieving erections. Fasano had found a doctor in New York who prescribed a plastic hand pump for genital stimulation, and recommended it to Balagula. The prosecution later played the tape at Balagula's trial in Philadelphia to prove the men had more than a casual relationship.

"Go out and get a ten-pound bag of shit and try to put it in a five-pound bag and that's Fasano," said Joe Ezra, one of the five defense attorneys Balagula brought to Philadelphia at a cost of nearly $1 million. Lead attorney Barry Slotnick, renowned for his successful defense of Bernhard Goetz, was dismissed on the first day of the trial by the judge because of a conflict of interest: his firm already represented one of Balagula's co-defendants, Benjamin Nayfeld. Slotnick, who received a $125,000 fee, camped out at the Hershey Hotel, where he debriefed Balagula's lawyers at the end of each session and advised them on their strategy for the following day.

Nevertheless, Balagula was convicted of credit card fraud, and there is even now a great deal of rancor among Balagula's defense team. Some charge that Slotnick's backseat lawyering hurt the case; others claim that one defense lawyer received a large bribe to fix the trial. Marat himself believed that the money was being used to grease the system. After his conviction, Balagula was taken by Rabbi Greenwald to attorney Alan Dershowitz to discuss an appeal. Instead, Balagula asked the esteemed lawyer to bribe the appeals judge. An indignant Dershowitz refused. Just three days before his November 1986 sentencing, the mobster fled to Antwerp with his mistress, former model Natalia Shevchencko.

Secret Service agent Harold Bibb admits he feared that Balagula "would turn rabbit" after the government rejected the crime boss's offer to ferret out Soviet spies in Brighton

Beach in return for setting aside his conviction. In addition to protecting the president and foreign dignitaries, the Secret Service investigates credit card fraud and counterfeiting. Ironically, Bibb, a born-again Christian from Tennessee, had once been assigned to the security detail protecting Israeli cabinet minister Moshe Dayan during U.S. fundraising trips on behalf of Soviet Jews in the early 1970s. He had now been given the task of hunting down the most dangerous of those Soviet Jews, the godfather of the Russian mob.

In February 1987, four months after Balagula left the country, Bibb tracked him down in Johannesburg, where he was living with his mistress and her daughter, who had enrolled at a local university. "You have to understand how to chase a fugitive," Bibb explained in his spartan Secret Service office in Memphis. "You either find the hole that they're living in, you find the people that they are talking to, or you find out how they are getting funded." In this case, Bibb found Balagula by tracing his girlfriend's credit card receipts. He also discovered that Balagula was receiving monthly deliveries of $50,000 in cash from his New York underlings. The money, stuffed in a worn black leather bag, was hand-delivered to Balagula's Johannesburg apartment by Balagula's driver, the ex-submarine commander.

Bibb had intended to tail the driver to Balagula's hideout. But the Secret Service was too cheap to pay for his plane ticket, the agent said. So he contacted the security officer at the American embassy in Pretoria, who in turn alerted the police, supplying them with photos of the driver and Balagula. However, Bibb suspects that the constable who was dispatched to make the arrest let Balagula go free when the Russian handed him the monthly payment. Again with his mistress in tow, Balagula next fled to Sierra Leone, where he bought Sierra Leonean and Paraguayan diplomatic passports for $20,000.

Over the next three years of Balagula's exile, he jetted to thirty-six separate countries, including Switzerland, Paraguay, and Hong Kong, where he worked "in the jewelry business," according to the Genovese family figure close to him. Bibb even heard that he was once spotted playing craps in Atlantic City. Finally, on February 27, 1989, an especially alert border guard at the Frankfurt airport recognized the Russian godfather from his picture on the "Red Notice," the wanted poster distributed by Interpol. After being apprehended, Balagula claimed, "It's very difficult to be a fugitive. I can't see my family. In the last year I started to work in the open. I wanted to get caught."

Balagula's close association with Efim Laskin earned him detention in a maximum security "terrorist jail" in Germany. (One of his cell mates was Mohammed Ali Hamadei, the Lebanese who hijacked TWA Flight 847, during which a Navy SEAL was brutally murdered.) The *New York Times* reported that, during his extradition hearing, rumors circulated about a large bribe that was to be paid to free the Brighton Beach mobster. The *Times* also noted that, according to informants cited in U.S. intelligence reports, Balagula may have had connections to Soviet intelligence—a charge Balagula denied in a sworn statement to the FBI.

Meanwhile, in New York, Barry Slotnick met with U.S. Attorney Charles Rose, hoping to broker a deal that would keep Balagula out of an American jail. Balagula proposed setting up a company in Europe to entrap traders in stolen American technology. "Marat also tried to present himself as a secret agent to help track down KGB spies in Little Odessa and Eastern Europe," says one of Balagula's attorneys Sam Racer. "He claimed Little Odessa was teeming with KGB and that they were using the gas stations as a front."

In return for his cooperation, said Charles Rose, Balagula "obviously wanted the authority to travel, which was important to him. We had FBI agents who were familiar with foreign counterintelligence stuff talk to him. It was all very cloak-and-daggerish. The theory was that he would be so valuable to us that we would not want him to be in jail. . . . We never really paid much attention, and said we wanted to prosecute the guy."

In December 1989, federal marshals wearing flak jackets escorted Balagula aboard a C-5A military transport bound for New York, where he was placed in the tomblike Metropolitan Correctional Center to await sentencing for his four-year-old conviction on credit card fraud. "He called me from MCC crying, 'Why am I in solitary?'" recalls Sam Racer. According to Racer, a contact in the Bureau of Prisons told Slotnick that "a group of terrorists from Europe was in New York to break Balagula out."

His rescuers never appeared, however, and Balagula received an eight-year sentence for the credit card fraud. In November 1992, he was sentenced to an additional ten years for evading federal taxes on the sale of four million gallons of gasoline. "This was supposed to be a haven for you," declared U.S. District Court Judge Leonard Wexler. "It turned out to be a hell for us."

Balagula was domiciled in Lewisburg federal penitentiary, situated on one thousand acres of rolling Pennsylvania farmland. The shady, tree-lined blacktop leading to the prison from the highway looks like the entrance to an elite country club. The maximum security prison, however, is a vast stone fortress, with thirty-foot-high walls and eight gun turrets bristling with automatic weapons. Balagula shared a dormitory room with thirty-six dope dealers, rapists, and murderers. He was one of only a handful of inmates at Lewisburg convicted of a white-collar crime, and he was also the only mob boss allegedly running "family" business from the facility.

I had always heard Balagula described as a man of King Kong–like proportions. But when prison guards ushered him into a smoky ground-floor visiting room, dressed in an orange jumpsuit and bound in manacles and chains, he looked haggard. He sat down heavily, a thick chain wrapped snugly around his soft paunch, and lit a Marlboro with yellow-stained fingers.

It was his twenty-fifth wedding anniversary, and Alexandra, his tall, elegant blond wife, was in another waiting room. She was in a foul mood. Prison authorities had just told her that Balagula had been receiving visits from his mistress, Natalia Shevchencko. "It was hell" when his wife found out, Balagula hissed.

Balagula was spending his days working as a prison janitor, practicing his English, reading Russian detective novels and academic books on economics. "They claim I made $25 million dollars per day bootlegging. It's crazy! I got nothing. What have I got? The government took my apartment in Manhattan, my house on Long Island, $300,000 in cash. They said, 'If you don't cooperate you'll go to jail for twenty years.' The prosecutors wrote a letter to the judge that I'm a Mafia big shot so they put me here.

"They want me to tell them about the Mafia, about gasoline [bootlegging], about hits," Balagula told me, glowering. "Forget it. All these charges are bullshit! All my life I like to help people. Just because a lot of people come to me for advice, everybody thinks I'm a boss. I came to America to find work, support myself, and create a future for my children."

Balagula, who is eligible for parole in March 2003, has not only refused to give the authorities any information about the Russian mob's activities in America, but denies that he ever heard of such an enterprise. "There is no such thing as the Russian *Mafiya*. Two or three friends hang out together. That's a *Mafiya*?"

OPERATION
RED DAISY

One after another, a parade of stretch limousines pulled up in front of an unremarkable two-story building squatting on the corner of a blighted stretch of Coney Island Avenue. Out of each stepped a massive Russian in a tuxedo, more often than not accompanied by a slender blonde in a low-cut gold lamé evening gown. As they entered the etched brown metal doors, they were ushered into another world, a world that resembled nothing so much as the set of a B movie made six thousand miles away.

Black-and-brown imported Italian marble covered the floor of the foyer where a hand-painted mural of St. Petersburg's skyline led arriving guests into a cavernous nightclub and to tables covered with rose-colored tablecloths laden with slabs of sable, skewers of beef, and ice-cold bottles of Stolys. As multicolored lasers crisscrossed the room,

Joseph Kobzon, a renowned Russian pop star, crooned Top 40 tunes from the motherland and, for the honored guests that evening, Sinatra ballads.

This was Rasputin, the Winter Palace of Brooklyn.

Off to the side stood two barrel-chested men, beaming, almost giddy. For the Zilber brothers, Vladimir, thirty-two, and Alex, thirty-four, everything had led up to this June 1992 gala opening. They had arrived in Brooklyn as penniless Jewish refugees from Odessa thirteen years earlier. Their father was a foreman in a New Jersey pillow factory, their mother a seamstress there. The boys, however, had quickly realized that the honest, hardworking immigrant was a chump game; they had made more than their parents ever dreamed possible from gasoline bootlegging, money laundering, and casinos and aluminum factories in the former Soviet Union. The Zilber brothers—Vladimir as informal head of U.S. operations, Alex as their Russian liaison—had become dons in the Brighton Beach mob; this was their Russian cotillion.

When the Zilbers took their place at the head table— where a row of dark-suited Italian-Americans, all members of the Genovese crime family, peered across nearly empty vodka bottles at an equal number of hard-faced Russians— it symbolized a new era in organized crime in America. The Russians had always loved films about the American Mafia and took great pains to emulate their predecessors' sense of sartorial style. But on this night, the two groups had more in common than a taste for heavy gold chains and open collars. The Russians had finally become powerful enough to sit at the same table with the Italians. No longer semicomic *Godfather* pretenders, the Russians were now arguably just as ruthless and, by many accounts, considerably wealthier than their more long-established counterparts.

The Italians were not entirely flattered by the gaudy

imitation; they had warned their Russian colleagues against indulging in glitzy nightclubs that might attract the attention of the FBI and the media. (Indeed, in November 1994, the *New York Times* featured Rasputin in its Living Section.) Not long after Rasputin's grand opening, investigators examined its books. The ledgers showed the restaurant had been renovated for $800,000, but according to one Genovese crime family figure, the men's bathroom alone cost half a million dollars. In fact, more than $4 million had been spent on upgrading Rasputin. "No legit guy is gonna invest that kind of money in a restaurant," said the Genovese source. "The Zilbers wanted a place to sit with a big cigar, and then fuck the broads that come in there.

"The restaurant is gonna be their downfall."

The Genoveses had good reason to be concerned about the Zilber brothers' ostentatious lifestyle. They had staked Vladimir Zilber's gasoline bootlegging operation in exchange for a percentage of the tens of millions of dollars he made evading state and federal excise taxes. But he had gotten reckless, shaking down a team of FBI/IRS undercover agents posing as gasoline distributors in Ewing Township, New Jersey, and then, in February 1992, allegedly ordering the torching of the undercover business when they refused to pay a "mob tax."

On November 20, 1992, Vladimir was summoned to a meeting in Manhattan with Genovese crime family figures, who accused him of jeopardizing the business. A huge man with a trip-wire personality, Zilber was not cowed. "If I go down, you go, too," Zilber told the Italians. "I'm not going to prison."

"Zilber had big balls," said the Genovese associate. "Unfortunately, he used them for brains."

Zilber's sour-tempered performance only stoked the Italians' fears. If he talked, he could implicate, among others,

Daniel Pagano, a forty-two-year-old Genovese capo who not only got a penny out of every 27 cents in gasoline taxes that the Russians stole, but was also involved in the record industry, loan sharking, and gambling. (An additional penny went to Gambino capo Anthony "Fat Tony" Morelli, who delivered a weekly cut to Gambino boss John Gotti at the Bergin Hunt and Fish Social Club. The cash reeked of gasoline.) Pagano was mob royalty. His late father, Joseph, a convicted narcotics trafficker, had been fingered by Mafia snitch Joseph Valachi as a hit man for the Genovese crime family in the 1950s.

After the acrimonious Manhattan discussions, Zilber was supposed to go to a sit-down with representatives of Pagano in Brooklyn, says a well-placed Russian mob source. According to the Genovese figure, however, on the day of the meeting, Zilber was actually heading to Brooklyn to work out the details of a new gasoline scam, which he was concealing from Pagano and Morelli. Whatever version was true, this much is known: although he often traveled with four Genovese bodyguards, Zilber was alone when he steered his father-in-law's battered 1989 Ford Taurus south toward the FDR Drive off-ramp onto the Brooklyn Bridge during rush hour. As he approached the ramp, a car braked in front of him. Another car with four Russians pulled up alongside. A shotgun blast hit Zilber in the side of the head, blowing away his optic nerve and filling his brain with bullet fragments. If his window had been open, doctors say, Zilber would have been killed.

After the shooting, Fat Tony Morelli materialized next to Zilber's bed in Bellevue Hospital's intensive care unit. Morelli whispered something to the wounded Russian, and Zilber subsequently refused to talk to the police, although sources say he had recognized the triggerman. Vladimir did rant to the staff that he had been the victim of a mob hit, although the police had initially told the doctors that he was the victim of road rage. His physician noted in his medical chart that Zilber was a "delusional, paranoid schizophrenic." Knowing better, Alex Zilber surrounded his brother's room with round-the-clock bodyguards.

The police found the shooters' car abandoned at South Street Seaport, a popular tourist attraction in lower Manhattan. Inside was the shotgun used to shoot Zilber, as well as a rifle, a baseball cap, and a hair band of the type that Russian gangsters fancy for their flamboyant ponytails.

Shortly after the incident, the real reason for Zilber's hit became clear. Through informants in the New York Police Department, the Italian Mafia had learned that federal indictments were being prepared. Zilber would be a serious liability when they were issued. "He's lucky his head wasn't blown off," said the Genovese figure. "Vladimir was a loose cannon. Shutting him up was an act of survival." Indeed, the hit could not have taken place, Russian and Italian underworld sources, as well as federal authorities, agree, if Pagano and Morelli had not sanctioned it. "The shooters would need somebody's permission on the Italian side to kill the primary goose that was laying the golden egg," says a federal prosecutor.

The attempt on Zilber's life prodded the authorities into action. On November 22, 1992, two days after the ambush on the FDR, an army of federal agents, under the code name Operation Red Daisy, fanned out across New York, New Jersey, Pennsylvania, and Florida, with more than two hundred search warrants, confiscating evidence and freezing assets of the alleged gasoline bootleggers. After years of neglect, law enforcement had finally begun to marshal its forces and pay serious attention to the Russian threat. Operation Red Daisy would be by far its most successful foray against the Russian mob to date.

But in general, state and federal law enforcement agencies were loath to go after Russian mobsters, instead devoting their energies to bagging Italian wiseguys, a traditional route to promotion. And because the Russian mob was mostly Jewish, it was a political hot potato, especially in the New York area, where the vast majority of refugees were being resettled by Jewish welfare agencies. As for the New York City Police Department, it had almost no Russian-speaking cops, and even fewer reliable informants in the Russian émigré community. For years, the NYPD's intelligence unit couldn't find a single detective to monitor the Russian mob, because many cops were scared. "The Russians are just as crazy as the Jamaican drug gangs," a Ukrainian-speaking detective, who declined to work the Russian beat, told me in 1992. "They won't hesitate to go after a cop's family."

The NYPD was apparently unaware of the existence of the Russian mob until December 7, 1982, when detectives were summoned to a luxury apartment building on Manhattan's East 49th Street, near the United Nations. There they found a middle-aged man sprawled across a bed on his back—his arms outstretched, feet dangling over the edge and touching the floor, his eyes wide open. At first glance, lead detective Barry Drubin, a gruff police veteran, believed the deceased was a heart attack victim. The body lay in peaceful repose. There were no signs of a forced entry or struggle, and the dead man was still carrying his wallet and wearing an expensive gold watch and a black leather jacket. When Drubin looked more closely, however, he noticed that the vessels in one eye had burst, filling it with a dollop of blood. Drubin gently raised the man's head and saw that blood had coagulated in the back of the man's hair. There was no blood on the bed. The victim had been shot once, execution-style, at close range above the right ear at the hairline with a .25 caliber handgun. "We traced the bullet hole from the back of the head to the entry wound," Drubin says. "It was a professional hit."

Drubin's men searched the three-room apartment, which was decorated with expensive artwork. Nothing appeared to be disturbed or missing and they turned up no shell casings or suspicious fingerprints. A large, open attaché case in the living room was empty, save for a jeweler's loupe, a magnifying lens used to examine gems. The briefcase was subsequently checked for trace elements of drugs, but the tests were negative. Inside a credenza in the den, the detectives found $50,000 wrapped in cellophane, tucked away next to a VCR and an extensive video porn collection. A small amount of recreational hash was nearby.

The victim was soon identified as forty-nine-year-old Yuri Brokhin—the man with whom Monya Elson had first teamed up with when he arrived in Brighton Beach, and with whom he had enjoyed a great deal of success robbing and smuggling precious gems. But as Drubin soon discovered, Brokhin had been leading a paradoxical double life. Most of the world knew him as a prominent Russian Jewish dissident, author, and filmmaker, who had immigrated to the United States with his wife, Tanya, on November 16, 1972. He lived in an expensive apartment on Manhattan's East Side, bought a small country home on Long Island, and frequently treated friends to dinner at Elaine's, a famous hangout for the city's literati, and evenings at jazz clubs in Greenwich Village. He also owned a black stretch limousine and a beat-up Mercedes-Benz that he spent thousands of dollars to refurbish.

While Tanya took a job at Radio Liberty, earning $20,000 a year, Brokhin worked to maintain his reputation as a writer of import. He had published two books, which received mixed to poor reviews, including *The Big Red Machine*, an exposé of corruption inside the Soviet sports establishment, which was published by Random House in 1978.

Brokhin's anti-Soviet diatribes soon brought him to the attention of New York Democratic senator Daniel Patrick Moynihan, then vice chairman of the Senate Intelligence Committee. Brokhin was introduced to Moynihan by his chief of staff on the Intelligence Committee, Eric Breindel, an avid cold warrior. Brokhin supplied the committee with information about alleged Soviet agents who had penetrated America posing as Jewish refugees. Although Moynihan has no memory of having met Brokhin, Brokhin and Breindel developed an enthusiastic friendship, according to David Luchins, the senator's longtime liaison to the Orthodox Jewish community.

When Brokhin was discovered murdered, Breindel leaked a story to the press that he had been killed by the KGB because he was at work on a devastating exposé of the personal life of Yuri Andropov, the newly installed Soviet general secretary, and onetime KGB head. Breindel told Moynihan that Brokhin's execution was reminiscent of the highly publicized assassination of a Bulgarian dissident and anti-Soviet writer in England, who was stabbed with the poisonous tip of an umbrella by communist agents and later succumbed to the lethal toxin.* "After he put a bee in

---

*Shortly after Brokhin's death, Breindel faced his own investigation. On May 23, 1983, the Senate aide was arrested at a Holiday Inn in northeast Washington after purchasing five bags of heroin from an undercover cop for $150. Breindel, who had top security clearance, was ignominiously fired by Moynihan. The senator said in a statement to the press that he had no reason to believe that there had been any "intelligence losses attributed to Breindel," somberly adding that "this is a matter for further and thorough investigation." Breindel's career miraculously recovered and thrived. The onetime *Harvard Crimson* editor went on to become the editorial page editor of the *New York Post* and vice president of Rupert Murdoch's News Corporation before he died in 1998.

Moynihan's bonnet," as Luchins recalls, Breindel encouraged the senator to publicly call on the FBI to probe
whether the Russian émigré had been slain by a foreign
intelligence agency. The bureau dutifully complied, assign-
ing William Moschella, one of its counterintelligence
agents, to help Drubin unravel Brokhin's homicide.
"Moschella was not one of their big brain trusts, I can tell
you that," observed Drubin dryly. The NYPD's Peter Grinenko, a Ukrainian- and Russian-speaking cop, was transferred from an auto theft detail to work with Moschella.

Brokhin's body had been discovered at 4:15 P.M. by his
girlfriend, Tina Ragsdale, who called 911 after returning
home from her photo editor's job. (Brokhin's wife, Tanya,
was found drowned in the bathtub in their apartment a year
earlier. Brokhin had recently taken out a $150,000 insur-
ance policy on her life. Police ruled the death an accident.
He collected double indemnity.) Ragsdale, a waif of a girl
from Little Rock, immediately aroused Drubin's suspicion.
"She was in her twenties and he was forty-nine," recalled
Drubin, a circumspect man with a careful memory. "You
had to really wonder what's wrong with this love-starved,
overly romantic young woman. He wasn't a particularly
good-looking guy. In fact, he was quite ugly. He was hard
and severe-looking. And she was relatively attractive."

"Yuri and I were interested in the same things: photog-
raphy and art," Ragsdale insisted when interviewed fifteen
years after her boyfriend's homicide. "That was our common meeting ground."

She had given Drubin precisely the same explanation,
but he didn't buy it. "We got bad vibes from Tina. We felt
she was holding back. We found the cash, hashish by the
television, and the pornography tapes, and we didn't feel
she was giving us information."

After hours of relentless grilling, a tearful Ragsdale

finally surrendered what the police wanted: the names of Brokhin's closest friends—people to whom she also had grown close and may have had reason to protect. Although Ragsdale had given him a long list of names, Drubin didn't recognize any of them. "There was nobody to tell you who these people were like there would be with the Italians," he explained.

At this point in time, Russian crime was recognized by the authorities as a growing problem, but not an organized one, and Russian criminals, when they were caught in petty food stamp scams or even quite large Medicare frauds, were treated as isolated cases. However, the NYPD had become sufficiently concerned with the rise in Russian arrests to have recently authorized setting up a two-man intelligence unit under detective Joel Campanella to begin monitoring the phenomenon. Though he had only just begun his investigation, Campanella was at the time the closest thing to an expert on the subject, and when Drubin eventually turned to him for assistance, he helped confirm that Ragsdale's list of names was a menacing collection of Russian underworld figures.

Drubin hauled in dozens of these men for interrogation, all of whom were coarse, Gulag-hardened thugs whom Ragsdale knew from smoke-filled parties, high-stakes card games, and vodka-laced nights in Russian cabarets. One suspect sat across Drubin's desk in the squad room, contemptuously chomping on a .22 caliber bullet. "He would remove the bullet from the shell and chew on it. I don't know what kind of lead poisoning he has. And when I asked him if he had any more of those, he showed me a whole box of bullets. And my next question was the same question that you would have asked. Do you have a gun that goes with the bullets? The next thing on the desk is the gun."

Drubin quickly realized that the Russians held him in

very low regard. "I had one suspect look me in the face and say, 'I did time on the Arctic Circle. Do you think anything you're going to do is going to bother me?'"

Even the godfather of the Brighton Beach mob at the time, Evsei Agron, was brought in for questioning after one informant claimed that it had been he who had killed Brokhin. Agron, however, had an alibi: he had been playing cards with his friends. "They all had alibis," Drubin complained. Before Agron exited the station house, Drubin did manage to relieve him of his favorite, ever-present electric cattle prod.

Although Drubin was having little success in identifying the killer, he and Campanella were unearthing a huge amount of information about the workings of the Russian mob, and Campanella quickly set up a database in his unit. One of Campanella's most shocking discoveries was that many of his fellow cops in Brighton Beach were on the *Organizatsiya*'s payroll. Employed as bodyguards, bagmen, and chauffeurs for Russian godfathers, the dirty cops made $150 a night or more for special jobs. "Everyone knew, including Internal Affairs, that cops in cheap suits who looked like gangsters worked the door as bouncers and sat in the front tables at Russian mob joints," said criminal defense attorney James DiPietro. In the late 1980s, Campanella wrote to Internal Affairs about the problem; his complaint was ignored.

Unaddressed, the problem persisted. In the summer of 1994, New York State tax investigator Roger Berger, acting on a tip from an underworld source, likewise contacted Internal Affairs, telling them about police working at the Rasputin and Metropole nightclubs, as well as traffic cops participating in phony-car-accident scams with the Russians. Instead of investigating the complaint, however, IA tried to browbeat him into revealing his sources. "I said,

'First of all, these cops are conduits of information between the precinct and the Russians,'" Berger recalls. "'And that would be just perfect, to turn my informant over to you so he can get killed.'"

"Russians [in Brighton Beach] still don't trust the local cops because they see them work as bouncers at the local mobbed-up restaurants," says Gregory Stasiuk, an investigator with the New York State Organized Crime Task Force. "The Task Force had me go out and do interviews with Russians rather than the NYPD. The Russian community thinks the cops are on the take. The 60th and 61st precincts are very corrupt. We can't even do surveillance because the local cops make us in our vans. Every move we make is reported to the Russian gangsters by the dirty cops."

Barry Drubin was also warned "to be careful about whom I talked to and what I said"— in Brighton Beach— "because a lot of cops were on the mob's payroll. Detectives were working as bodyguards, they were making collections, they were doing a little strong-arm shit, and I said forget about this stuff here. I'm not going near this with a ten-foot pole. These cops weren't going to lead me to the guys that shot Yuri Brokhin."

The Moynihan-inspired investigation by the Moschella and Grinenko team wasn't much help in Brighton Beach either. Drubin considered them buffoons, and recalled one incident in which he crashed a bar mitzvah with them just to show their faces and apply a little pressure to the mobsters. "It was at the Sadko restaurant," Drubin recalled, an infamous mob joint. "Grinenko and Moschella got shit-faced, and Peter [Grinenko] starts dancing with all the Russian women, even breaking in on the husbands." The situation was only exacerbated by the deep animosity between Grinenko and Drubin, which stemmed from Grinenko's supposed anti-Semitism. Grinenko allegedly told Drubin that he believed Jews were "genetically inferior." When Drubin countered that Grinenko was an anti-Semitic Cossack, the cops nearly came to blows.*

Despite the numerous obstacles, Drubin and Campanella were making some progress, at least in uncovering the truth about Yuri Brokhin. Beneath the facade of a Soviet critic and intellectual lay a mobbed-up international drug dealer, jewel thief, and confidence man. Brokhin was constantly in debt, and the paltry income from his writing career, which could amount to no more than a few thousand dollars a year, certainly did not account for his rather affluent lifestyle, which included frequent trips to Atlantic City gaming tables and the Aqueduct Race Track. A compulsive gambler, he also spent many evenings playing cards with his friends in the Russian mob—godfathers, future

---

*In an August 1994 interview with the *New York Times*, Peter Grinenko, by then an investigator in Brooklyn DA Joe Hynes's office, downplayed the threat posed by Russian organized crime: "As organized crime in America, they are a flea on a horse." In an interview with the author, Grinenko said, "My assessment is that there are too many fucking reporters out there that are making [Russian] godfathers. How does that sound? Would you quote me on that?"

Grinenko openly admits that he has had extensive business ventures in the former Soviet Union, including a project to manufacture an American cigarette there. Law enforcement officials experienced in Russian crime remark that it can be difficult to conduct such business without working out an accommodation with organized crime. According to *The Economist*, cigarettes are a gangster-ridden industry in Russia. "Two Philip Morris executives had to leave Moscow in a hurry in 1997 after they trod on the toes of the tobacco mafia," the magazine reported.

"If Grinenko is making money in Russia, I mean, how do you do that without playing the [mob] game?" pondered an assistant U.S. attorney in New York who believes that his activities in the former Soviet Union create the potential for a conflict of interest. Grinenko responded: "They don't know what they are talking about. You can work over there if you know what you're doing." The Brooklyn DA's office declined to comment.

godfathers, hit men, and extortionists, who gathered to gamble in a fortified Brooklyn "social club." "He made a lot and he played a lot," said Ivan, a Russian mobster whose friendship with Brokhin dated back to Moscow, where Brokhin specialized in robbing copulating couples in public parks. "Yuri was very close with the godfather Evsei Agron," explained Ivan, who remembered how happy Brokhin was when Agron invited him to Canada to attend the godfather's younger sister's wedding.

But there was an even more duplicitous side to Brokhin, Drubin later learned from federal counterintelligence agents. Brokhin and his criminal cronies took frequent trips to Bulgaria. Its spas were a favorite hangout for Brighton Beach gangsters, KGB agents, and Soviet black marketeers. The spas were cheap, conducive to conducting business, and within close proximity to the U.S.S.R. A great deal of contraband, such as narcotics, flowed in and out of the Soviet Union through Bulgaria, as did intelligence information. Sofia was also a principal money laundering center for the KGB and the Brighton Beach mob. Brokhin was frequently observed by U.S. intelligence agents slipping in and out of the Soviet Union from Bulgaria and then returning to New York. U.S. counterintelligence officials believed that he was not only trading in contraband, but supplying the KGB with information about his new homeland. If he was a Soviet mole, as these officials believed, he could easily use his status as a dissident intellectual and friend of the Senate Intelligence Committee to provide valuable information he may have gleaned through his relationship with Breindel.

But Brokhin was killed, not because of Cold War intrigue, but because of a dispute among thieves. On the morning of Brokhin's homicide, he had had breakfast at the National restaurant in Brighton Beach with Ivan. Then the men drove into Manhattan, where Ivan dropped him off at his home. "Yuri did something wrong," Ivan recalled. "Yuri told me that he was going to go and live in Europe. 'I'm finished over here. Wednesday I'm going to get a lot of money, sell the apartment, and I'm going.'"

Sometime that afternoon, two unidentified men entered Brokhin's apartment. "He knew the people he let in," Drubin said. "He did not know he was getting hit. Everything was laid out—the briefcase, the jeweler's loupe—like he was doing business. He was a burly guy, about five ten. He would have put up a struggle if he knew he was about to get it. And he laid down so nicely on the bed after he was killed, he hardly rumpled the bedcover."

Drubin, who had interviewed more than a hundred suspects, concluded that Brokhin had probably been killed in a jewelry scam gone wrong, and that Balagula's old nemesis, Vladimir Reznikov, had been the triggerman. "Yuri was pulling some con on West 47th Street and maybe there were some diamonds involved," Drubin suggested. "Brokhin owed some money and pissed somebody off and he was killed."

Incredibly, in the years between Brokhin's homicide and the launch of Operation Red Daisy, law enforcement did little to stem the rising red tide of the Russian mob. Despite the efforts of individuals like Drubin and Campanella, and despite the glaring evidence that came to light in a few scattered prosecutions, such as that of Marat Balagula, there were still few authorities who understood, or even believed, that the Russian mob was a deadly threat. "Nobody takes the Russian mob seriously," the soft-spoken Campanella said a few years after the Brokhin incident. "The lack of interest of law enforcement has given the Russians time to grow."

A large part of the problem was political: the Russian

mob was predominantly Jewish. It was for that reason, asserted Campanella and other New York State and federal law enforcement officials, that seven years after Campanella's two-man Russian mob unit in the NYPD was inaugurated, it was shut down in a highly politicized, characteristically New York City type of reaction. The effort had come under considerable criticism from the Jewish establishment, which complained that the adverse publicity generated in the hunt for Russian Jewish criminals would foster anti-Semitism and jeopardize the continued emigration of Russian Jews to Israel and the West.

In Germany, where the arrival of the Brighton Beach mob was quickly recognized as a serious problem, police formed a task force of one hundred specially trained investigators in the early 1990s to combat the Russians, according to a classified report prepared by the German Federal Police in Wiesbaden. The Russian crime wave, which included bloody rubouts in fashionable restaurants on Berlin's Fasanenstrasse, forced authorities to overcome their "supersensitivity . . . to the Jewish aspect of emigre crime," said the report. But in the United States, according to several top law enforcement officials, Jewish organizations continued to lobby the Justice Department to downplay the threat posed by the Russian mob. "The Russian Mafia has the lowest priority on the criminal pecking order," admitted FBI spokesman Joe Valiquette during a 1992 interview.

Some of Valiquette's colleagues were harshly critical of the bureau's lack of attention to the threat. They believed that the *Organizatsiya* had already developed into a new version of the Mafia; one that was just as ruthless as the Italian brand but potentially very much more difficult to tackle. "The Italian mobsters play boccie ball, the Russian gangsters play chess," said one law enforcement source who marveled at their growing sophistication. And while the Russian mob may not have had the cumulative force of seventy years of tradition behind it, like La Cosa Nostra, by the early 1990s, some five thousand hard-core Russian criminals had already established themselves in the New York region, a criminal presence that was as large as all the Italian Mafia families combined.

"The Russians are an emerging crime group," Justice Department prosecutor Patrick J. Cotter, a member of the team that convicted John Gotti, said in 1992. "They make tons of money, they kill people, they are international, they are moving into drugs—but we don't have a single unit of the FBI that's devoted to going after them. We've got a Bonanno squad, we've got a Lucchese squad, but we don't have a Russian squad—so there is your problem. If we don't begin to address the problem now, we'll be running around asking ourselves how the hell this Russian organized crime got so big and how we can get rid of them.

"Money is power in crime as in everything else in this world," Cotter continued. "If you ignore the fact that the Russians are reaping huge profits, you're making a bad mistake. They're not going to invest in IRAs. They're going to buy businesses, they're going to buy power. If we want to stop these guys, we better do it before they buy those things. If I've learned one thing from prosecuting the Mafia the last five years, I've learned that that's the toughest kind of mob influence to rub out. It's relatively easy to get the drug sellers, the gun sellers, the protection racketeers. It's real tough to get the corporation that's partly owned by the mob, or the union that's been corrupted."

There was, in fact, one official at FBI headquarters in Washington, D.C., who did believe that if the government didn't quickly launch a full-scale assault on the Russian mob, it would become untouchable. James Moody, a strapping six-foot-three organized crime expert, spent his youth in the backwoods of Oklahoma—a large, barefoot boy in overalls, hunting and fishing with his brothers. His great-grandfather was the first chief of police in Stroud, his tiny hometown. Moody joined the FBI at age twenty-nine in 1970 after a six-year stint in the military that included two tours in Vietnam.

In August 1989, Moody was appointed chief of the FBI's organized crime section. Examining the bureau's past record, he realized that former director J. Edgar Hoover had not paid sufficient attention to the Italian Mafia, having instead devoted the majority of his resources to his corrosive obsession: combating domestic subversion and the perceived communist penetration of America. In the 1960s, when New York's five Italian crime families controlled labor unions, the garment industry, and the docks, there was only one FBI field agent in Manhattan assigned to organized crime, whose very existence, Hoover had proclaimed, was "baloney." The FBI had to wait until Hoover's death in 1972 to undertake a serious investigation of La Cosa Nostra, but by then, it had become a criminal colossus. Moody didn't want to repeat that error with the surging Russian mob.

Still, he was having trouble convincing colleagues of the seriousness of the threat; the FBI continued to be allowed to pursue individual Russian crimes only when it came across them. Then, in 1992, during the heady first days after the fall of communism, Moody received a visit from Mikhail Konstantinovich Yegorov, the first deputy minister of the interior for the Russian Federation. The Russian proposed an immediate cooperation agreement with American law enforcement to combat jointly the Russian mob.

"I can't do it because we have so much of a past history of being enemies," Moody told Yegorov, after spending a day chauffeuring him around the American capital. "We're going to have to kind of take it a step at a time."

But Yegorov would not be so easily dissuaded, and asked, "Okay, what can I do to improve the relationship and get it moving a little faster?"

"I don't know of a specific thing right now, but whenever I identify one, I'll get back in touch with you," Moody replied.

It didn't take Moody long to propose a specific plan. Two fugitives from Red Daisy — David Shuster and an accomplice — were known to be hiding out in Moscow. Moody wanted them, but Yegorov reminded him that the countries didn't have an extradition treaty.

"That's true," Moody admitted. "We don't have any treaties whatsoever. But expel those guys from your country as being bad," he urged him, as a way to jump-start relations.

"About two days later, maybe three," Moody recalled, "I come walking into my office and there's a handwritten fax on my desk."

"Mr. Moody, we've got them," the note said. "Please come and get them."

The previous day, a Russian commando unit wearing sky blue ski masks and bulletproof vests had stormed Shuster's "import-export" firm in downtown Moscow; a furious gun battle ensued. When the shooting stopped, Shuster was on his back, being pummeled by members of the Russian Special Forces, but putting up an impressive fight all the same. "My understanding is that Shuster broke two sets of Russian handcuffs," Moody said. "He's not a very tall guy, but he's strong as hell."

At first, the Russians didn't know what to do with him; Shuster was, in fact, being illegally detained. If they put him in jail, the Russian federal prosecutor's office would learn that the Ministry of Interior was covertly working with the FBI and the event could spark a Cold War–style political firestorm. So in typically brutal Russian style, Shuster was transported to a dense forest outside of Moscow, dumped into a hole, and buried up to his neck in gravel.

The Russians informed the FBI that they would have to retrieve Shuster within three days, at which point he would be released. The bureau scrambled, but obtaining a Russian visa on short notice wasn't easy in those days, even for a U.S. government agency. Finally, Klaus C. Rohr, an old organized crime hand and the FBI's assistant legate in Bonn, made it into Russia, and was taken directly to Shuster. "We don't have any jurisdiction in Russia," Rohr told him, after identifying himself as an agent of the FBI. "But we're going to put you on a plane and take you back to the United States, and I'm going to arrest you once we get back to America. If you give me any problems, I'm going to leave you in the hole."

"No problem," Shuster replied.

Moody immediately took the fax from Yegorov relaying the news of Shuster's capture to Larry Potts, the assistant director of the FBI's Criminal Investigative Division. He hoped to use the document to make a case for starting a Russian organized crime squad and for cooperating with Russian police and security officials—initiatives vociferously opposed by the foreign counterintelligence side of the FBI, which considered the Russians to be an everlasting threat to national security, perestroika or not.

"You might say all of our obstacles suddenly disappeared" after the Shuster snatch, Moody explained. With the strong backing of Attorney General Janet Reno, the FBI set up a Russian organized crime subsection at its Washington, D.C., headquarters in early 1993, which would report directly to Moody, and which received full authority to investigate the Russian mob as an organized criminal cartel.

Entrenched bureaucrats with Cold War hangovers continued to fight the new initiatives. It was only in May 1994 that the FBI office in New York, commanded by William A. Gavin, finally set up a squad specifically targeted to fighting Russian organized crime, and even then, he didn't seem to realize just how late he had entered the battle. "I had a problem getting Gavin's attention," Moody explained, citing Gavin's resistance to setting up a Russian force. "He said he liked to do his own thing. I said, 'Okay, you go do your own thing, but you're not going to do it with my manpower.'" It wasn't until Moody started shifting personnel out of the New York office that Gavin capitulated. "I basically forced him into setting up the [Russian] squad," Moody acknowledged. It was dubbed the C-24 squad.

With few informants and only a superficial knowledge of New York's 300,000-strong Russian émigré community, the FBI realized how handicapped it was in this effort. Based on its early reports, Raymond C. Kerr, the head of the new Russian unit under Gavin, believed that there were three or four major Russian crime families operating in Brighton Beach, with outposts in at least five other U.S. cities. The largest family consisted primarily of Jewish émigrés, many of them from Odessa; a second family was from Tashkent, in Uzbekistan. The FBI had identified them as Muslim; people in the community insisted they were Jews. A third family was from Ekaterinburg, in Russia. As far as the FBI's Gavin and Kerr could determine, each of the families had a Cosa Nostra–like pyramid structure with bosses or godfathers poised at the top, and beneath them the consiglieres, or advisers, and then the crews.

But virtually everyone else in law enforcement with a knowledge of the Russian mob challenged the FBI model.

"You can't put them in a family," one DEA official explained. "One day, two guys are trying to kill each other, and the next day they are doing a dope deal together." He added that while Italian wiseguys often specialized in particular criminal enterprises, the Russians tended to be generalists. "Whatever opportunity affords itself—that's what they do that day."

Meanwhile, with Shuster in hand, federal prosecutors moved forward with trying the Red Daisy case. Bootlegging czar Vladimir Zilber and six other Russians, as well as five Gambino crime family figures, had been indicted in Newark, New Jersey, for federal excise tax fraud, money laundering, and racketeering. But to solidify the case, the prosecutors still needed members of the criminal enterprise to cooperate and so they offered Shuster a deal he couldn't refuse: if he agreed to testify against members of the massive bootlegging conspiracy, he would be given a letter that promises to petition the judge for leniency at sentencing as a reward for cooperation.

As part of his proffer agreement, or deal with the government, which required him to confess to every crime he had ever committed, Shuster admitted that he was an international pickpocket, gasoline bootlegger, and had dabbled in dealing Turkish heroin. The government confiscated $6 million from him, as well as seventeen cars and real estate, then stashed him in a safe house until the trial.

Local police were furious that Shuster had gotten a deal. They suspected that he had ordered a jewelry store heist in Lodi, New Jersey, that had led to the shooting death of an off-duty cop. The investigating officers had several witnesses, including gang members who were at the scene of the execution. The federal prosecutors were given the information, but chose to ignore it. As far as the police were concerned, Shuster—who vehemently denied his involvement in the affair—had lied to get his letter, and had gotten off the hook for killing a cop.

Zilber's case was severed from the others; his attorneys alleged that brain damage from his attack on the FDR left him incompetent to stand trial. Whether or not he went to court hardly mattered. The government seized $550,000 in cash from his safe deposit box, and his $1.2 million house in New Jersey was put in foreclosure. His wife walked out on him. His brother, Alex, fled with the family fortune, heading first for Brazil, and then to Moscow, where he eventually ran an aluminum factory and a casino for the Genovese crime family. Vladimir spends his days on a bench on the Coney Island boardwalk gazing absently out to sea, or holed up in his meager apartment, listening to CNN. He receives free meals at Rasputin and his old gang pitched in to buy him a live-in whore. "The one thing I hear that's still functioning well without any inhibitions is a lust for women of all ages," a federal prosecutor related. "Vladimir has no control over himself. If his grandmother was in the room, he'd go after her. I think, no pun intended, his brain is really shot." Even with Zilber's forced retirement, however, his crowning achievement, Rasputin, continued to be a magnet for wiseguys from Little Italy to the Volga.

With Vladimir Zilber excused from testifying, Gambino capo Anthony "Fat Tony" Morelli became Red Daisy's marquee defendant. Morelli was accused of directing subordinates to use intimidation and violence to collect the "mob tax" from the Russian bootleggers. A wealthy shylock and fence who was notoriously stingy, Morelli had retained high-priced attorney Barry Slotnick to represent his bagman Edward Dougherty, but then refused to pay his full fee. Slotnick's enthusiasm for the case understandably waned, and when Dougherty deduced that Morelli was setting him up to be the fall guy, he joined the government's growing cast of cooperating witnesses.

Although Morelli could afford to hire the best criminal lawyer in New York for himself, he retained a second-string Gambino house attorney by the name of Richard Rehbock, who regularly annoyed juries with his constant, seemingly irrelevant objections and bombastic speeches. It hardly helped Morelli's cause when, about one month into the Red Daisy trial, Rehbock was the subject of a humiliating, front-page exposé in the *New York Post*. Star gossip columnist Cindy Adams quoted Rehbock's estranged wife, Sylvia DiPietro, as alleging that her husband had hidden $100,000 of mob cash in a suit in his clothes closet, and kept three sets of accounting books.

Having already angered Morelli as a result of his wife's vexatious accusations, Rehbock further put himself in disfavor with his questionable trial strategy. Early in the case, for example, he made a colossal blunder when the government introduced Colombo soldier Frankie "the Bug" Sciortino's personal phone book into evidence. The book was valuable to the prosecution's case in that it listed Morelli's various private phone numbers, as well as the telephone numbers of numerous Russian bootleggers and Italian gangsters involved in the Red Daisy bootlegging scam, and therefore helped establish the web of relationships in the Russian-Italian bootleg combine about which Dougherty, Shuster, and others were going to testify. The FBI had arrested the Bug on September 29, 1989, initially for witness tampering; the agent responsible for his apprehension was called to the stand merely to place the confiscated phone book into evidence.

In his cross-examination of the agent, however, Rehbock inadvertently helped prove the government's case. Apparently unaware that the FBI agent was a well-known expert on organized crime and, moreover, had investigated every name in the Bug's thick black book, Rehbock asked, "Agent, this doesn't say, Phone Book of Frankie Sciortino's Mob Friends, does it?"

"No, it just says address book, or telephone book," the agent replied.

"Is the book entitled *All My Gangster Friends?*"

"No."

"The first entry, is he in the gas business?"

"I don't know."

"Is he a gangster?" Rehbock asked, his confidence growing.

"I can't tell you."

"Is he a person that's listed on the little charts that you have on the wall in the F.B.I. office as an Organized Crime member?"

"I don't know."

Emboldened even further, Rehbock ventured forth. "How about the next one, Artie Goldstein, do you know him?"

"I believe he is in business on Long Island—a shylock victim."

"That's what, a customer of Mr. Sciortino? Is that what you're saying?"

"He had a loan with Mr. Sciortino."

By asking the witness to characterize whether the people listed in Sciortino's book were mobsters, Rehbock had opened the door for the government to do the same thing on redirect.

"Let's go through some of the names," said prosecutor Robert Stahl. "Anthony in Florida."

"I believe that's Anthony Trentascosta—a made member of the Gambino crime family," replied the G-man.

"Go to page forty-five. Benny A."

"That would be Benny Aloi. I believe he's a Colombo made member."

After identifying a number of wiseguys, as well as Frankie "the Bug's" loan shark victims, Stahl stopped just before Morelli's name, by which point, "the jury was just laughing," Stahl recalled. "We took a break, and Morelli says loud enough for us to hear, 'Hey, Richie, whaddaya gonna do, the fuckin' twenty years for me now?'"

The gangster's prediction proved to be all too accurate; he was convicted and sentenced to exactly twenty years. In addition, eleven defendants were also convicted. Shuster was released from custody not long after the trial and is living somewhere in Brooklyn. Since he only testified against Italians, he has nothing to fear from the Russians.

However groundbreaking an effort the Red Daisy prosecutions—and several successful bootlegging prosecutions thereafter—they scarcely had any repercussions on the Russian mob, which continued to make tons of money as it spread across America. "The cancer is beyond the lymph nodes," New York State taxman Berger glumly noted in 1994. Nevertheless, recognizing the severe destabilizing effect that organized crime was having on Russia's tenuous democracy, FBI director Louis Freeh told a Senate subcommittee in May 1994 that the war against the Russian mob "is critical—not just for the Russians but for all of us, because the fall of democracy there poses a direct threat to our national security and to world peace." Freeh traveled to Russia, where he proposed launching "a lawful, massive, and coordinated law enforcement response" against Russian organized crime. He suggested setting up an international databank and training Russian police in American investigative methods. That year, the FBI established such an academy for ex-Eastern bloc law enforcement officials in Budapest.

The relationship Moody worked so hard to forge quickly foundered. "There is a great distrust on the American side of the integrity of Russian law enforcement," says Rutgers criminologist James Fickenauer, who was awarded a grant from the Justice Department to study Russian organized crime. "They want to sell their information. They think if the information is valuable, it must be worth something. These are badly underpaid people who are looking for money from wherever they can get it." And, as the Genovese crime figure who backed Rasputin says, "We'll always be able to pay more than the FBI."

However short it fell of its goals, the Red Daisy campaign did mark the belated recognition by American law enforcement of how serious a threat the Russian mob actually posed. But although the FBI, along with other local and federal agencies like the DEA and Customs Bureau, could now focus some of its energies on penetrating the *Mafiya*'s extensive web of influence and corruption, the effort may have come too late. For looming just over the horizon was a force that dwarfed the Brighton Beach *Mafiya* in size and power, and it was headed directly for U.S. shores.

RED TIDE

I n May 1991, while eating breakfast at the National restaurant in Brighton Beach, Emile Puzyretsky was shot nine times in the face and chest. Fifteen diners witnessed the execution. *"Ya nechevo ne znayu,"* they all told detectives, "I don't know anything"—even though the killer had carefully rummaged around the restaurant floor on his hands and knees, looking for the spent cartridges, some of which had become lodged under their tables. The reason for their silence was simple: no one in the restaurant wanted to be branded a *stukatch*, a snitch, and risk a surprise visit from the killer—Monya Elson. After a six-year absence, the fearsome hit man had returned to Brighton Beach to claim his warm spot in the Russian mob.

"There are a lot of rumors in Brighton Beach that I killed Puzyretsky," Elson said with a laugh. "You can say that I killed him to take care of business."

Elson had spent most of his years away stewing in filthy, ovenlike Israeli jails, to which he had been sentenced in 1984 after his effort to seek fame and fortune in the cocaine smuggling business had not gone as planned. Being marooned in an oppressive, flea-infested tent city for convicts in the barren, lunarlike Negev Desert was hardly what Elson had in mind when he set out to claim his place in the criminal hierarchy. To make matters worse, he heard stories about his contemporaries in Brighton Beach making big names for themselves in the Russian underworld. He yearned to return "home" to Brighton Beach and establish himself as one of the most respected men in the Russian mobs' power structure. Prison did bestow on Elson one piece of good fortune: he became the cell mate and body-guard for convicted spy Shabtai Kalmanovitch, cementing a criminal alliance that would pay big dividends for both men.

On August 19, 1990, Elson was released from jail, bursting "with a lot of ideas" about bringing some order to the mobocracy that ruled Brighton Beach. But first, he had some unfinished business to attend to in Moscow. Elson had learned while in prison that a well-known Russian hood had been spreading word that Elson was a *musor*, a rat. Supposedly, Elson had exposed some Russians running an international gun ring, a charge that, though he vehemently denied it, had circulated rapidly throughout the criminal grapevine. Elson was furious that his reputation was being maligned. "If he doesn't like one word that comes out of your mouth, you're dead," says an acquaintance of Elson's. "I said, 'Hey Monya, you can't kill people for that.' He said, 'Yes I can!'"

"He said I was a *musor*." Elson recalled of the man who was bad-mouthing him. "I wanted to kill him. He thought that because I was a Jewish guy, and I had presumably left Russia forever, that it would be okay to play with Monya."

As soon as he arrived in Moscow Elson quickly tracked down the malefactor and, with a single swing of an ax, hacked off his arm, leaving him to bleed to death. "Half the criminals will think I killed for revenge," Elson remarked. "The other half will think that maybe he knew something, and I killed [him] to shut his mouth." Citing an old Russian proverb, Elson explained his motive as: "Revenge is the sweetest form of passion!"

His business in Moscow complete, Elson, then thirty-nine, returned at last to Brighton Beach. This time, he knew precisely what he wanted to achieve, and he knew how to do so. He quickly assembled a team of experienced hit men, master thieves, and extortionists—a group the FBI dubbed "Monya's Brigada"—and dispatched them to take over a large swath of Brighton Beach. He established his headquarters in Rasputin, where he received $15,000 a week from the Zilbers and a percentage of the raucous cabaret's revenues. "I was the new epicenter for Russian organized crime," Elson boasted. "Before, it was bullshit! It wasn't fucking so tough."

Elson's braggadocio had a deadly bite. One of his first deeds was to murder Puzyretsky, who had been employed to defend a large Russian bootlegging combine that competed with the Zilber brothers for dominance in the gasoline business. Elson then methodically slaughtered many of the Zilbers' rivals, propelling the three men to the top of the Russian criminal pyramid.

This was Monya's golden age—a few short years between 1990 and 1993. With a small army and his savage determination, he seemed unstoppable, extorting and killing with impunity. "Monya was a nut," said Gregory Stasiuk, the investigator for the New York State Organized Crime Task Force. "On one wire, Elson said to a tardy loan shark victim, 'You are making me so crazy, I don't know whether I should come over and kill you now or later.'"

"Monya loves to kill," said a Genovese wiseguy. "He was a goon on a short, hot leash."

Monya's Brigada was soon becoming immensely wealthy, dealing in everything from coke to precious gems, which he allegedly smuggled from Manhattan's jewelry district to Moscow. A December 1994 secret FBI intelligence report noted that "Elson is a principal player in the control of the export of diamonds, gold and other jewelry from the United States and other countries to Russia. A carat of diamonds can be obtained for $1,500 in New York, and sold for $10,000 in Moscow. Elson receives a kickback on every diamond and gold deal he brokers in Moscow. An unknown Austrian front company has been set up to receive the kickbacks. This concern has a permit from the Russian government to import these items. Elson believes this situation gives him 'leverage' with other O.C. [organized crime] players."

At least one rival Russian mobster, however, refused to accede to Elson's growing power. Boris Nayfeld, once the underling of the Little Don Evsei Agron and of Marat Balagula, had emerged as an estimable force in his own right while Elson was still confined in his Israeli prison cell. By the time Elson resurfaced in Brooklyn, Nayfeld was shuttling between Antwerp, where he lived in a luxury apartment with his mistress, and Staten Island, where he resided with his wife and children in a sumptuous home on Nevada Avenue across from a nature preserve.

Nayfeld came to prominence by running a heroin ring of French Connection proportions. He obtained the drugs in Thailand, smuggled them into Singapore, and then stashed them in TV picture tubes and shipped them to Poland through a Belgium-based import-export company, M&S International. From there, Russian couriers from Brighton

Beach with valid U.S. passports "bodied" the heroin into the United States through New York's Kennedy Airport. "Customs never looked," said a DEA official. "Poland wasn't an obvious transshipment point for drugs. It's not Bogotá or Bangkok. They shotgunned each plane with three, four, or five couriers, all unknown to each other. They moved eight to ten kilos per flight, and it went on a good year before we caught on to it." Eventually, the couriers expanded their operations to Boston, Chicago, and elsewhere, while the drug smugglers continued to make millions of dollars a planeload.

In New York, part of the drugs was sold to Sicilian mobsters out of a dive in Coney Island, while another faction of the ring dealt the heroin to Hispanic customers out of the S&S Hot Bagel Shop, next to Katz's Delicatessen on East Houston Street in Manhattan. The DEA was impressed with the sophistication of the mobsters' business. "What's unique," said one official admiringly, "is that these guys were actually controlling it from the source to the street."

Elson, however, viewed his rival's expanding empire with displeasure. "I knew when I got out of jail that Biba [Boris Nayfeld's nickname] would still be in the ballpark. He would be a fucking problem," Elson said derisively. "Everybody said Biba, Biba. *Biba Shmeeba. I said he was a piece of ass. He's a fucking nobody.* And somebody sent word to Biba that I'm cursing him. And I said yes, I want to meet the motherfucker. He was a piece of shit! For this reason, I declared the war! I said, he cannot be what he wants to be! He's a *musor* in his heart. He wanted to be somebody. He was never nobody. You know to be a godfather you have to have leadership qualities. He don't have any qualities."

Nayfeld responded to these taunts with a $100,000

contract on Elson, setting the stage for a massive gangland war. "They were like two gunslingers," said Stasiuk, "who had to prove themselves top gun."

On a frigid night shortly before the Russian New Year in January 1991, Elson's men taped a powerful bomb under the muffler of Nayfeld's car. The following afternoon, Nayfeld drove the car to Brooklyn to pick up his children at school. As the engine idled, the youngsters piled into the backseat. Just then, a maintenance man pointed to an object hanging from the chassis. The bomb, which was designed to have been activated by heat from the muffler, had become dislodged and failed to explode. "It could have taken out a city block," said an assistant U.S. attorney.

Nayfeld wasted no time in seeking revenge. On May 14, 1991, Elson was speaking with some friends on the corner of Brighton Beach Avenue and Sixth Street in front of the Cafe Arabat, a Russian mob haunt. At exactly 3:00 P.M., a hit man sauntered up and pumped five dumdum bullets into Elson's belly. "I never lost consciousness," Elson insisted. "I wanted to shoot this guy. You can't imagine how hot and painful the wound was. But I saw the guy, a black man, run away. I was going to shoot him. I didn't have the strength to shoot him." A friend rushed Elson to Coney Island Hospital. "The bullets made two holes in my stomach. My liver was severed. My pancreas was shattered. One bullet lodged in my left kidney and exploded." Doctors removed the kidney, along with twenty feet of intestine. "If I had gotten there twenty seconds later, I would have been on a slab. They put me on a stretcher and I lost consciousness."

Elson developed peritonitis. "There was a lot of puss in my pancreas, which was abscessed. There was a lot of puss in my stomach. And the doctors said to my wife: 'He's going to die now.' And they put a tube into my heart." Elson claims he was pronounced dead and wheeled into the morgue, but when "I heard 'morgue,' somehow I reacted. I twitched my toe as if to say I'm alive. They put me back in ICU. Then I had an operation. They told my wife I had a fifty-fifty chance; if I survived the first forty-eight hours, I might live. . . . I spent twenty-eight days in intensive care; my wife was advised to say her farewell to me."

Elson recovered and quickly made another attempt at getting even with Nayfeld. One of Nayfeld's paid assassins, Alexander Slepinin, was a three-hundred-pound, six-foot-five-inch veteran of Russia's Special Forces, who had served in Afghanistan during the war against the Mujahedeen, the Islamic fundamentalist rebels. Nicknamed the "Colonel," he had tattoos of a panther and a dragon on his upper torso, signs that he was a veteran of the Gulag. He was an expert in a variety of martial arts, and kept a large collection of swords and knives, which he used to dismember his victims in his bathtub before disposing of the body parts. He carried a business card that said he specialized in the techniques of mortal combat.

On a June morning, three shooters, including Elson, according to eyewitnesses and police officials, ambushed Slepinin as he sat in his 1985 Cadillac Seville on a residential street in the Sunset Park section of Brooklyn. "He started crying, the big motherfucker, and admitted that Nayfeld had paid him to kill me," Elson snorted gleefully. Breathing convulsively, Slepinin "asked for forgiveness."

"We are not in the church," growled one of the hit men.

The enormous man tried to squeeze his bulk through the passenger door, but was shot three times in the back, the bullets carefully aimed to ensure that his death would be agonizing. Thrashing and moaning, he continued to beg for his life, but two bullets to the back of the head finished off the Colonel. "He was huge, big, and mean," Elson said.

"He was a monster, a cold-blooded killer. The FBI has to give me an award."

A few months after the Colonel was butchered, Elson received a tip that Nayfeld was planning to attend a meeting in a trendy part of Moscow. Elson's informant knew the exact time and location of the conclave, as well as Nayfeld's route to and from the gathering. Elson gave the contract to kill Nayfeld to Sergei Timofeyev, who was nicknamed "Sylvester" because of his resemblance to film star Sylvester Stallone, and his lieutenant Sergei "the Beard" Kruglov, two of the most vicious gangsters in Moscow. According to Elson's informant, Nayfeld's car was supposed to pass a high-rise apartment tower that was under renovation. Because its windows were covered with cardboard, an Olympic marksman, hired by Timofeyev and Kruglov, had to take aim at Nayfeld as his car approached the building by squinting through a peephole. But Nayfeld must have had a premonition, for at the last moment he pulled a hasty U-turn and disappeared into traffic. "It was Biba's miraculous escape," said a still bewildered Elson. "He had a lot of miracles."

As did Elson. On November 6, 1992, Elson arrived in Los Angeles's Plummer Park, a meeting place for Russian émigrés who gambled their welfare checks and drank cheap vodka. Elson, who was there to meet a friend, suddenly decided to return to his car to retrieve something he had forgotten. As he walked back to the parking garage, a black man crept up behind him and shoved a pistol against the base of his skull. Elson heard the click of its trigger, but the weapon jammed. "Can you imagine if the gun went off?" Elson asked. "My brains would have been scrambled eggs." Elson spun around and wrestled the man to the ground, kicking away the gun. The assassin grabbed it back and, this time, successfully fired it repeatedly, backpedaling until he was able to escape. Elson was hit in the left hand, severing a tendon. At the hospital, he gave a fictitious name, and told detectives that he had fought off a mugger who was trying to steal his $75,000 Rolex watch. He later slipped out of the hospital without paying his bill and traveled to Arizona for painful reconstructive surgery. Before he left Los Angeles, however, another would-be assassin attempted to place an explosive inside his car. "The shnook couldn't figure out how to wire the bomb," says a law enforcement source. "The device exploded in the man's hands, blowing them off."

As the Elson-Nayfeld war raged on, dozens of gangsters were massacred. Some were gutted like sheep; others had their throats cut. Some were castrated with crescent-shaped knives; both the implements and the body parts became favorite gangster souvenirs. Though Elson and Nayfeld tried to enlist other influential gangsters to their respective sides, neither could gain a decisive advantage, and the bombs and bullets continued to explode from Brighton Beach to Moscow.

At one point Rafik Bagdasaryan, nicknamed Svo, a mighty *vor* from Soviet Armenia, tried to intervene on Nayfeld's behalf. Svo was known as the diplomat of the Russian underworld, and he was so highly respected that, when he was poisoned to death in prison some years later by Chechen gangsters, his body was flown from a secret military airstrip near Moscow to his native home in Yerevan, the capital of Soviet Armenia. Svo's funeral was held with a degree of pomp usually reserved only for members of the Politburo. His countrymen thronged his coffin, and the streets were showered with rose petals. Mob bosses and politicians came to pay their last respects. Lights were turned on for forty-eight hours in Yerevan, where the power supply was erratic at best.

Seeking to put an end to the deadly struggle, Svo tele-phoned Elson's vaunted ally, the Beard. "I love you like a son," said Svo. "I know you had a meeting with Monya in Yerevan, and I had a meeting with him in Yerevan. And Monya spoke about killing Biba. I'm asking you like my son, I like Biba, and please don't get involved in this."

The plea went unheeded. Elson learned from another informant about the impending arrival in Moscow of Shlava Ukleba, who worked for Nayfeld as an international heroin trafficker. On a blistering cold day, Ukleba's hotel room was rocked by a thunderous explosion, which obliterated five adjoining rooms. "But nobody was hurt. It was wintertime, and Ukleba ran out of the rubble in his underwear. He ran all the way to Austria," chortled Elson.

Then, on July 26, 1993, as Elson, his wife, and his twenty-five-year-old bodyguard, Oleg Zapivakmine, were emerging from a black Lexus in front of the couple's Brook-lyn apartment, a car careened toward the curb. The trio was sprayed with a "Streetsweeper" shotgun and Uzi subma-chine gunfire. Elson, who was carrying a briefcase with $300,000 in watches and jewelry from New York's dia-mond district, was shot in the back and thigh. His wife, Marina, bolted from the Lexus and hid in a crawlspace, behind two garbage cans. A masked man leapt from the attacker's vehicle and pumped two shotgun blasts into the cowering woman from several yards away. Seventeen pel-lets tore through her face, throat, chest, and shoulder.

An all-out gun battle ensued with shotgun pellets pep-pering the entire length of the seventy-five-foot apartment house, penetrating neighbors' cabinets and walls. "It was like the Persian Gulf War," Elson recalls. More than a hun-dred rounds were exchanged between the hit team and Elson and Zapivakmine, who was only lightly grazed in the stomach.

Evsei Agron, Russian organized crime's first American don.
(*New York Times* Pictures)

Agron was gunned down inside his Brooklyn vestibule on May 4, 1985.
(Courtesy of James Rosenthal)

Boris Nayfeld, a strong-arm man for Agron who later became a global heroin dealer and Monya Elson's nemesis.
(*New York Times* Pictures)

Monya Elson, the Russian *Mafiya*'s most fearsome hit man.
(Courtesy of *Novoye Russkoye Slovo*)

Marat Balagula, Brighton Beach's second godfather. He took the American Russian *Mafiya* global.
(Courtesy of James Rosenthal)

Yuri Brokhin and his wife, Tanya.

The floor show at Rasputin, a cabaret owned by the Zilber brothers and also Monya Elson's headquarters.
(© Eli Reed/Magnum Photos)

Hockey superstars the FBI and the Royal Canadian Mounted Police have connected to major Russian crime figures:

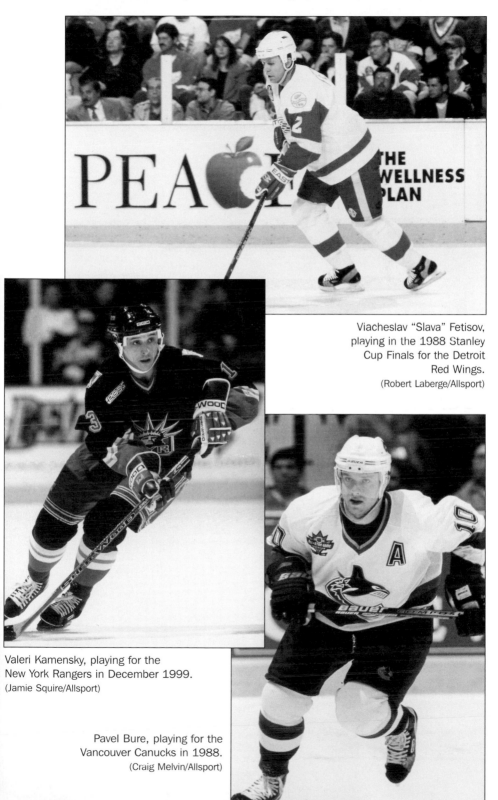

Viacheslav "Slava" Fetisov, playing in the 1988 Stanley Cup Finals for the Detroit Red Wings.
(Robert Laberge/Allsport)

Valeri Kamensky, playing for the New York Rangers in December 1999.
(Jamie Squire/Allsport)

Pavel Bure, playing for the Vancouver Canucks in 1988.
(Craig Melvin/Allsport)

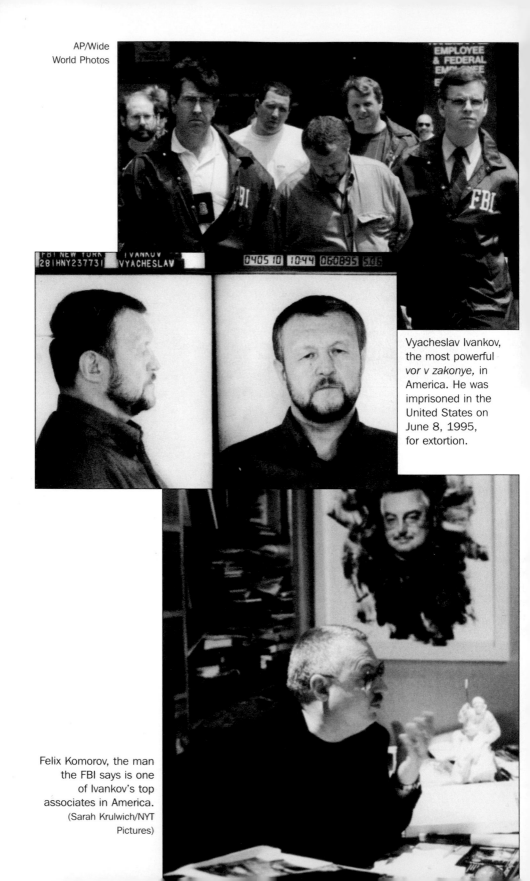

FBI NEW YORK 281HNY237731 IVANKOV VYACHESLAV 040510 10:44 060895 506

Vyacheslav Ivankov,
the most powerful
vor v zakonye, in
America. He was
imprisoned in the
United States on
June 8, 1995,
for extortion.

Felix Komorov, the man
the FBI says is one
of Ivankov's top
associates in America.
(Sarah Krulwich/NYT
Pictures)

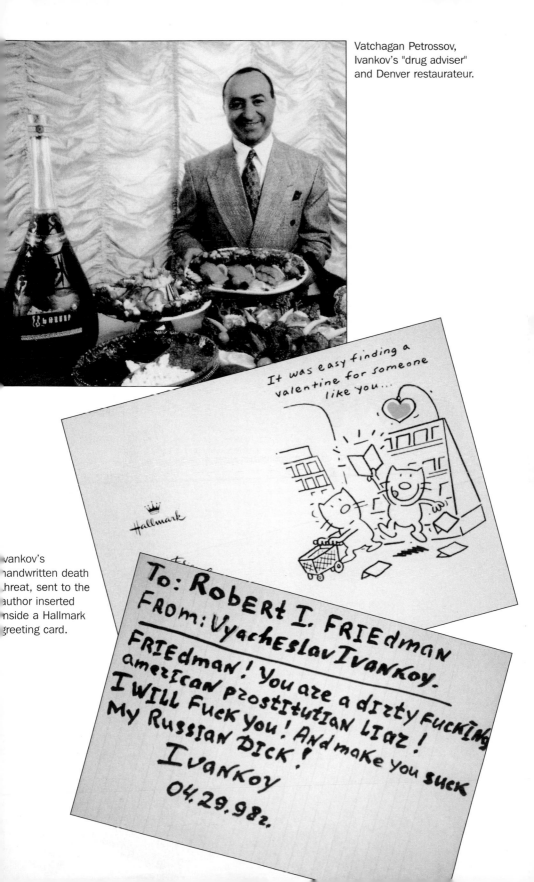

Vatchagan Petrossov, Ivankov's "drug adviser" and Denver restaurateur.

Ivankov's handwritten death threat, sent to the author inserted inside a Hallmark greeting card.

It was easy finding a valentine for someone like you...

Hallmark

To: RobeRT I. FRIEdmaN
FROm: Vyacheslav IvanKoy.

FRIEdman! You are a diRTy FuckIng
ameRican pRostItutIaN LIaz!
I WILL Fuck you! And make you suck
My RussIan DIcK!
IvanKoy
04.29.98z.

Porky's Strip Club in Miami, owned by Ludwig "Tarzan" Fainberg.

SPECIAL GUEST

APPEARING LIVE, NUDE ON STAGE!

GINA LAMARCA

'95 PENTHOUSE PET OF THE YEAR
INTERNATIONAL SUPER MODEL

As seen on
Howard Stern / Salley Jesse Rafael / Montel Williams
and in over 75 issues of Penthouse

3 SHOWS DAILY

6:30 pm • 9:30 pm • 11:30 pm
COME EARLY FOR BEST SEATING!

Thursday, May 11
EVENTS
Arm Wrestling Contest
Banana Eating Contest
Beer Drinking Contest
Best Fake Orgasm
(Cash Prizes)

Friday, May 12
EVENTS
Arm Wrestling Co
Beer Drinking Co
Best Fake Org
Best Lesbian S
(Cash Prize

SPECIAL THANKS TO PORKY'S FA
AND MR. BILL SEIDLE FAMILY
FOR GIVING ME THE OPPORTU
TO CREATE PORKY'S
LOVE YOU ALL
TARZAN

Porky's
ALL-GIRL REVUE

4th ANNUAL

PIG OUT PARTY
(2 Day Event)

THURSDAY, MAY 11, 1995
AND
FRIDAY, MAY 12, 1995
(With Invitation Only)

FREE DRINKS ★ FREE GIFTS
FREE GIRLS ★ FREE SEX
FREE BUFFET (Includes Our Famous Roast Pork)
BE FREE!!!
YOUR INVITED

Flyer from Porky's

Tarzan and Juan Almeida sampling the stock in a Swiss wine cellar.

Tarzan being shown subs in Kronstadt.

Tarzan and friend in Russia.

An armored car bringing sacks of $100 bills for the Russian *Mafiya* to be loaded on a Delta flight to Moscow at JFK Airport, New York. (© A. Tannenbaum/SYGMA)

Semion Mogilevich, the man the CIA calls the most dangerous gangster in the world. Mogilevich took out a hundred-thousand-dollar contract to kill the author, according to the *New York Times*. (Courtesy of ABCNews World News Tonight)

Incredibly, the two men managed to fend off their assailants. "You missed me! You missed me! You missed me!" Marina shrieked all the way to the hospital. "She had seventy stitches," Elson says. "You won't believe how many bullets and pellets she has in her chest." To this day, Marina has so many bullet fragments lodged in her body that she sets off metal detectors at airports.

Marina had been deliberately targeted. "We know she joined Monya on killing sprees," observed the DEA's Louis Cardenelli. "Our CIs [confidential informants] said that's the only way you could hit a woman." Moreover, if she had survived her husband, Cardenelli added, Marina had the authority to order Monya's Brigada to exact a swift and terrible revenge. (Mrs. Elson refused to comment.)

Having learned of the shootout, Major Case Squad detective Ralph Cefarello raced to the hospital. "Elson was laying there waiting for the docs to work on him, and I'm trying to question him," Cefarello recalled. "He played his usual game. He said politely, 'I'll tell you anything. I want to know who did this to me. But I didn't see the shooters.'" Before exiting the room, Cefarello brushed by Elson's bed, intentionally pulling off the bed sheets. The gangster was stark naked. The word MONYA, framed by two green bands, was emblazoned around Elson's penis.

"I had a kid in uniform who spoke Russian standing guard. They had no way of knowing he was Russian-speaking. As soon as I left the room, Elson turned to his wife and said, 'Don't tell these pigs a thing!'"

A short time after the incident, the FBI visited their bullet-marred apartment complex. Zapivakmine was sitting on their front porch, carefully surveying the street. In a confidential report of the meeting, the FBI wrote, "Elson indicated that he knew who was behind the shootings. Elson was particularly angry because of the shooting of his wife, and he stated that he would not rest until he gets his revenge. He said that his revenge will not occur in the United States but will happen somewhere overseas."

Unbeknownst to Elson, his bodyguard had been warned in advance of the shooting. A representative of the People's Court—the authoritative group of Russian organized crime leaders in Brighton Beach—told Zapivakime that Elson was going to be killed because he had committed too many unauthorized murders and extortions. They cautioned him not to interfere, according to a classified FBI report, but Zapivakmine ignored the admonition and had seriously injured a member of the "Streetsweeper" hit team who was brought to the same Coney Island hospital that was treating the Elsons. Two weeks later, Zapivakmine was shot in the back of the head while changing a flat tire in Brooklyn.

With Zapivakmine's execution, the balance of power began to shift. "Elson had very capable guys that he brought in as reinforcements from Israel and the former Soviet Union," said a Russian wiseguy. "But every week, one of them would get their heads blown off by a shotgun blast. Even Monya realized it was time to get out."

However, it was not Boris Nayfeld who finally convinced Elson to flee to Europe in November 1994. The force behind the "Streetsweeper" incident, the man who posed the first serious challenge to Elson's hegemony and had more resources than any other Russian gangster who had come before him, was Vyascheslav Kirillovich Ivankov, and the dreaded *vor* had come to the United States from Moscow to take over the Russian Jewish mob in America.

Ivankov had begun his outlaw career in the back alleys of Moscow in the early 1960s. By age fifteen, he was a cocky, bare-knuckled street brawler who beat up people for the fun of it. His hooliganism eventually attracted the attention of a large criminal organization headed by a notorious gangster named Gennadiy "the Mongol" Korkov, who specialized in turning Soviet star athletes and martial arts masters into extortionists. Under Korkov's tutelage, Ivankov was trained to shake down black marketeers, bribe-taking bureaucrats, and thieving store managers—all of them underground millionaires who could hardly risk reporting thefts to the State. Ivankov's crew invaded their homes, dressed as Soviet militiamen, armed with forged identification papers and search warrants. This "militia" would confiscate the victim's valuables, inventory the goods, and order the owner to show up in court the next day for further questioning. Of course, the merchandise would disappear along with Ivankov. A sophisticated racketeer for his day, the Mongol also added intelligence and counterintelligence wings to his operations, a lesson Ivankov would not forget.

With a taste for theatrics, the young Ivankov set out to build a mystique around himself. He expropriated the name of the legendary Russian bandit Yaponchick, which literally means "the little Japanese" in Russian. The original Yaponchick, whose given name was Mishka Vinnitsky, ran the seamy Jewish underworld in the pre-revolutionary Black Sea port of Odessa. Yaponchick and his gang became folk heroes when they joined the Red Army during the Revolution. Gang members tattooed their chests with the communist Red Star. Instead of being rewarded for their revolutionary zeal, however, they were imprisoned by the Bolsheviks soon after the war. (Yaponchick has since been the subject of many books and films, most notably *Benya Kirk*, a 1926 Soviet, Yiddish-language, silent film written by Isaac Babel.)

Ivankov's own career was temporarily derailed in 1974,

when the manager of a Moscow café complained to the real militia about his extortion demands. An entire detachment of Soviet militiamen was dispatched to apprehend Ivankov, who was found hiding in his car in a Moscow suburb. A sensational gun battle ensued, and Ivankov made a daring getaway. The shoot-out only enhanced his growing legend as a social bandit who stole from the wealthy parasites living off the workers. Ivankov also distinguished himself for his bravado, for while the U.S.S.R. had plenty of common criminals, they virtually never used weapons against the authorities.

Ivankov quickly became the target of one of the biggest manhunts in Soviet history. After six months on the run, the weary brigand finally turned himself in, claiming that he was not a criminal at all, but a paranoid schizophrenic. The more serious charges against him were dropped, and he was sentenced to five years in a Soviet psychiatric detention hospital. Eventually wearying of feigning mental illness, Ivankov asked to be retested and was subsequently sent to a penal colony. There he was quickly inducted into the brotherhood of the *vor v zakonye.*

After he was released from prison, Ivankov went back to work for the Mongol, becoming his senior associate. During the next two years, Ivankov committed hundreds of extortions and armed robberies, leaving behind him a long trail of mayhem and acts of mindless savagery. In 1981, for example, Ivankov and his crew broke into the apartment of a well-to-do black marketeer, brandishing their weapons. Handcuffing the terrified man to a bathroom radiator, Ivankov threatened to douse him with acid if he didn't pay back an alleged debt. With a gun jammed to his forehead, he was forced to sign a promissory note for 100,000 rubles; Ivankov then stole a Dutch Masters painting, a stamp collection, and 3,000 rubles. Ivankov was arrested for the home invasion in 1982 and charged with robbery, aggravated assault, and extortion, for which he was sentenced to fourteen years in a maximum security prison camp in Siberia. Because several of those arrested with him were famous Soviet athletes who had turned to crime, the authorities saw to it that the case received no publicity.

Back in prison, the despotic Ivankov once again became the top *vor*, enforcer, and kingpin. He stabbed one inmate in the back and clubbed a prison guard over the head with a metal stool. After several of his victims died, he was placed in a brutal punishment cell for a year. But the murders did not add time to Ivankov's prison sentence, because in the code of the "Zone," or the Gulag, the victims had brought their deaths on themselves by failing to obey the code of ethics of the thieves-in-law.

Even from prison, Ivankov was able to maintain control over the vast Vladivostok region in the Russian Far East, and increased his criminal power by establishing business enterprises as far away as Moscow, from which he received regular and substantial income. Once, with the help of two Russian accomplices from Toronto, he persuaded several major Russian banks and investors to buy $5 million worth of shares in a phony Siberian gold mining company. (One of the Russian banks sent a hit man to Toronto to terminate Ivankov's co-conspirators, but the Mounties arrested him.)

While Ivankov served out his sentence in the frigid wastelands of the U.S.S.R.'s vast penal colonies, major changes were taking place behind closed doors in Soviet crime and government. As early as the mid-1980s the KGB had notified the gray cardinals around Politburo boss Konstanin Chernenko that the Soviet Union's socialist economy was doomed; chronic corruption, inefficiency, and the enormously expensive arms race with the United States had bankrupted Lenin's revolution. The KGB recommended two options: one was a first-strike nuclear attack against the West, which was seriously considered by xenophobic elements who couldn't bear the prospect of losing the Cold War. The second option was to loot the bountiful motherland of its remaining wealth.

During Gorbachev's reign, the KGB began to hide communist party funds abroad, according to top-level Western and U.S. intelligence sources. The KGB consequently set up some two thousand shell companies and false-flag bank accounts, some as far away as Nevada and Ireland. Over the next eleven years, perhaps as much as $600 billion was spirited out of the country, in the greatest looting of a nation in world history. No matter what happened to Russia during a political transition from communism to a quasi-market economy under perestroika, the party bosses had effectively guaranteed that they would continue to control key state resources and property. Stealing such a massive amount of wealth, however, turned out to be a larger job than anyone had expected. The KGB ran out of people to sequester assets, so they expanded their operation to the criminal *Mafiya*, explained Richard Palmer, a twenty-year veteran of the CIA, whose final assignment was as a station chief in the former Soviet Union from 1992 to 1994.

In its haste to stash party funds, the KGB modernized the relatively small Soviet *Mafiyas*, which had previously been based along neighborhood, regional, and ethnic lines. They were outfitted with everything from the latest high-tech computers to sophisticated communications gear. After communism crumbled, many KGB men, military officers, and government officials went to work for the emerging *Mafiya* organizations. Young Russian entrepreneurs sporting MBAs from the best schools in Russia and the West also swelled their ranks.

By the early 1990s, organized crime in the Soviet Union

had evolved into a diabolical troika consisting of gun-wielding mobsters and *vors;* nomenklatura types and the black marketeers that tailed them like pilot fish; and many current and former members of the government, military, and security services. Nevertheless, *vors* like Ivankov still represented the pinnacle of organized crime. Like made guys in the American La Cosa Nostra, Russia's eight hundred thieves-in-law held varying degrees of position and power depending on their abilities. A *vor* could reign over a region as vast as Siberia, with a representative or supervisor (*smotryashchiy*) accountable to him in every regional city in which he had influence. A *vor* might control many *Mafiya* groups simultaneously, head an association of gangs, or lead a single gang. Some thieves-in-law might be part of the supply group (*obespechenie*) or the security group (*bezopasnosti*) in a *Mafiya* organization.

By the mid-1980s, there were nearly nine thousand criminal gangs in Russia with 35,000 members. During "privatization," the period when the government put everything from the great oil and gas giants to hotels in downtown Moscow up for sale, organized crime and the Russian government continued their mutually beneficial relationship. The criminals needed export licenses, tax exemptions, below-market-rate loans, business visas, and freedom from arrest and prosecution for their crimes. All of this and more was available from corrupt bureaucrats, especially since inflation had wiped out the savings of everyone in Russia who wasn't participating in the grab. A dozen or so "oligarchs" took over vast state properties and became among the wealthiest men in the world. As for law and order, police officers, for example, who didn't steal or take bribes were unlikely to be able to feed their families. A survey of Muscovites conducted in September 1994 by the Russian Academy of Sciences revealed that 70 percent of the respondents would not ask a Moscow police officer for help when threatened by a crime.

Soon nine leading *Mafiya* organizations controlled more than 40 percent of Moscow's economy. (Some experts say the figure is at least 80 percent.) Practically every business, from curbside kiosks to multinational corporations, paid protection money. "In 1917 we had the Bolshevik revolution, and all the rules changed," a Russian banker declared. "In the late 1980s, we had a *Mafiya* revolution, and the rules changed again. If you're a businessman you can either pay the mob, leave the country, or get a bullet through your brain." Russian criminal groups penetrated virtually every level of the government, from Russia's parliament, the Duma, to President Yeltsin's inner circle. Even the immense arsenals of the Soviet armed forces were plundered.

But in the gold rush years of the late 1980s and early 1990s, competition for the Soviet Union's booty inevitably led to gangland turf wars. The Chechen *Mafiya*, which had always been a powerful force in Moscow's turbulent under-world, called in reinforcements from their mountain redoubt in the republic of Chechnya. Relentless as the Golden Horde that had thundered across the Russian steppes and sacked the city in the Middle Ages, the group came close to gaining control over the city's rackets, leaving the formerly dominant Jewish, Georgian, Armenian, and Slavic mobs in disarray. Corrupt Soviet oligarchs started preparing their departure in order to avoid the carnage.

Ivankov's panicky colleagues desperately concluded that they, too, needed additional troops and that, more importantly, it was time to spring the powerful *vor* from jail. Ivankov's release was scheduled for late 1995, but in early 1990 two of the nation's most powerful mafiosi orchestrated a letter-writing campaign in support of his early parole. One of them, Otari Kvantrishvili, was a brawny, forty-six-year-old native of the former Soviet republic of Georgia. A national sports hero, Kvantrishvili had been a wrestler on the Soviet Olympic team, an all-European champion wrestler, and chairman of the prestigious Russian Athletes Association, a government-sponsored union. In the late 1980s, he set up the Twenty First Century Association, ostensibly as a charity to aid needy Russian athletes. Although the association also established banks, casinos, and other enterprises, in fact, "this notorious company has never had any legitimate business interests and was structured only as a front to conceal proceeds of extortions of Russian businessmen" and other crimes, as a secret FBI report revealed.

Ivankov's other powerful patron was Joseph Kobzon, the dapper, sixty-year-old Russian pop singer. A cultural icon, Kobzon was a household name to generations of Russian music lovers. He frequently brought Soviet leader Leonid Brezhnev to tears at public functions with his soulful renditions of patriotic ballads. But for decades, Kobzon had been using his star persona to hide a sinister criminal identity. According to the CIA, Kobzon was Russia's "crime Czar"; a secret FBI document described him as the "spiritual leader" of the Russian *Mafiya* in Moscow, who was "highly respected . . . because of his intelligence, contacts, shrewdness and ability to help when [organized crime] groups get into trouble. Not just anyone can gain his assistance, however; only high-level [mobsters]. He settles disputes between groups and belongs to no particular organization."

"Kobzon," says the FBI's James Moody, "is definitely one of the most influential criminals in Russia. He is very, very high-ranking. And very dangerous."

In the crime-addled Soviet Union, Kobzon's true status as a top crime boss didn't dissuade the Soviet government from appointing him to the Russian Olympic Committee, making him the dean of the School of Popular Music at Moscow's Music Academy, as well as Moscow's minister of culture, among other prestigious positions. The singer has twice been elected to the Duma. During his first stint in the late 1980s, he was formally introduced to the U.S. Senate by New Jersey Democrat Frank Lautenberg. Kobzon was elected to the Duma a second time in 1998 from a tiny, impoverished autonomous district in eastern Siberia near Russia's border with Mongolia, despite never having lived there—or even campaigning there during the election. Vladimir Grishin, the rival candidate, claimed that Kobzon's campaign manager doled out 100 million rubles in donations to local charities, 35 million rubles to a local hospital, and allegedly promised additional cash and a new fleet of buses for the district if he were victorious. Grishin filed fraud charges with the Central Election Commission, but nothing ever came of it.

One of Kobzon's most lucrative activities, however, was smuggling arms. For example, he was allegedly able to help maneuver a corrupt Russian Defense Ministry official, Viktor Atiolkin, into the top job at the Rossvoorvzheniya, the only government agency that can authorize the export of weapons from Russia. "This position can greatly assist OC figures in arranging sales of tanks, rocket-propelled grenades, surface-to-air missiles and possibly even nuclear materials," explains the FBI report. In one instance, Kobzon brokered the sale of surface-to-air missiles to Iran, according to a federal wiretap affidavit and a top investigator for U.S. Customs who specializes in the Russian mob.

Thanks to the efforts of Kvantrishvili and Kobzon, President Gorbachev and Supreme Soviet Chairman Boris Yeltsin received hundreds of additional letters from famous Russian scientists, artists, and politicians asserting that

Ivankov had been successfully rehabilitated. Even the warden of his Gulag prison grudgingly acknowledged that Ivankov "is not the worst inmate." To assure his release, the judge handling Ivankov's case was bribed by Semion Mogilevich, the Budapest-based don who has been implicated in laundering billions of dollars through the august Bank of New York; other payoffs went to a former Russian minister of internal affairs and an unidentified state prosecutor, according to classified FBI reports, U.S. court documents, State Department records, and interviews with senior U.S. and European law enforcement sources.

The campaign succeeded and Ivankov was freed in February 1991. His liberators quickly put him to work at their most critical task: to destroy the barbarians at the gate, the Chechen *Mafiya* invaders. Ivankov duly mounted an awesome offensive, employing a brigade composed of hundreds of hardened criminals. In typical Ivankov fashion, he went above and beyond the call of duty, wantonly massacring rival gangsters. His methods were, as always, cruel. Car bombings rocked the capital, casualties mounted, and the bloodbath became so violent that it began frightening away Western investors. Ivankov's excesses were infuriating the very politicians who had helped free him, for while stemming the Chechen tide, he had become a liability. "Ivankov had big problems," says the DEA's Cardenelli. "He had to leave. The Chechens were coming to kill him. Friends in the government told him that they wanted an end to the high-profile gangland war."

As a result, in early 1992 the Bratsky Krug, or the Circle of Brothers, the ruling council of the *vors*, is said to have ordered Ivankov to "Go to the New Land and invade America!"

INVASION OF AMERICA

Vyacheslav Kirillovich Ivankov's arrival in America on March 8, 1992, was tantamount to the coming of a great white shark. He was met at JFK airport by an Armenian *vor* who handed him a suitcase packed with $1.5 million in cash. Swiftly setting up offices in Brighton Beach, Ivankov recruited two "combat brigades" led by an ex-KGB officer and composed of 250 former athletes and Special Forces veterans of the Afghanistan war. He put the combat brigades on a $20,000-a-month retainer to kill his enemies, collect tribute from legitimate businesses worldwide, "arbitrate" disputes among Russian businessmen, and establish "an international link closely connecting thieves-in-law to the United States," according to a classified FBI document.

"When Ivankov came into town, I never saw such fear," remarked a Genovese wiseguy.

Soon after Ivankov appeared in New York, Alex Zilber,

still one of the most powerful forces in Brighton Beach, asked one of his Genovese partners to arrange a sit-down with him. The mobster offered to have the Italians kill Ivankov, but Alex pleaded with them not to go to war. "I'll be okay here in Brighton Beach," he said, "but they'll take me out in Russia [where he had extensive business interests]. Let's pay him." Ivankov celebrated his new partnership in Rasputin by hosting a lavish champagne party there.

The Old Guard of Russian Jewish gangsters had little choice but to cooperate with Ivankov. He was regarded as a prolific moneymaker, and many ranking members of the Brighton Beach mob were by then aging, quasi-legitimate businessmen who no longer had the fortitude for an extended gangland war. And as the Zilber brothers realized and hit man Moyna Elson soon discovered—resistance was futile. The "Streetsweeper" shooting, which precipitated Elson's flight, "put the fear of God" into the Old Guard, commented Elson's lawyer, James DiPietro. "We were amateurs compared to Ivankov and his men," observed Brighton Beach–based Jewish gangster Vladimir Ginzberg. "We had a criminal past, but not so rich like them."

Indeed, much of the fear that Ivankov inspired was due to the fact that he came invested with the full backing of Moscow's most powerful crime lords. Made affluent and powerful by the fall of communism, their gangs had grown unprecedently large and fierce, and enjoyed a wealth of resources in the corrupt former Soviet Union that dwarfed that of even the most significant Russian mob operations in the United States. Now, as perestroika bloomed, the *Mafiyas* based in the former Soviet Union began to reach across suddenly unrestricted national boundaries, sending their soldiers and bosses like Ivankov out around the globe to either reconnect with or conquer their comrades who had emigrated a generation earlier.

In fact, in the post-perestroika years, thousands of Russian thugs were easily slipping into the country. The understaffed and ill-equipped Immigration and Naturalization Service seemed helpless to stop them. Ivankov landed in the United States traveling under his own name, with an official foreign-travel passport. His visa, good for two weeks, had been obtained directly from the U.S. embassy in Moscow. He was sponsored by Manhattan-based shipping magnate Leonard Lev, a fifty-eight-year-old émigré who had started his career in time-honored fashion as a master pickpocket in Kiev before becoming a partner in Marat Balagula's gasoline operations and the Odessa restaurant.

Lev's Park Avenue company controlled a massive fleet of deepwater ships in Panama, which the government suspected of smuggling everything from coke to the latest model Ford Bronco, and of obtaining American visas for any number of mafiosi. "Bullshit," said Lev about the alleged smuggling. "I move chicken parts." If a ship's captain smuggled contraband, he was completely unaware of it, he told me.

Lev had created a "film" company called Twelve-LA, and wrote the U.S. embassy requesting a visa for Ivankov, saying he was a film consultant. Then Lev helped the recently arrived Ivankov enter into a sham marriage so he could apply for a green card and, after that, U.S. citizenship. Over drinks at the Odessa, Lev introduced Ivankov to an aging Russian lounge singer. She agreed to marry the *vor* for $15,000, getting her first installment from Lev in a cigarette box stuffed with $5,000 in crumpled greenbacks. Part of the deal was to get a quickie divorce in the Dominican Republic after Ivankov got his Social Security card.

Ivankov's criminal domain in the New World rapidly expanded into gambling, prostitution, and arms sales, as well as participation in gasoline tax fraud. In Brighton Beach, he had shrewdly placed reliable members of the Jewish *Organizatsiya*'s Old Guard like Lev as prime facilitators, using their knowledge about the American banking and criminal justice systems to obtain crooked lawyers, government contacts, passports, visas, and green cards.

"Ivankov brings with him the tradition of hard-core Russian criminals' dedication to their own authority and their experience in deception and corruption practiced under Communism," commented a classified FBI report. "While not abandoning extortion, intimidation and murder, Ivankov also incorporates more subtle and sophisticated modern methods which enable cooperation with other groups, the exploitation of weaknesses in legal and financial procedures, and the use of current Eastern European and Eurasian political and economic instability to further his empire."

In Miami, Ivankov allegedly took over a hidden share of Porky's, a strip club where he "was shown great homage" by the club's owner, Ludwig "Tarzan" Fainberg, a Russian crime lord, said U.S. intelligence sources, and also entered into a deal to provide heroin and money laundering services to the Cali cartel in exchange for cocaine, which was earmarked for Russia. In Denver, he obtained a hidden interest in a sprawling Russian restaurant from Vatchagan Petrossov, an Armenian *vor*, who was Ivankov's international drug adviser, asserts the FBI. Ivankov also bought large parcels of real estate in the Rocky Mountains. In Houston, he purchased a used car dealership for money laundering. In New Jersey, he met with Russian bankers about possible deals in Thailand, Brazil, and Sierra Leone, where he wanted to steal diamonds. Ivankov was fascinated with the complexities of Western banking, and listened intently as the bankers explained to him the intricacies of a financial instrument known as American depository receipts. In Manhattan, meanwhile, financial wizard Felix Komorov became his chief money launderer, according to the FBI.*

Outside the borders of North America, the cagey *vor* constantly traversed Europe, the Middle East, and Eurasia as restlessly as a nomad, keeping close links to his own formidable organization in Russia, which the Circle of Brothers allowed him to maintain. "It seems like I go from meeting to meeting, flying around," he wearily told an associate over a government wire. In the summer of 1994, Ivankov presided over two Appalachian-style sit-downs in Tel Aviv with his son Eduard, where dozens of gangsters gathered at the plush Dan Hotel to discuss their invest-

---

*Komorov, who headed a vicious extortion ring, also allegedly ran a complex advance fee scheme in which five Russian-American "salesmen" were sent to a trade show in Moscow in 1992, where they sold nonexistent electronic equipment and foodstuffs to some twenty Russian enterprises. It worked in this manner: In January 1992, according to a classified FBI report, a number of Russian and Ukrainian émigrés affiliated with a major Eurasian crime group "established an agreement with a scientific center in Russia for the use of the facilities and a bank account. They also established a front company and a respective commercial bank account in New York City. The bank account was opened with a false New York State driver's license. The address was a mail drop. Seized documents revealed approximately thirty other bank accounts associated with the New York front company. False identities of prominent U.S. citizens were used to open the accounts and establish short-term credit for the fraud scheme in Russia.

"Five persons acting as representatives of the front company subsequently perpetrated an advance fee scheme at a business exposition in Moscow," says the FBI report. "They sought out buyers of computer equipment and consumer goods, offering low prices. More than 20 Russian enterprises were victimized, making advance payments of over $6 million to the scientific center account. The front company then transferred the money to their other accounts without fulfilling contract obligations. The FBI and MVD [The Russian Internal Affairs Ministry] have traced $1 million of the illicit proceeds to New York City."

Of the five "salesmen," one accepted a plea bargain and received a five-month jail term. Two others cooperated with the government and entered the Federal Witness Protection Program. Another "salesman" was captured by the Russian authorities and imprisoned, and a fifth is still waiting to be sentenced in New York. Komorov was never charged.

ments in the Jewish state, according to U.S. and Israeli intelligence sources. During his global travels he also recruited the most intelligent, ruthless, and boldest young Russian criminals for his U.S. operations. Wooing them with promises of the "good life," according to a classified FBI report, he opened bank accounts for them and provided credit cards and automobiles for their use. Ivankov himself "seems always able to reenter the United States undetected after each trip," declared an FBI report.

Ivankov also reinforced old relationships with leaders of various Eurasian criminal underworld groups, such as the Budapest-based Mogilevich organization and the *Solntsevskaya* family, Moscow's mightiest criminal enterprise, which had more than 1,700 members. Its neighborhood stronghold in the suburbs of southern Moscow was where the communists released criminals when they were freed from the Gulag. These hoodlums and their offspring grew into tough mob leaders who flourished during perestroika when they seized more than eighty commercial companies, prime real estate, hotels, and other property. The *Solntsevskaya* organization is divided into ten- to twelve-member combat brigades, which are headed by criminal *avoritets*. Each unit controls assigned banks and business concerns in Moscow and the suburbs. At the same time, the group has a shared fund, or an *obshchak*, to which all brigades allocate money on a regular basis. When friction arises, members of several brigades come together to negotiate.

With other crime groups, however, Ivankov battled for territory. He was particularly determined to dominate the nascent Russian trade in cocaine, a drug that had quickly soared in popularity among the nation's nouveaux riches. Two Russian criminals stood in his way. One was the Georgian *vor* Valeri "Globus" Glugech, the first gangster to set up large-scale drug importation to Moscow from suppliers in the United States, a venture that made him a wealthy man. Ivankov invited Globus to visit the United States in early 1993 and "offered" to buy out his operation, a proposal Globus refused. In March 1993, Globus was shot to death by a sniper outside a discotheque he owned in Moscow. Three days later, his principal lieutenant, Anatoly Semionov, was gunned down in front of his Moscow apartment. Two weeks after that, another top aide, Vladislav Wanner, was killed at an open-air gun range in Moscow. At a May 1994 sit-down in Vienna, the heads of several Russian organized crime groups officially awarded Ivankov the remnants of Globus's drug business.

The next Russian drug kingpin to fall was Elson's friend Sergei "Sylvester" Timofeyev, who directed his mob's activities from Cyprus. Timofeyev and Ivankov had had a long-standing beef. Ivankov had an illegitimate son, Viktor Nikiforov, also known as Kalina, who had become a thief-in-law and a powerful figure in the Moscow underworld while his father was in prison. Just before Ivankov was released, Kalina was murdered. Most underworld figures believed Sylvester had ordered the hit, although no one could prove it.

Typically, however, Russian gangsters do not let their personal animosities stand in the way of their business, and the two men continued to make deals. In July 1994, Sylvester and Ivankov completed a drug transaction, after which Sylvester complained that he had been shortchanged by $300,000. A few weeks later Sylvester traveled to New York to work out the dispute with Ivankov. The meeting ended with the two cursing and shouting at each other, Ivankov accusing Timofeyev of having murdered Kalina, as well as assassinating his friend Otari Kvantrishvili outside a Moscow bathhouse. One month after the altercation, Sylvester was blown apart in Moscow by a car bomb placed in his Mercedes, and he had to be identified by his dental records.

Ivankov also nurtured his high-level contacts with corrupt Russian government leaders, as well as with former leaders of Russian intelligence and military services. He employed high-profile former foreign government officials as his international "diplomats." One such figure was Tofik Azimov, the former principal representative of the Republic of Azerbaijan to the European Economic Community. Azimov was handpicked by Ivankov to provide a "legitimate" front for Atkom, a "consulting firm" that allegedly laundered tens of millions of dollars out of a $10,000-a-month office suite in Vienna. The city is popular with Russian mobsters because of its strict banking secrecy laws, its three-hour flight time from Moscow, and its abundance of corrupt state bureaucrats. The money laundering operation was, in fact, directed by Ivankov's son Eduard, who "conducts a wide array of financial and banking transactions throughout Central and Western Europe (including England) in an effort to launder proceeds of Ivankov's illegal activities," according to the FBI. Atkom employed two female secretaries, a former member of the Austrian Special Forces who worked as an armed bodyguard, and a Russian emigrant and an Austrian citizen who did nothing but process banking transactions and money transfers, according to a classified Austrian police document. Azimov came in handy when two *Solntsevskaya* crime lords had to leave Russia because of attempts on their lives; it was he who arranged for the mobsters' visas through Atkom. As stunned FBI officials later learned, the Russian gangsters were even welcomed into the country by Viennese police officers with gifts of semiautomatic Glock pistols "for self-defense."

Within just a year after he arrived in the "New Land,"

Ivankov had succeeded in extending his insidious influence from Austria to Denver to the icy Baltic republics. His organization was visionary, well managed, efficient, wealthy, merciless, and expanding. He muscled into Russia's oil, aluminum, and arms businesses. Tens of millions of dollars of illicit proceeds was laundered through the U.S. banking system. He frequently used front companies, through cooperation or extortion, to facilitate money laundering and the sponsorship of "business associates" for visas to enter the United States. It was said by his associates that he could provide millions of dollars in credit to finance a deal with a single phone call. His vast power was "propelled by a network of influential contacts and seemingly unlimited funds," said a classified FBI report. "Ivankov is a shrewd and respected leader over a group of ruthless members knowledgeable in business, financial, legal, and government operations. In addition to extortion, money laundering, drug trafficking, Ivankov is suspected of not only arranging numerous murders but bragging about them."

By January 1995, Ivankov and the Russian mob had grown so bold that they even convened a summit in the U.S. commonwealth of Puerto Rico, at the San Juan Hotel and Casino. Shortly before the rendezvous, Toronto-based Russian crime figure Joseph Sigalov was overheard on a Royal Canadian Mounted Police wiretap boasting that he was going to Puerto Rico "with Yaponchick [Ivankov] . . . to discuss who we will kill, fuck!" Known by his gangland friends as Mr. Tomato because of his oversized head, Sigalov was the publisher of *Exodus*, an influential Orthodox Jewish newspaper in Toronto sponsored by the Chabad movement, which was active in resettling Russian Jewish refugees. Sigalov also owned a bakery and was a venture capitalist.

Robert Kaplan, Canada's solicitor general in charge of the Royal Canadian Mounted Police and the Canadian

Security Intelligence Service (the nation's CIA) from 1980 to 1984, and a member of Parliament for twenty-five years until he stepped down in 1993, was Sigalov's business adviser for thirteen months beginning sometime in 1994. Kaplan said that charges that Sigalov was a mobster were "ridiculous . . . and hard to believe. . . . It was never an issue for me while I was working for him . . . because there was nothing reported about it then or said about it. No one in the community said this is someone to stay away from and no one did say that. He was very active in the Russian Jewish community in Toronto, which was rapidly growing," adding that Sigalov helped the émigrés join synagogues and rediscover their religion.

But Sigalov's good deeds and legitimate business affairs were little more than a cover for international heroin smuggling, arms trafficking, and extortion. In one incident, Ivankov ordered Sigalov and Vyacheslav Sliva, the godfather of Russian organized crime in Canada, to have their henchmen visit the mayor of Kharkov in Ukraine. The thugs not only strong-armed the mayor into paying protection money to operate the city-run casino, but for good measure also took over control of Ukraine's state-sponsored lottery, according to the RCMP.

Sigalov and Ivankov were joined at the Puerto Rican concalve by the elite of the Russian underworld: along with Joseph Kobzon and mob leaders from Georgia, St. Petersburg, Miami, and Brighton Beach were Viktor Averin and Sergei Mikhailov, heads of the *Solntsevskaya* organization. Although the Puerto Rican meeting was supposed to be a discussion about "who we will kill, fuck," the mob bosses seized the occasion to express their ire at Ivankov. They were incensed over his reckless behavior, accusing him of gratuitously murdering dozens of Russian cops, customs officers, and tax police in his unbridled quest to dominate Rus-

sia's drug trade. The violence was attracting too much attention from the law and ruining everybody's business, they
complained. When they patiently tried to work out an equi-
table division of the drug spoils, an implacable Ivankov simply refused. Miraculously, the mobsters did manage to agree
on several mutually beneficial rubouts without a quarrel.

Not surprisingly, Kobzon offered a far different version
of the events in Puerto Rico to a Russian newspaper. He
claimed that he had traveled to the Caribbean to enjoy an
old-fashioned vacation with several family members and
close friends, including Valery Weinberg, publisher of the
Manhattan-based *Novoye Russkoye Slovo*, the largest and
most influential Russian-language daily newspaper in America. With a circulation of some 180,000, it reaches nearly
every Russian émigré home in New York, Pennsylvania,
New Jersey, and Connecticut, where more than 300,000
now live. The paper is unique among the dozens of Russian
publications in America for its routine glorification of the
Russian mob and its vilification of U.S. law enforcement,
especially the FBI, further contributing to the alienation of
an émigré group that has bountiful enough reasons to suspect authority. The paper's editorial slant has helped to
keep the émigré community insular and suspicious. Nevertheless, in March 1999, Weinberg received the prestigious
"outstanding leadership" award for his work on behalf of
Soviet Jewry from the UJA-Federation, a large, nationwide
Jewish philanthropic organization. Weinberg's wife, Lilly, is
the UJA's New York Russian division chairwoman. The
awards dinner was held at Manhattan's luxurious Plaza
Hotel and the featured speaker was Senator Charles
Schumer, the junior Democratic senator from New York,
who said that "as you better yourselves, you better America. Those who say you should close the doors to immigration should come into this ballroom." The ballroom included

Weinberg's friends, some of whom have used business success and philanthropy to, in effect, launder their questionable pasts, and rub shoulders with the unwitting elite of the American Jewish community.

Weinberg's philanthropy extended to writing character references for Kobzon after the United States State Department revoked Kobzon's visa and banned him from entering the country in June 1995 because of his *Mafiya* ties. Although Weinberg says he never met Ivankov or any other mobster while vacationing in Puerto Rico, Kobzon recalled socializing with the engaging *vor*. "When he recited [Russian poet Sergei] Yesenin by heart, I thought, 'well, this is a swell guy.'"*

"We spent a wonderful time with our families," Kobzon went on. "I have a photograph where we are all together in Puerto Rico," recounted the singer, who favors pancake makeup, eyeliner, and a thick black toupee shaped into a pompadour. "We spent days on the beach. In the evenings we relaxed. We had a daily regimen. We went to restaurants—then to the casino. . . . This was all in one hotel. And that's how it lasted for several days straight. Then Slava Fetisov [the former NHL superstar and now a coach for the New Jersey Devils] came to see us for two days. Then Anzor Kikalishvili [who succeeded Otari Kvantrishvili as president of the mobbed-up Twenty First Century Association, which helped Ivankov win his early release from the Gulag] called from Miami and said: 'Guys, it's very dull here. How is it where you are? Can I join you for a day?'

"'Come, Come.' So he came for a day."

FBI agents monitoring the summit loitered around the

---

*Disillusioned with the Russian Revolution and his failed marriages to the American dancer Isadora Duncan and to Sophia Tolstoy, Yesenin committed suicide in 1925. His poetry celebrated peasant life and nature.

hotel wearing paisley shirts, trying to look inconspicuous, and filming as much as they could from behind potted plants. After the Russians departed, agents scoured Kobzon's hotel room for incriminating evidence and retrieved a matchbook in a wastepaper basket with Ivankov's name and Brooklyn phone number on it. They also discovered that calls had been placed to Ivankov's cell phone from Kobzon's hotel room.*

This is what the FBI was reduced to. Scrounging around Kobzon's room, looking for clues, and picking up matchbooks out of garbage cans. The FBI had inaugurated its Russian organized crime unit only some eight months earlier. Already playing a bad game of catch-up, it was ill prepared for the tidal wave of Russian criminals unleashed on the world by the dissolution of the Soviet Union. Apart from what it learned from a few scattered prosecutions, the bureau was still largely in the dark about how this new Red Menace operated, who controlled it, and steps that might be taken to stop it. The FBI did realize, however, that it had to act fast.

Unfortunately, the chronically turf-jealous FBI barely cooperated with the government's other investigative bodies who were also investigating the Russians, such as the INS, the IRS, and the DEA. To make matters worse, local police forces were kept almost completely in the dark. (In 1999, relations between the influential FBI office in New York and the Manhattan district attorney's office—which were conducting separate investigations into money laundering charges at the Bank of New York by the Russian mob—became so hostile that the bureau announced that any agency that got in its way would be slammed with

---

*In the summer of 1999, Kobzon's suite of luxury offices at the Intourist Hotel inside the same building that houses the Twenty First Century Association was bombed. Kobzon escaped injury.

obstruction-of-justice charges, according to the *New York Times*.) The FBI preferred to operate independently, poring over wiretap transcripts of suspected mobsters, tailing suspects, recruiting informants, and generally trying to gather intelligence on the burgeoning Russian *Mafiya*.

Despite Ivankov's flagrant, multinational criminal activities, during his first years in America, the FBI had a hard time even locating him. "At first all we had was a name," says the FBI's James Moody. "We were looking around, looking around, looking around, and had to go out and really beat the bushes. And then we found out that he was in a luxury condo in Trump Towers" in Manhattan.*

But almost as soon as they found him, he disappeared again leaving nothing but vapor trails for the FBI to follow. "Ivankov," explained an FBI agent, "didn't come from a walk-and-talk culture," like Italian gangsters who take walks to discuss family business so they can't be bugged or overheard by the bureau. "As soon as he'd sniff out the feds, he'd go into hiding for days at a time," a trait that made him harder to keep tabs on than Italian mobsters.

"He was like a ghost to the FBI," says Gregory Stasiuk, the New York State Organized Crime Task Force special investigator. Stasiuk picked up Ivankov's trail at the Taj Mahal in Atlantic City, the Trump-owned casino that the real estate magnate boasted was the "eighth wonder of the world." The Taj Mahal had become the Russian mob's favorite East Coast destination. As with other high rollers, scores of Russian hoodlums received "comps" for up to $100,000 a visit for free food, rooms, champagne, cartons of cigarettes, entertainment, and transportation in stretch

---

*A copy of Ivankov's personal phone book, which was obtained by the author, included a working number for the Trump Organization's Trump Tower Residence, and a Trump Organization office fax machine.

limos and helicopters. "As long as these guys attract a lot of money or spend a lot of money, the casinos don't care," a federal agent asserted. Russian mobsters like Ivankov proved a windfall for the casinos, since they often lost hundreds of thousands of dollars a night in the "High-Roller Pit," sometimes betting more than $5,000 on a single hand of blackjack. "They're degenerate gamblers," says Stasiuk. Although the FBI still couldn't find Ivankov, Stasiuk managed to tail him from the Taj Mahal to shipping mogul Leonard Lev's sprawling home on a dead-end street in Far Rockaway, Queens, and on another occasion, from the Taj to the Paradise Club, a notorious Russian mob haunt in Sheepshead Bay, Brooklyn, then managed by godfather Marat Balagula's youngest daughter, Aksana, the onetime aspiring optometrist.

So wily did Ivankov prove to be that the FBI couldn't gather enough evidence against him to convince a federal judge to grant a wiretap. The Canadian Mounties eventually came to the bureau's aid, for they had recorded numerous conversations between Sliva and Ivankov plotting various crimes. The grateful feds used the recordings to win a court-authorized wiretap to listen in on his multiple telephones, which provided the fullest picture yet of the *vor*'s world.

In one monitored phone conversation, Ivankov was barely able to conceal his rage when a colleague in Russia described how several mob associates were shot to death in an ambush in downtown Moscow by a rival gang. In another transatlantic call, an accomplice told Ivankov that two deputy mayors in Moscow who were on Ivankov's payroll were becoming too independent-minded. "They are trying to get involved in politics and they are fucking wanting to get rid of us," complained Ivankov's comrade. "These people are our tribe."

"I'm trying to solve the problem with the deputy mayor," Ivankov brusquely replied.

In another call, an underworld confidant told Ivankov that he had an Israeli gangster "beaten severely" for trying to cheat him on a diamond deal.

"It's not enough just to beat him . . . this fucking animal," Ivankov growled.

When Ivankov learned that a piece of property in Russia he had coveted was taken over by a rival mob, he screamed, "No fucking way! I'll fuck them all, the living and the dead!"

Ivankov had many prosaic conversations about the philosophy of the *vors* with Moucheg (aka Misha) Azatian, an imposing enforcer type who lived in Los Angeles. The code of the *vor*—which Ivankov called "human law"—was pure, honest, and uncorrupted by politics. He ridiculed the political pretensions that were the foundation of perestroika, declaring that it was merely a cynical plot devised by the ruling class to control the populace. After perestroika "they'll invent something different, again and again, and this is an endless process," he told Misha. "But in any case, everything is fine, brother. We live according to human law. And according to the law of our mini-state, everything is done in an honorable and honest way. And that's it."

"Of course, brother," Misha replied. "There is nothing better than human law, and that's the only important thing in the world."

"Of course, conscience and honor—that's the only law we keep," Ivankov reminded him.

The FBI got particularly lucky in the autumn of 1994 when Bank Chara in Moscow collapsed under suspicious circumstances, costing its depositors more than $30 million. Some $3.5 million of the money had been invested in Summit International, a New York investment house that had been founded by two of Chara's Russian board members, Alexander Volkov and Vladimir Voloshin. The Summit executives were no strangers to organized crime. Volkov, Summit's president, is a thin, wiry, chain-smoking ex-KGB officer with a noxious temper. Voloshin, Summit's VP, is a member of the *Lyubertskaya* crime family in Moscow, where he had once mixed up a target's address and torched the wrong apartment, as well as its female inhabitant. Their unlicensed Wall Street investment firm was actually a giant Ponzi scheme, preying mostly on Russian émigrés who were promised up to 120 percent per annum returns on phony companies with names like "Silicon Walley." To cover itself in a cloak of fiscal respectability, Summit entered into a contract with Prudential Securities vice president Ronald Doria to serve as its financial adviser. (Doria was later terminated by Prudential, and took the Fifth, refusing to testify, during a National Association of Securities Dealers arbitration hearing.) Between 1993 and 1995, Volkov and Voloshin took in $8 million from investors, spending nearly the entire sum on their own lavish entertainment: beautiful women, long weekends in the Caribbean, and gambling junkets to Atlantic City. In one night alone, Voloshin lost $100,000 at Bally's Hotel; he covered it with his investors' money.

In the spring of 1995 Bank Chara's new president, Roustam Sadykov, flew to New York to ask Summit's directors to return the bank's missing funds. When the men refused, Sadykov turned to Ivankov to collect the debt. "This should be fairly simple," Ivankov told an accomplice over a government wire. "If you call the men and use my name that makes people do what they are supposed to do." When Ivankov and two henchmen paid a visit to Summit's Wall Street offices, Volkov and Voloshin fled in terror to Miami. But Ivankov's men caught up with them when they returned to Manhattan, kidnapping them at gunpoint from the bar of the Hilton Hotel and forcing them to sign a contract promising to pay one of Ivankov's associates $3.5 million. "You understand who you are dealing with?" snarled Ivankov to the Summit officials. As an inducement to honor their commitment, Voloshin's father was stomped to death in a Moscow train station.

Unbeknownst to Ivankov, however, the pair had informed the FBI of the extortion. Voloshin had initially flown to San Francisco to implore members of the Moscow-based *Lyubertskaya* crime family, which had a modest contingent in California, to help him rid himself of Ivankov, but when they declined, Voloshin and Volkov were left with the FBI as their only recourse.

On the morning of June 8, 1995, a squad of FBI agents yanked a sleepy-eyed Ivankov from his mistress's bed in Brighton Beach. They found a gun in the bushes outside the apartment and $75,000 in cash on the kitchen table. One of the documents that was seized contained the name of a Russian banker who was hiding in the United States with his wife and children. Although the FBI would have preferred to arrest Ivankov on bigger charges, and had been trying to gather evidence to assemble a racketeering case against him, they had no choice but to arrest him for extortion before he could kill the Russian bankers. As he was being led into the FBI building, a defiant Ivankov kicked and spit at reporters. "I eat my enemies for dinner," he sneered.

Ivankov might actually have avoided conviction had he shown his six co-defendants that same degree of loyalty he demanded from them. Incarcerated at the Manhattan Correctional Center awaiting trial with his underlings, Ivankov tried to bully them, dictating which attorneys they should hire, and instructing them how to subordinate their defense strategy to his. He warned that anyone who did not follow his orders would be his "enemy for life."

Still, there were rebellions. One day, Ivankov and his cohorts gathered in a tobacco-filled day room at MCC to figure out how to spin incriminating wiretap conversations. According to FBI interviews with Ivankov's gang, Yakov "Billy Bombs" Volovnik, a nervous cokehead, who had a prior conviction for his role in a Russian mob jewelry theft ring, pleaded with Ivankov for funds to hire a decent attorney. Ivankov refused, ordering him to get the money from Leonid Abelis, the man who had been in charge of the day-to-day operations of the extortion plot.

"I have no money to spare," complained the six-foot, 220-pound, thirty-seven-year-old Abelis, a former machinist in Russia. "I'm paying for my own lawyer. I have my own family to think about."

"What, I do not have a family?" Ivankov angrily replied.

When the hulking Abelis started to rise from his chair, the 150-pound, five-foot-four-inch, fifty-seven-year-old *vor* grabbed him by the shoulders and growled, "Sit down, you whore! I will settle everything with you shitheads!"

Billy Bombs pulled the men apart, warning them not to quarrel in prison where they were undoubtedly under surveillance.

Ivankov spared no expense for his own defense, hiring Barry Slotnick for a sum of $750,000. The fee was underwritten by the sale of property in upstate New York owned by shipping magnate Leonard Lev; the proceeds were routed through a company in Monrovia, Liberia, according to a U.S. Customs agent. (Lev denies that he had anything to do with the defense costs and, in fact, didn't even control the property at that time.) Whatever the case, Ivankov left his co-defendants to fend for themselves. But Abelis — who had fought with Ivankov over money — believed that he was being set up by Slotnick and Ivankov as the fall guy, and turned state's evidence. Billy Bombs Volovnik quickly followed suit.

Still, the government's case had holes. Ivankov had carefully insulated himself by generally staying on the sidelines while his henchmen made the extortion threats, invoking his name to induce terror. Furthermore, the Summit executives scarcely fit the role of sympathetic victims. Not only had they stolen millions of dollars from their Russian-American clients, but according to court testimony, they had also taken more than $30 million from Russian banks before coming to America.

Slotnick, who had just concluded a long mental competency hearing for his client Genovese crime boss Vincent Gigante, seemed unprepared during the crucial opening stages of Ivankov's trial. He unconvincingly tried to portray the Russian godfather as a kind of Robin Hood who was guilty of nothing more than defending Bank Chara from greedy career criminals. Indeed, Slotnick argued, Ivankov was a Russian national hero who had been defying communism since grade school, spending half his life in the Gulag rather than being forced to sing the "Internationale."

But Abelis's testimony proved devastating. Not only did he establish Ivankov as the mastermind of the Summit extortion, but for good measure, he described Ivankov's shakedown of the Rasputin nightclub. After a five-week trial, the jury took just three hours to convict Ivankov and his associates of extortion. Voloshin and Volkov went into the Federal Witness Protection Program. In a subsequent trial, Ivankov and Leonard Lev were convicted for conspiring to arrange the sham marriage that allowed Ivankov to stay in the United States.

At the sentencing for the second case, Slotnick's partner, Jay Shapiro, compared Ivankov to Soviet Jewish

refuseniks, Jews in Nazi Germany, and Alexander Solzhenitsyn. ("To use his [Ivankov's] name in the same sentence as
Solzhenitsyn is a sacrilege," the FBI's Raymond Kerr later
remarked.) Ivankov was nevertheless smacked with a nine-
and-a-half-year jail term for the two convictions. "Let them
put me on the chopping block — let them crucify me on a
cross," snarled Ivankov. "I'm tough. I will survive!"

In many respects, Ivankov does survive. Not only did he
pave the way for the Russian *Mafiya*'s second wave to
invade America, putting in place a significant web of businesses and criminal relationships, a legacy that could later
be exploited by other mobsters, but, according to several
North American law enforcement agencies and Italian
crime bosses, Ivankov continued to run a sophisticated
crime empire from the federal prison in Lewisburg, giving
orders in ancient dialects like Assyrian and using criminal
codes the FBI has yet to master. "The FBI, the MVD, the
FSB [the former KGB] have stolen my life from me," he
told a Russian newspaper. "I have a list of who committed
these crimes — both on the side of Russia and on the side of
the FBI. . . . I know who all these people are. And I warn
them that they will answer for their crimes."

In the winter of 1999, Ivankov was found with heroin in
his cell and traces of the narcotic were detected in his
urine. He was transferred to a maximum-security wing at
Allenwood Federal Penitentiary.

TARZAN

In the middle of Miami's shabby warehouse district near Hialeah Race Track stood a squat, windowless one-story building. As its name implied, Porky's was a strip club, though it was much seedier than its namesake in the movie of the same title. In its dimly lit corridors, working-class Cuban men from the nearby rough-and-tumble neighborhoods pawed topless dancers, or received jiffy blow jobs for a few dollars a pop. In a filthy, dungeonlike office, away from the ear-splitting disco music and the smoky bar where strippers solicited lap dances, Rocky, the forty-two-year-old day manager, remembered better days, when Porky's was run by a brawny Russian gangster known as Tarzan. "Ivankov was here surrounded by three goons," Rocky told me. "I saw Ivankov with my own eyes. Did Ivankov and Tarzan know each other? Oh, yeah! Did they do business together? No question. The Russian mob came in all the time."

Porky's was once a howling, hedonistic beacon for Russian wiseguys from Tashkent to Brighton Beach. Gangsters craving sultry young, $1,000-a-night Eurasian prostitutes, Colombian cocaine, and Soviet-era weapons knew Porky's was the place to come to. Recreational drugs, bootlegged boxes of Philip Morris cigarettes, and stolen bottles of ice-cold Stolichnaya vodka could be procured just as easily. The club was abuzz with so much Russian mob activity that even local policemen jokingly referred to it as Redfellas South.

Rocky pointed out a memento from Tarzan's glory days: a framed photo of the club's most famous stripper, mega porn star Amber Lynn, who charged $25,000 a week to perform. "The regular dancers [at Porky's] didn't get paid," said Rocky, who was once a bodyguard for one of the biggest Colombian drug lords in Florida and had emptied a thirty-round Mac-10 clip into a nightclub during a gangland dispute. "They worked on tip money, much of which I suspect was kicked back to Tarzan." Adorning the wall was also a promotional flyer for Porky's fourth anniversary party, featuring a photo montage of Tarzan fondling a series of exotic dancers. In one shot, he leered directly into the camera, while two big-haired, blond strippers pressed their enormous bosoms into each side of his face. Rocky said the flyer used to hang in the office next to a photo of Tarzan's four-year-old daughter. "Tarzan doesn't care about anyone except himself. He has no loyalty to anyone. One night he cut the commissions the girls get on drinks. They went ballistic. I said, 'Wait till the end of the shift. They are threatening to go on strike.' He backed off. I said, 'Why do you always have to screw everything up?' He was a piece of shit!"

On a September day at the tail end of Hurricane Floyd, when rain was still soaking the blacktops, I took a taxi to

the Federal Detention Center in downtown Miami to interview Tarzan. His real name is Ludwig Fainberg, and he was,
until the feds nabbed him, the flamboyant ringleader of the
South Florida Russian mob. When I got to the prison, the
guards relieved me of my passport, my keys, and a pack of
chewing gum. "It'll cost us $2,000 to unjam a lock from
that gum if an inmate gets ahold of it," I was told by way of
explanation. After passing through a metal detector and
two machines that monitored my hand, which had been
coded with incandescent ink, I was led to a large, open rec-
tangular room where prisoners in gray jumpsuits silently
waited for their lawyers and guests.

In a glass-walled cubicle at the back of the room, I spotted Tarzan, a huffy, thirty-eight-year-old man with a grim
glare, slumped over a brown Formica table. He used to have
wild, acid-rock-size hair, but it was shorn now; he once took
pride in a steroid-enhanced, muscular physique, but when I
saw him he looked like a deflated inner tube. He slammed
a thick document down on the table. It was his indictment,
and it was a heavy load. Conspiracy to distribute cocaine
and heroin. Weapons trafficking. "It says, 'The U.S.A. vs.
Ludwig Fainberg,'" he griped. "Who can fight the U.S. government?" He sounded like an adolescent. "I already spent
a million dollars on lawyers," he said.

Tarzan first became conspicious in Miami in the early
1990s. He had all the makings of a successful mobster: he
was greedy (he held numerous fund-raisers for various
charities and the state of Israel, pocketing 85 cents of every
dollar, according to the DEA; Tarzan is adamant that he
never stole from Jewish charities); he was ruthless (he once
forced a woman to eat gravel); and he was ambitious (he
once brokered a complicated negotiation involving the
transfer of a Russian military submarine to Colombian nar-
cotraffickers).

In Russia, Tarzan told me, dishonesty is a trait that's bred in the womb. Deprivation teaches Russians to be cunning predators—it's the only way to survive, he said. Americans, on the other hand, are trusting souls. Their rules, Tarzan figured, were made to be broken.

Ludwig Fainberg was born in Odessa in 1958. When he was three, his family moved to Chernovtsi, a small city in western Ukraine. He sang in a national boys choir, and was trained in a boxing program set up by the Soviet military. "When I was a kid everything that I did made people laugh," he said. His inspiration was a Soviet comedy team that was similar in style to that of the Three Stooges. His stepfather, who manufactured Persian rugs and thick fur hats for a Soviet factory, was a dealer on the burgeoning black market. He'd trade rugs and fur caps for choice cuts of meat, some of which he'd barter for hard-to-get items, such as theater tickets. Then he'd trade the tickets for something more valuable—fresh vegetables.

One day in 1972, when Ludwig was thirteen, his parents announced that they were moving the family to Israel, where they hoped to increase their already considerable wealth. Ludwig, who had never known the family to identify with Judaism in any way, was confused. "Jew" was just something stamped on their passport, he thought, signifying their ethnic group. To him, being Jewish simply meant having certain privileges. "Jews were the richest people in town," he told me. "Jews had cars, Jews had money, Jews lived in nice apartments. We were comfortable. My mother had nice clothes and jewelry. We took a vacation once a year to Odessa, a stunning city with a boardwalk and gorgeous beaches. It was filled with mobsters and entertainers. It was a city with a Jewish flavor."

In Russia refuseniks—Jews who had denounced communism and were denied an exit visa — were sometimes accorded a touch of grudging respect. But in many cases Jews like the Fainbergs, who left for economic reasons, were despised. When Ludwig's teachers learned that he was moving to Israel, he was forced to stand in front of the six-hundred-member student body and denounced as a traitor. On the way home, he says, he was beaten by classmates. "Why do we have to be Jewish," Tarzan cried to his parents.

Before leaving, the Fainbergs converted their money into gold and diamonds, stashing some in shoes with false bottoms and hiding the rest in secret compartments of specially built tables and chairs, which they shipped to Israel. There, Ludwig lived on a kibbutz. According to his friends, that's where he got his nickname — he bestowed it upon himself after jumping off the fourth floor of a building to attract attention.

Tarzan, who soon stood at six feet one, joined the Israeli navy and applied to the elite Navy SEALS commando unit. But he washed out during basic training, and served the remaining three years of his service in the main weapons room of a destroyer. He wanted to be an officer but failed the exam. "I did not have enough brains," he told a reporter. "It was a very difficult exam."

In 1980, a restless Tarzan moved to East Berlin. He had one Russian friend in the city who had official-looking medical diplomas — just one of the many varieties of forged documents the Russian mob had for sale. The friend asked Tarzan if he wanted to be a doctor, too. "Are you crazy?" Tarzan said incredulously. "Do you think I want to kill patients?" He settled for a dental technician's license, but his gross incompetence got him fired from seven jobs in a row.

Like many young Russian émigrés in East Berlin, Tarzan

joined a mob crew. He specialized in credit card fraud and counterfeiting. Then the brawny lad decided to try his hand at extortion. Working for a mob group run by the notorious Efim Laskin — who had sold weapons to the Red Brigades — Tarzan was ordered to nab a German banker. Tarzan and two accomplices accosted the banker as he ate lunch at an expensive restaurant and forced him into the trunk of their car. But when the man swore he could get no money until his bank opened after its lunch break, the hapless extortionists agreed to release him, and arranged to meet him at the bank at four o'clock. Moments before the rendezvous, Tarzan stepped out of the car and walked to a nearby pillar for a smoke. Suddenly, a group of rival gangsters in four Mercedes-Benzes pulled up in front of the bank and beat his accomplices severely. A terrified Tarzan fled all the way to Brighton Beach.

Tarzan found Brighton Beach to be an unsavory haunt for murderers and thieves. "It was the Wild West," he recalled. "I took my gun everywhere." His fortunes improved markedly when, soon after arriving in Brooklyn, he married Maria Raichel, a wastrel Russian *Mafiya* princess. Her grandfather, her ex-husband, and her brother-in-law were all known by the same sobriquet — *Psyk* — the Russian word for "psycho." Her grandfather earned the name after he cold-bloodedly stabbed a man to death in Russia. Her first husband, Semion, and his brother Naum eventually became big-time extortionists, and ran their own crew; but because of their irrational behavior they were shunned by other Russian gangsters. Semion, for instance, threw a Ukrainian prostitute into a bathtub and threatened to toss in an electric appliance until she promised him a share of her earnings. Then, for good measure, he forced her to give him a blow job. The woman subsequently told her tale to the cops and Semion was arrested. A few days later, she received a long-distance phone call from a deep-throated man who told her that someone wanted to speak to her. "Mommy, Mommy, Mommy, they will kill me!" a voice cried. It was the woman's three-year-old child, who was living with relatives in Ukraine. The woman dropped the charges. "He's an evil, horrible person," says a New York City detective who worked on the case.

Although Tarzan had married into mob royalty, the relationship had its downside. Maria wanted him to live off the fortune left behind by Semion, who was serving a seven-year prison sentence in Germany for extortion. She bought Tarzan $3,000 tuxedoes for nights on the town, and expected him to stay home and watch game shows. He felt like a sissy and found refuge in the criminal exploits of Grecia Roizes. Their families had been close friends in Chernovtsi, and later in Israel. In Russia, Roizes had spent three years in a prison in Siberia for hitting someone so hard in the stomach that his guts came through a recent medical incision. Now he headed one of the most feared Russian crews in Brighton Beach and owned a wholesale furniture store with branches in Coney Island, Italy, and Russia. (The DEA and a knowledgeable figure in the Genovese underworld say that the store fronted a heroin business that involved the Gambinos, the Geneveses, and a host of Russian mobsters.)

Tarzan helped Roizes's crew with torch jobs and extortion, and soon developed an interest in furniture. After a young couple in Bensonhurst, Brooklyn, refused to sell their wholesale furniture store to Roizes for a fire sale price, they permanently disappeared. Tarzan claims that he was shocked when they vanished, but he happily took over their business.

Inevitably, the Russian mobsters crossed paths with their Italian counterparts. By intuition, or perhaps a sure knowledge of the territory, this happened to Tarzan on a day when an old woman walked into his new store and asked to buy a cheap bedroom set on credit. "This ain't a bank, lady," a clerk named Vinny curtly replied. Tarzan overheard the conversation and gave her the set for free. He even loaded it on his truck and drove it to her house. Tarzan said that he felt sorry for her, and that besides, he liked catering to old people and "kibitzing" with them.

The following day, a powerfully built Italian man sauntered into a video store that Tarzan ran and introduced himself only as Frankie. "I'm the son of the old woman," he said, offering Tarzan coffee and pastries. "I owe you. Anything you want is yours."

Tarzan says he was awestruck. "You could feel his power," he recalled. "He was the kind of man who wouldn't take no for an answer."

Over the next few years, if the rent at Tarzan's video store was raised by the landlord, he'd call his friend Frankie, and it would be taken care of. When an Italian extortionist tried to shake down Tarzan, Frankie's boys had him pistol-whipped in front of his wife. "They are going to find you in a car cut in little pieces," the wife shrieked at Tarzan.

Tarzan claimed he never knew the identity of his Italian patron until one day in 1987, when he saw a picture of him in the tabloids. The papers identified him as the late Frank Santora, a notable in the Colombo organized crime family, and reported that he had been shot twice at close range outside a dry-cleaning store on a quiet Brooklyn street.

Soon, many of Tarzan's friends were coming to grief:

Vladimir Reznikov, one of Brighton Beach's most successful professional killers, was shot to death in front of Marat
Balagula's popular restaurant and nightclub Odessa. Then
Tarzan lost his crewmate Alexander Slepinin—the three-
hundred-pound, six-foot-five-inch tattooed hit man
known as the Colonel who was brutally executed by
Monya Elson. "My mother loved the Colonel," Tarzan
gloomily recalled.

Fainberg decided he should move to a safer neighborhood. In 1990, he left his wife and Brighton Beach behind,
and headed south.

In America, Miami had become the Russian mob's
second city. Like Brighton Beach, it had a large Russian
immigrant population. In the early 1970s, the Miami
Beach Police Department began to notice that an inordi-
nate number of Russian émigré taxi drivers were commit-
ting criminal acts. These Russians didn't fit the cops'
preconceived notion of crooks, however. "They were
always neatly dressed and very clean-cut and gave the
appearance of wanting to fit in and learn the American
way of life," says a federal law enforcement report, written in 1994. Gradually, the Miami police learned that
these taxi drivers were involved in many of the same
crimes that had made the Italian Mafia so powerful:
extortion, narcotics, gambling, and prostitution. "They
were a very tight group of criminals who had a code of
silence that even the threat of arrest could not break,"
the report added.

By the 1980s, the Miami Beach police noted that
crimes involving Russian criminals were growing craftier;
their schemes, more involved—well-organized narcotics
trafficking, burglary and counterfeiting rings, and sophisticated bank and jewelry frauds. Even as the Russian mob-

sters graduated to white-collar crime, a continuing influx of Russians allowed them to control the streets. "Russian Organized Crime is a new and serious threat to South Florida," warned the 1994 report. "This is a well-educated group of active, young criminals."

By the time that Tarzan arrived in Florida, the Russians pouring in were not the taxi-driving sort. "Miami was a boomtown for the Russian mob, which came after pere-stroika with the hundreds of millions they had looted during privatization," says Assistant U.S. Attorney Diana Fernandez. They used their vast war chest to buy row after row of pricey condominiums in North Beach, and paid tens of millions more for the gated mansions on Fisher Island, the city's most fashionable residential area. Many of the buyers were high-ranking Russian military officers and ex-KGB officials. "These were the people who held together the Evil Empire," one real estate agent said. "These were the assassins and the spies." The Versace-clad Russians loved the balmy, palm-studded tropics, where each new day brought the potential for a multimillion-dollar score. Who needed a *shvitz* in a century-old, grime-encrusted Brighton Beach bathhouse when wiseguys could go for a steam and a sit-down at the dégagé Art Deco Hotel Delano's rooftop spa, and maybe even spy a movie star? In Miami, the Russians found their ideal dacha: a base for money laundering that was also close to South American cocaine. "Porky's became the focal point where Russian gangsters could get their bearings when they came to South Florida," said Fernandez.

Tarzan had opened Porky's with the help of William Seidle, whom he latched on to shortly after arriving in Miami. Seidle, a seventy-one-year-old, longtime Floridian, owns a hugely profitable Nissan dealership, as well as the largest Suzuki dealership in America, and is said in Russian mob circles to have a criminal lineage that could be traced to Meyer Lansky, the mobster who once boasted that the Mafia was bigger than U.S. Steel. According to Brighton Beach gangster Vladimir Ginzberg, the Russian mobsters, out of deference, call the energetic, silver-haired Seidle *Stariyk*, the Russian word for "old man." (Seidle denies that he knew Lansky or has ever done business with organized crime.) Brent Eaton, a veteran DEA agent, says that Seidle has been under investigation by numerous federal agencies for more than twenty years, although he has never been indicted. "Bill Seidle is a great guy," William Lehman, a former Democratic congressman, told me. Lehman, who represented South Florida for twenty years, said Seidle "enjoyed Tarzan's outrageousness. I've know Bill for fifty years and he's always run a kosher business. There are no blemishes."

Seidle took a shine to Tarzan the moment they met. "Tarzan was a boisterous, big-mouthed Yiddel," Seidle told me in a Yiddish drawl, one hot, buggy day in Miami. "He's a Jewboy, you know. Just a big-mouth kid, always bragging, boisterous, but very nice, very kind . . . I would describe him as a very, very dear friend. I was close to him. He was close to our family. They loved Tarzan. They think a lot of him. They still feel the same."

Seidle saw in Tarzan a younger version of himself: a bold risk-taker, not adverse to crossing the line. The men decided that there was a lot of money to be made in the "pussy" business so Seidle staked the young Russian to Porky's for a hidden share of the off-the-book profits, assert court documents. Seidle admits only that he collected rent from the club as its landlord, and he denies receiving club profits.

Tarzan's criminal ambitions did not stop with Porky's. According to government wiretap affidavits, Tarzan cultivated vast fields of hemp in the Everglades, with giant grow

lights and a landing strip. Tarzan boasted to at least two government undercover agents that he was using aircraft to
ferry in tons of marijuana from Jamaica. He allegedly even
recruited his geeky-looking younger brother, Alex, to mule
seven large, green garbage bags stuffed with marijuana from
New York City to Porky's. "Alex was so afraid of being
robbed that immediately after receiving the drugs, he spent
the night in a New York City hotel rather than at his own
home; he then drove the entire trip without stopping for
the night because he was convinced that he would be
apprehended carrying the drugs," asserts a federal wiretap
affidavit.

Marijuana was, for Tarzan, a gateway drug. Before long,
he had moved on to cocaine. At the time, the Russian
Mafiya had little contact with the Colombian drug cartels,
though they were eager to remedy that failing. Tarzan
helped forge a connection, brokering cocaine deals between
the Colombians and the most powerful mob family in St.
Petersburg. In one instance, according to the DEA, he
smuggled more than one hundred kilos of cocaine in crates
of freeze-dried shrimp that were flown from Guayaquil,
Ecuador, to St. Petersburg. He also ran coke directly out of
Miami, a charge he hotly denies. The street price for
cocaine in Russia was $60,000 per kilo; for every kilo,
Tarzan made a thousand dollars.

Tarzan's principal link to the Colombians came
through two men, Juan Almeida and Fernando Birbragher.
Almeida, thirty-seven years old and the son of a Por-
tuguese-born Miami real estate and construction mogul,
had been a major cocaine dealer since the mid-1980s. He
supervised the tricky contacts with the Colombian drug
cartels using his luxury car rental shops, a posh marina,
and other businesses he owned as covers for his illicit
activities. Birbragher, meanwhile, was a Colombian and a

friend of Seidle, and had had excellent ties to the Cali cartel. In 1982, he admitted in a plea bargain that he had
washed $54 million for them. "Birbragher was very close
friends with Pablo Escobar," says the DEA's Brent Eaton.
"He [Birbragher] used to buy him [Escobar] sports cars
and luxury boats and do a lot of other things for him." Top
DEA officials assert that Birbragher also laundered drug
money for Manuel Noriega, the former Panamanian
leader, who was convicted in 1992 of drug trafficking.

Working closely with Almeida, who assured him that
they wouldn't run afoul of the law as long as they didn't sell
drugs in America, Tarzan vaulted, precociously, to the top
tier of his profession. His cocaine business was doing so
well that he found himself fending off hostile takeovers
from other Russian mobsters eager to exploit the new
cocaine trade with the Colombians. One of them was the
man in charge of Ivankov's street operations in the United
States, who tried to move in on Tarzan's thriving business
shortly after the *vor*'s arrest. His name was Alexander Bor,
otherwise known as Timoka. During a sit-down at the Russian *banya*, or bathhouse, at Miami's Castle Beach Hotel,
Tarzan turned the tables on Timoka, declaring that he
wanted Timoka to pay him $15,000 a month in protection
money to do business in Miami. "Get fucked," Timoka
sneered.

Luckily for Tarzan, Timoka made a grave error while
in Miami when he put out the word that he was looking
for professional hit men to rub out the two New
York–based FBI agents who had captured Ivankov. A
snitch passed the death threats on to the FBI, which put
so much heat on Timoka that he abandoned his recently
built $500,000 house in Massapequa, Long Island, and
fled to Germany.

Unchallenged, Tarzan proudly sat astride a dominion

of crime, smugly holding court for visiting Russian dons,
who often sought relief in Miami from the vicious mob
wars raging at home. One of the most powerful dons was
Anzor Kikalishvili, who bragged over an FBI wire that he
had more than six hundred "soldiers" in South Florida. In
May 1994, Tarzan introduced Kikalishvili to the owners of
a local bagel shop and deli. Kikalishvili, flaunting gold
chains, gold rings, and an Armani suit, bragged about his
powerful *Mafiya* connections in Moscow. He then "persuaded" the couple to sell him 49 percent of the deli for a
very low price, and to pay him $25,000 every month, for
his protection. "That's how it's done in Russia," he said.
Terrified, the owners sold their share of the deli for
$50,000, a fraction of its worth. Three months later,
Kikalishvili visited the couple and ordered them to buy
the restaurant back for $450,000. He assured them that if
he left their home empty-handed, there would be an additional $100,000 penalty, and warned that he could "find
them anywhere in the world and skin them like an animal." The couple fled in terror to Canada with their children. Tarzan took over the deli with Kikalishvili as his
silent partner.

After extortion, Tarzan's second favorite sport was
degrading women. He once bound onto Porky's stage during a burlesque show and dove into the muff of a blond
stripper. He was arrested for performing a "lewd and las-
civious" act, and fined $250. In his defense, Tarzan claimed
that the stripper had opened her legs "a little more than the
law allows." In an incident filmed by the FBI from the roof
of a building across the street from Porky's, Tarzan chased a
dancer out of the club and knocked her cold. On another
occasion, he slammed a dancer to the ground in Porky's
parking lot, stomped on her face, and forced her to eat
gravel. He once beat his mistress's head against the steering

wheel of his Mercedes until the space under the gas pedal pooled with blood. After he impregnated another woman, he ordered his cousin to threaten to slit her throat if she didn't have an abortion. He also regularly abused his common-law wife, Faina, a frail, thirty-three-year-old beauty. When the police arrived at their home in response to 911 calls, she'd quiver in fear, sometimes huddled inside a locked car with her daughter. Faina never pressed charges, however. In 1997, a few minutes after dropping her daughter off at day care, Faina was killed when her car plowed into a tree traveling at a speed of more than 90 miles an hour in a 30-mile-per-hour zone. Her blood alcohol level was double the legal limit. The coroner's office ruled that the death was an accident, although the feds initially suspected that Tarzan had murdered Faina and arranged her death to look like an accident.

Tarzan denied that he killed Faina, but conceded that his behavior drove her to her death. If that behavior perturbed him, however, he didn't show it, but rather bragged that he was a sex machine, and Faina couldn't accommodate it. For instance, he claims he owned a "couples club" where he often spent evenings servicing wives in front of their voyeuristic husbands. He'd take out four or five buxom strippers at a time sailing on his thirty-four-foot yacht; while his baby daughter scooted around the galley, the adults orgied. He boasted that he could thumb through any adult magazine—*Hustler, Playboy, Penthouse*—"call my agent, get the girl to the club, and then take her out and fuck her brains out. . . . You can't believe the ego boost this gives you. I was addicted to sex."

Meanwhile, Tarzan and Juan Almeida saw a way to get even tighter with the Colombians—by hooking them up with Russian gear. They had access to Russian military hardware, from aircraft to armored personnel carriers to submarines. Such goods were shockingly easy to come by in the armed forces of the former Soviet empire if you knew who to talk to. Russian armories, stored in physically deteriorating facilities, and guarded by indifferent, bribable soldiers, were easy pickings for the *Mafiya*.*

On Halloween day 1992, Tarzan traveled to Latvia, where he told the Colombians that he had Russian organized crime contacts who could help him procure six heavy-lift Russian military helicopters for Pablo Escobar, who wanted the machines to ferry chemicals to jungle labs that refined coke. Tarzan bragged to DEA undercover agents that Seidle financed 10 percent of the trip, an assertion Seidle denies. Tarzan was escorted by Almeida, Fernando Birbragher, and a host of Colombian and Cuban cutthroats.

---

*Russian military matériel moving through organized crime channels has already begun to result in the spread of former Soviet weapons to militants, nationalists, and criminals throughout the world, says a confidential threat assessment report about the Russian *Mafiya* prepared by the U.S. Department of Energy. In the first half of 1992, 25,000 firearms were reported missing from military depots, including 2,000 AK series rifles, AK-74SU assault carbines, and medium and heavy support weapons. In December 1992, police seized 768 firearms, including seven grenade launchers, 574 submachine guns, and 159 pistols. Near the Black Sea port of Adler, police detained a high-speed boat carrying two missile launchers, a machine gun, two grenade launchers, and four submachine guns.

In 1997, two Lithuanians linked to the Russian mob were arrested in Miami trying to sell tactical nuclear weapons and Bulgarian-made shoulder-held antiaircraft missiles to U.S. Customs undercover agents posing as drug smugglers. The Lithuanians were caught on audio- and videotape negotiating the sale in a series of meetings in seedy hotels in London and Miami. The Customs agents didn't have the $330,000 asking price for the antiaircraft missiles, so the mobsters sold the weapons to Iran.

Russian mobsters have also attempted to traffic weapons-grade fissionable material, using a global distribution network to smuggle it to renegade states and drug cartels, say officials from the Energy Department, the FBI, and the CIA. There have been at least sixteen cases in which police have interdicted plutonium or highly enriched uranium coming out of the former Soviet bloc since 1992. In one instance, approximately six pounds of fissionable material stolen from Russia was seized in Prague in December 1994. On September 24, 1999, a cache of stolen uranium was intercepted by Georgian authorities near the Georgian-Turkish border.

The trip was a bust, and Almeida and Birbragher blamed it on Tarzan. "Tarzan is an idiot," Almeida told me with disgust. "He didn't know anybody."

But in mid-1993 Tarzan scored in Moscow. According to the DEA, he and Almeida succeeded in purchasing up to six MI8 Russian military helicopters for $1 million each. Tarzan later boasted to government undercover agents that he had bought the helicopters to traffic coke for "Colombian drug barons" headed by Pablo Escobar, and, after the deal was completed, he stayed behind in Moscow to oversee the final details. At the request of the Colombians, the helicopters' seats were removed and fuel bladders were added to extend their range, Tarzan later told a government undercover agent. With everything set, Tarzan escorted the helicopters to an airport outside Moscow. But just as they were being loaded into the belly of a cargo plane bound for Bogotá, according to one of the key participants, half a dozen jeeps carrying men armed with automatic weapons roared onto the tarmac, encircling the transport. Tarzan was ordered to disgorge his precious shipment immediately. He had foolishly neglected to pay the local airport *Mafiya* for permission to purchase the helicopters. They threatened to kill him for it. He was hauled into a conference room at the airport to meet the two main mobsters. "They were like heavy weightlifters," he told me. "Their shorts were small on them. They were incredible hulks. I was in deep shit." But the Colombians held a certain mystique for the Russians, and by alluding to his close connections with them Tarzan was able to buy some valuable time.

Desperate, Tarzan called Anzor Kikalishvili in Miami. Kikalishvili said he'd make some calls and try to smooth things over, but Tarzan would have to explain why he hadn't cut the "boys" in for a share. In another series of frantic transatlantic phone calls, Tarzan related the mess to a smoldering Almeida. Almeida advised Tarzan to tell the Russians that the helicopters were for the legendary head of the Medellín cartel, Pablo Escobar, and that no one had told him that he was required to pay a bribe to get the equipment. Tarzan and Almeida hoped that the Russians, who still had little direct experience with the Colombians and the cocaine trade, might make an exception for Escobar—especially since Tarzan had dangled the carrot of future cocaine deals. If Escobar wanted the choppers, they replied, he'd have to show his face in Moscow and recover them himself.

Almeida decided that the only way to retrieve the helicopters—and save Tarzan—was to go to Moscow posing as Pablo Escobar. At Sheremetyevo airport in Moscow, Almeida was welcomed by a motorcade of thick-necked men driving big black Mercedes. He was escorted like a head of state to a five-star hotel in the center of the city, and led into a dark-paneled room, where more thick-necked men sat around a long conference table. Almeida walked past them to the head of the table where the don presided. There was a nervous silence. Suddenly, the Russian seized him in a bear hug, and cried, "Pablo, Pablo Escobar. What took you so long? Let's do some real shit. Cocaine."

To celebrate their new friendship, the Russians took Almeida and Tarzan out for a night on the town. They went to a dingy boxing ring called the Kamikaze Club, where chain-smoking mobsters and their girlfriends, dressed in American designer gowns, had gathered to watch a match. Young men dressed in street clothes were led into the ring. *Mafiya* rules: only one could walk out alive. Blood spattered the crowd as spectators placed bets on their favorite combatant, and swilled vodka. In order to show that he was a high roller, Almeida ordered Tarzan to bet $500 on every fight, which was a lot of money in Russia at the time. The spectacle went on through the night. There was no air-conditioning in the club and the stench of blood, Tarzan says, nearly made him vomit. Mortally injured boxers, their mouths half open, their ribs broken, were dragged from the mat and dumped in a landfill somewhere outside the city. The following day, Tarzan was permitted to fly the valuable cargo out of Moscow. Tarzan claims that the helicopters were immediately delivered to the drug barons.

Tarzan's crime wave was not passing unnoticed back in the United States. Alarmed at the scale and rapid expansion of his and other Russian mobsters' operations, the state of Florida and a slew of federal law enforcement agencies, working with liaison officers from the Royal Canadian Mounted Police, the German Federal Police, and the Russian Ministry of Internal Affairs, set up a task force called Operation Odessa to try to stem the criminal red tide.

Operation Odessa's guiding force was a Russian-born sergeant on the Miami police force, who posed as a corrupt undercover narcotics cop. He had succeeded in winning the mob's confidence, infiltrating some of its most closely guarded sit-downs. What he discovered horrified him. In a few short years the Russians, through an unprecedented combination of brains, brawn, and chutzpah, had replaced the Gambino family, which had been decimated by years of relentless prosecutions, as one of the top crime groups in South Florida. "Their obvious sophistication far exceeds that of the La Cosa Nostra at its infant stage," the bearded, professorial Miami assistant U.S. attorney Richard Gregory, one of Operation Odessa's founders, told me in Miami. "Tarzan was the original top Russian figure in Miami as far as law enforcement was concerned."

Operation Odessa's agents had so far been unable to infiltrate Tarzan's close-knit world. That assignment fell to Tarzan's old friend from Brighton Beach, Grecia Roizes, who had by this time acquired his nickname "the Cannibal." (A booking sergeant in Brooklyn had called him "a fucking dirty Jew," and he'd bitten off the tip of the man's nose.)

Roizes had also acquired a debt to the DEA. In 1992, he was arrested in Romania for trafficking heroin for Boris Nayfeld's French Connection–sized operation based in Antwerp. Rather than rot in a Romanian prison, where he claimed to have been beaten and denied his heart medication, the Cannibal made a deal with the DEA. First, he ratted on the members of the heroin-smuggling operation, helping the feds shut it down. After that, the DEA dispatched him to the Adriatic port town of Fano, Italy, where he became partners with his longtime friend Monya Elson. Elson was running a vast money laundering business out of a furniture store for Semion Mogilevich. Thanks to the Cannibal, Elson was arrested by Italian authorities in 1995. He was held for murder, money laundering, drug trafficking, and for having ties to the Italian mob. "They kept me in total isolation for eighteen months," Elson bitterly complained. "Five times a day, seven days a week, they shook my cell. They drove me nuts. I never spoke on the phone. I never had an American or Russian newspaper. Psychologically, they destroyed me."

While Elson was incommunicado, the Cannibal's next assignment was in Miami. He had no trouble getting close to Tarzan. "The Cannibal and I were like brothers," Tarzan told me. "We grew up in the same town in the Ukraine and lived on the same street in Israel. Our families were close. He's the one who helped me when I arrived in Brighton Beach. He loved me."

Using $72,000 in cash supplied by the DEA, the Canni-
bal bought a managing partnership in Tarzan's restaurant
Babushka. Situated in one of Miami's many strip malls,
Babushka had a loyal following among Russian émigrés who
were homesick for borscht, caviar, and kabobs. A local
reviewer once described Babushka's staff as "direct from
Petrograd central casting. . . . A man/bear who resembles a
general. A Ural-sized cook. A Rasputin-look-alike waiter."

But even in this theme park of a Russian mob joint, the
Cannibal's conduct stood out as ostentatious and vulgar.
Not only did he bring in his friends, flirt with the wait-
resses, and pay for everything on the house, but he seemed
to be trying to bring Babushka down, according to Paul, a
slender, Russian-born piano player and songwriter who performed at Babushka with his wife, Nelli, a singer.

"On New Year's Eve, he came in drunk and high on
cocaine, and was crude and loud," said Paul. "His behavior
was unbelievably bad. New Year's Eve is a big, big celebration for the Russians. They buy presents, new clothes, jewelry. He had nothing ready for the restaurant." Babushka's
New Year's Eve parties were renowned for generous
spreads of seafood, caviar, grilled meats, plenty of champagne and vodka, and great Russian music. "For 250 people,
we had fewer than a hundred lobsters, almost no shrimp,
no bread. There was almost no food on the table. Some
people left at 12:30, 1:00 A.M. I said to Tarzan, 'You let him
be partner for this?' And Tarzan said, 'I'm desperate for
money.'

"Tarzan had a big boat," Paul went on. "I'm the only one
who knew how to use the fishing rod. One day the three of
us"— Tarzan, Paul, and the Cannibal— "were going fishing,
and I said we needed to buy lines and hooks. We went into
a bait shop and the Cannibal didn't buy too much. He got
on the boat and he emptied his pockets, which were filled

with lines, hooks, all kinds of things which he had stolen," including a fisherman's cap. "My face went red. He said, 'Ah, I always do it. It's fun for me.'"

Paul and Nelli weren't the only ones who were disturbed by the Cannibal's corrosive presence. The Brooklynite gangster Vladimir Ginzberg, who, according to court documents, was a key operative in Tarzan's large-scale cigarette bootlegging operation on the East Coast, had repeatedly alerted Tarzan that the Cannibal was working for the feds.

"I warned Tarzan about the rumors—that he did in Elson, and the others," Ginzberg said. "Tarzan didn't listen. So I asked Tarzan why he trusted him. He said they were both from the same town. He knew his father. He had his friends checked out. And he had a cruel criminal past. That counts for a lot. And Tarzan didn't have a comparable past—and Tarzan wasn't so smart. He had steroids for brains. He had a big-muscle peanut brain."

With Tarzan's confidence secured, the Cannibal began his work. One day, a man named Alexander Yasevich walked into Babushka. The Cannibal embraced him like a long-lost comrade. "Hey, how ya doing?" he said over hugs and kisses. Tarzan, who was in the restaurant, sauntered over to meet the stranger. Tarzan recognized Yasevich from the old neighborhood in Brighton Beach. Yasevich had moved there from Odessa as a teen. But unbeknownst to Tarzan, Yasevich had joined the Marines, and then became an undercover agent for the DEA.

"The agent's cover was that he was an arms dealer and heroin dealer out of New York," says Miami-based DEA spokesperson Pam Brown, who was once part of an elite squad that interdicted drugs in the jungles of Peru and Colombia. "Tarzan immediately started running his mouth, telling him what a big shot he was, that he and his associates had politicians in their pockets." Many of their gab fests were on Tarzan's boat or in upscale restaurants. The men consumed a prodigious amount of a volatile concoction of ice-cold vodka and Japanese saki poured over a raw quail's egg. The first time Yasevich's girlfriend, who was also an undercover agent, drank the potion, she puked.

The drinking and kibitzing paid off. Yasevich learned that Tarzan was in the midst of executing his biggest caper yet: the purchase of a $100 million, Soviet-era, diesel-powered submarine for Pablo Escobar.

When Tarzan was first asked to procure the submarine, it unnerved him. The Russian helicopters had nearly cost him his life. But this time, he made sure to clear the deal through Anzor Kikalishvili, and he traveled to the former Soviet Union with Almeida dozens of times, looking for a submarine. Finally, through the most powerful crime boss in St. Petersburg, they met corrupt, high-ranking Russian military officers who took them to the front gate of Kronstadt, a sprawling naval base in the Baltic, where numerous untended diesel submarines bobbed on their sides, spewing waste into the polluted ocean. Anything is available in Russia, former CIA official Richard Palmer told me. The Soviet fleet is rotting and the sailors haven't been paid for months.

Initially, the Miamians wanted to buy a huge attack submarine for the Colombians' East Coast drug trade. But a retired Russian captain told them they should instead operate on the Pacific Coast, where America's anti-submarine net was less effective. He suggested that they buy a small, diesel-powered Piranha-class submarine, which is made of titanium and is much quieter. The Piranhas, with a range of one thousand kilometers, are used to plant saboteurs, troops, and spies behind enemy lines. The captain told

Tarzan that he had slipped the submarine past the Americans during the Cuban missile crisis.

They finally agreed on a ninety-foot-long Foxtrot-class attack submarine that drug lords calculated could carry up to forty tons of cocaine. The Colombians planned to base the sub, which would be demilitarized and retrofitted to resemble an oceanographic research vessel, in Panama. From there, it would transport the drugs underwater to a mother ship near San Diego and outside the United States's territorial waters. The mother ship would then deliver the coke to ports along the Pacific coast. A consortium of St. Petersburg mobsters and two active-duty admirals wanted $20 million for the vessel, which was built in 1992 for $100 million. Tarzan negotiated its price down to $5.5 million, of which he was to take home $1 million. The Russians wanted the money passed through a dummy company in Europe in order to give the Russian politicians who okayed the purchase plausible deniability. Tarzan hired the retired captain for $500 a month and secured a crew of seventeen for a two-year contract. Tarzan even got permission to take several photographs of the vessel to send to the Colombians. At a party at a dacha, the godfather of St. Petersburg, a man called Misha, made a side deal with Tarzan to procure cocaine from Miami for $30,000 a kilo, far above Tarzan's $4,000 cost. To Tarzan, everything looked good.

On Tuesday, January 21, 1997, just after Tarzan dropped off his daughter at the William and Miriam Tauber Day Care Center, he was stopped in his gleaming white 1996 Jaguar convertible by a marked Metro-Dade Police Department vehicle in the Aventura area of Miami. As he spoke with the officers, DEA agent Brent Eaton and Detective Joseph McMahon, who had been trailing him in an unmarked car, approached. Eaton and McMahon introduced themselves and invited him to join them in their car.

They told Tarzan that he was in trouble and would be arrested. They asked him to take a ride with them to a secure location, where they and a few other officers could speak with him confidentially about his predicament. Tarzan agreed, saying, "I'm a nicer person than you probably thought. I haven't done anything wrong."

When they arrived at the interview site, a DEA training room near Miami International Airport, Tarzan was offered a seat at a table and given a cup of coffee. He was not handcuffed or restrained in any manner. Michael McShane, a DEA inspector, offered him a chance to work with the government rather than be arrested. Tarzan replied that he could be very useful to the government, but was not well acquainted with U.S. laws and preferred to consult with his attorney before making a decision. Eaton told Tarzan that wasn't a wise decision since his lawyer represented other targets of the investigation. "I thought you would tell me what you have and ask me questions," Tarzan said, according to a transcript of the interrogation. "I don't know what to say because I don't know what you think I have done."

McMahon asked Tarzan if he had ever bought liquor for Porky's or for Babushka from any source other than a legitimate wholesaler or liquor store. "Never!" Tarzan declared emphatically.

"What about your relationship with Anzor Kikalishvili?" the detective asked.

"Anzor, I know nothing about what he does in Russia," Tarzan claimed. "I met him at my club. He is a sex maniac, always looking for girls. I helped him once when he opened a bagel store in Aventura." Tarzan did admit that he had once picnicked with Kikalishvili.

"Tell us about your activities with Juan Almeida," McMahon said.

"I don't know what he is up to," Tarzan said. "He speaks Spanish most of the time."

"You mean you travel all over the world with Almeida and you don't know what he's up to?"

"Yes," Tarzan replied.

"You know that those airplanes and helicopters you get go to Colombian drug traffickers," McMahon said angrily.

"They go to legitimate people," Tarzan insisted.

When the officers accused him of lying, Tarzan replied, "Maybe I should go to jail, then find out what you have." The agents had had enough. They handcuffed him, placed him under arrest, and drove him to the DEA processing room, where he was fingerprinted, photographed, and allowed to call his attorney.

Almeida surrendered to the authorities several days later. Not only had Tarzan talked about his activities with Almeida to various undercover agents, but he had even introduced Almeida to Yasevich, the DEA undercover agent, at La Carreta restaurant, in Miami. At the time, Almeida told the agent that he represented a client with unlimited funds who was interested in buying a Russian diesel submarine for illicit purposes, although he said with a laugh that the vessel was going to be used to transport stolen gold from the Philippines. Almeida, a suave man with a salesman's charm, told me the sub was intended for an underwater museum in South Florida. After he was arrested, his lawyer, Roy Black, said that the sub was intended to carry tourists around the Galápagos Islands. As for the Russian helicopters, Almeida claimed the aircraft were actually contracted by Helitaxi, a legitimate Bogotá-based company, to do heavy lifting at oil rigs in South America. Helitaxi's president, Byron López, is banned from the United States by the State Department because he has allegedly laundered money for drug lords.

The investigation produced 530 wiretapped conversations in Russian, Hebrew, Yiddish, and Spanish. On the tapes and in conversations with the undercover agents, Tarzan constantly implicated himself and others in numerous crimes. "We caught Tarzan bragging to our undercover agent about how he was hooked up with the Colombian drug lords, and how everything he was doing was for Colombian drug lords, and that he was getting the submarine for the same people that he got the helicopters for," DEA agent Eaton says. "A lot of that is on tape."

Louis Terminello, Tarzan's civil lawyer, insists that the only thing that Tarzan is guilty of is having a big mouth. "It's the high school kid who wants the high school girl to believe that he's got the biggest dick in the world."

After months of sullen denial, Tarzan decided to cooperate. "He's admitted to everything," DEA agent Pam Brown told me several months after his arrest. "He keeps saying, 'Well, this would have all been legal in Russia.'" For eleven months, Tarzan was kept in the snitch ward at Miami's Federal Detention Center blabbing about Russian mobsters and Latino drug lords. After negotiating at least six proffer agreements, the galled feds cut him loose to stand trial. Not only couldn't they corroborate much of his information, but he said that he would never testify unless he was released on bail. There was little likelihood of that happening. The feds had a good idea what Tarzan would do: a government wiretap picked up several powerful Israeli drug dealers in Miami discussing plans to help Tarzan flee to Israel, which does not extradite its nationals.

Finally, Tarzan, who faced a possible life sentence, pleaded guilty to racketeering charges, including conspiracy to sell cocaine, heroin, and a submarine, and sundry other crimes. He testified against Almeida—who was convicted of importing and distributing cocaine and attempting to buy a Russian submarine for Colombian drug kingpins to further the drug conspiracy. (The charge of purchasing heavy-lift helicopters for the Colombians was dropped.) "Tarzan's big mouth ruined my life," Almeida says mournfully. According to a well-placed government source, Almeida, who is awaiting sentencing, has taken out contracts on the judge and the prosecution team.

As for the man who helped the feds the most, Grecia Roizes, the Cannibal, looked as if he had not a care in the world as he stood erect, his Popeye-like arms bulging through a lime green knit polo shirt, calmly awaiting sentencing in the ornate marble courthouse in lower Manhattan. On July 8, 1998, Federal District Court Judge John Keenan waived his jail time as a reward for services rendered to the government, and Cannibal set up a furniture business outside Naples, Italy.

About a year later, Roizes was in trouble again: he was arrested by the Italian police in Bologna for associating with the Italian Mafia, money laundering, extortion, kidnapping, and smuggling. Most of his victims were small-time Russian entrepreneurs in Italy. Some of his illicit gains were allegedly passed through the Bank of New York. Apparently, while working for the DEA, the Cannibal had also been running a thriving criminal empire in Italy.

The Russian mob in South Florida today is the hub of a sophisticated and ruthless operation. But Ludwig Fainberg is no longer a participant. On October 14, 1999, after living in America for seventeen years, Tarzan was deported to Israel, with $1,500 in his pocket. He had served a mere thirty-three month prison term. His light sentence was in return for his cooperation, which reportedly included providing intelligence on several alleged Russian mob heavyweights.

Even as he awaited deportation, Tarzan's enthusiasm was irrepressible. "I love this country!" he told me. "It's so easy to steal here!" He was already cooking up a new scheme. "I'm going to Cuba," he said. "A few of my Russian friends already own resorts there." He said that with what he knows about the sex industry, he'll soon be rich again.

PART TWO
COLONIZATION
AND CONQUEST

POWER PLAY

onetsk, a bleak industrial city in the southeast corner of Ukraine, is not known for producing world-
class hockey players. And when Oleg Tverdovsky, a
scrawny seven-year-old, tried out for a local peewee team
in 1983, he didn't show much promise: his ankles were
weak—the result of a joint-swelling disease called Reiter's
syndrome—and he was one of the worst skaters in the
bunch. At first, he didn't even like the sport much. Still, a
coach spied some potential in him and encouraged the boy
to keep at it.

He did. By sixteen, Tverdovsky had blossomed into one
of the highest-scoring defensemen in Russia, playing for a
team called the Soviet Wings. But with the fall of communism, Soviet hockey also began a steady collapse. Arena
freezers frequently broke down, melting the ice. Stadiums
that once drew five thousand fans were lucky to lure several

hundred. "People had a lot of problems in their lives," recalls Tverdovsky. "Hockey tickets are not very expensive, but if you can't feed your family, well, you don't think about going to a hockey game."

Like most of Russia's best players, Tverdovsky was eventually discovered by NHL scouts, and in 1994, at the tender age of eighteen, the Mighty Ducks of Anaheim made him their first-round draft pick. He had awesome power and blazing speed, drawing comparisons to Bobby Orr — all the right stuff, said the scouts, to become a superstar. "I was excited to get drafted," he remembered. "To play with the best players in the world." When he arrived in Anaheim, he bought himself a house and a sports car. After a fine rookie season, he was traded to the Winnipeg Jets and signed a three-year deal worth some $4.2 million, a staggering sum for a young man whose countrymen were earning an average of $74 per month.

Tverdovsky's prosperity did not go unnoticed, however. One night, a former Russian hockey coach of Tverdovsky turned up on his California doorstep and demanded a share of his good fortune. The young phenom was terrified, for he knew, as did everyone in Russia, that hockey in the former Soviet Union was overrun by the *Mafiya*, and that it frequently brought its sadistic extortion methods to bear on successful players. "They'll take out a whole family," said a U.S. law enforcement official who specializes in the Russian mob. "But they'll torture victims first to send out a message — they'll cut off fingers, use acid, decapitate heads. It's gruesome."

In fact, the Russian mob's sinister grip on sports in the Soviet bloc dates back to well before communism's demise. In the Soviet era, sports stars — along with singers, artists, apparatchiks, and black marketeers — were all part of the Soviet Union's privileged elite. In this heavily criminalized society, top athletes and mobsters sought out one another's company to mutually enhance their image and prestige. They ate at the same choice restaurants, vacationed together at luxurious spas, and dated the same women. They also did business together. "The *Mafiya* has made the sports business one of its sources of revenue," a Russian sports historian has said. "Bribes, extortion, and killings are common."

Hockey — one of Russia's most popular sports — was no exception. From the small-town peewee leagues up to the powerhouse national teams, the *Mafiya*, by force or cooperation, had penetrated every level of the enterprise, just as it had most other businesses in Russia. "Many local teams in Russia are associated with the mob," said a Western law enforcement source, noting that they often used them for money laundering, as well as for many other illicit profits that could be sucked from stadium contracts, concessions, equipment procurement, ticket sales, player and management salaries, and tens of millions of dollars of untaxed vodka and cigarettes that the government gave to the teams.

When communism fell, the former Soviet Union's rich reservoir of hockey talent — the same players who had so often demonstrated their astonishing skills against the world in the Olympics — suddenly became available to the West. The NHL's U.S. and Canadian teams went on a buying binge, snapping up the country's current and future superstars, signing players like Tverdovsky to extraordinarily lucrative contracts. But the NHL teams discovered soon enough that they weren't importing only expert skaters and stickhandlers; they were also importing the brutal extortionists and gun-toters of the Russian *Mafiya* who followed in their wake. "Hockey in the former Soviet Union is controlled by Russian organized crime," said a top FBI official.

"They control the players who play there and they control the players who play here. They can stay in Russia and make 2,000 rubles a year or kick back $1 million of a $2 million American contract."

Although Tverdovsky was well aware that being in America did not guarantee his safety, he nevertheless refused the Russian coach's demands to be paid off. But the gangsters did not come for him. Instead, on January 30, 1996, four goons — carrying a tear gas pistol, handcuffs, and a snapshot of Tverdovsky's forty-six-year-old mother, Alexandra — seized his parents outside an apartment building in Donetsk, where they had gone to visit relatives. Tverdovsky received a message from his father: the gangsters wanted $200,000 for his mother's safe return.

While his mother sat imprisoned in a dank apartment outside Donetsk, Tverdovsky suffered severe anxiety, causing his ankles to swell up. "I had a terrible time," recalled the lanky, six-foot player during an interview at a Tex-Mex café across the street from the hockey stadium in Phoenix, where he then played for the Coyotes. "I didn't have many details about what was going on." Still, he didn't inform team or league officials about his ordeal, nor did he reveal his problem to his own teammates, fearing that, if word leaked out, his mother would be killed. "We [Russian players] won't even tell each other" about extortion plots, said Tverdovsky. "Not even our best Russian friends."

A few days later the kidnappers escorted Alexandra Tverdovsky onto a train bound for Moscow, confident that they were on their way to make a trade for a few suitcasesful of cash. Suddenly, in a rare case of Russian law enforcement competence, the police stormed the train and rescued the captive, arresting all four kidnappers in the process. Tverdovsky, however, wasn't taking any more chances. He spirited his parents out of the country and hid them away in a house he bought for them in a town in California that to this day he will not name.

In the NHL, where ex–Eastern bloc players make up 10 percent of team rosters, the list of hockey players who have been secretly shaken down, beaten, and threatened by voracious Russian mobsters reads like a Who's Who of the NHL. (In a few years that proportion will grow to 40 percent, and most of these players will be tied to the Russian mob, asserts the FBI.) Alexander Mogilny of the Vancouver Canucks, Alexei Zhitnik of the Buffalo Sabres, and Vladimir Malakhov of the Montreal Canadiens have all been targets of extortion. Even Detroit Red Wings superstar Sergei Fedorov was rumored to have had to pay gangsters to be left alone when he first came to America. Mike Barnett, Fedorov's agent, denies the story, though he admits: "If there was an incident, I probably wouldn't tell you. It's not something we would prefer to have publicized." Still, Fedorov doesn't go home to Russia unless he's accompanied by a swarm of bodyguards.

According to a May 1996 congressional investigation, as many as half of the league's ex–Eastern bloc players have been forced to buy a *krysha*, or "roof"—the euphemism for protection. "All the NHL teams are aware of the extortion," says an American law enforcement source. "It's a huge problem," Mike Smith, associate general manager of the Toronto Maple Leafs, has told the *Vancouver Province*. "There have even been players who have been roughed up."

During the 1996 congressional hearings on the *Mafiya*, a Russian mobster who testified explained precisely how the system worked: "Often when a Russian criminal demands money, the threat is not explicit but is clearly understood," he said, speaking from behind a black felt curtain. "Alexei Zhitnik used to play for the Los Angeles Kings.

He showed up at a Russian club in Los Angeles one night with a new car, expensive clothes, and a beautiful woman. He was young and naive.

"A man named Sasha, whom I know is connected to a Russian organized crime group, approached Alexei and demanded money from him. Sasha was sending Alexei a warning, to make sure he thought about his future in Los Angeles. Alexei did not go to the police." According to several knowledgeable sources, Alexei was later hauled under an L.A. pier and beaten. Eventually, the mob witness testified, "[Zhitnik] went to a more powerful criminal group to take care of the problem."

Zhitnik, for his part, tried to shrug off the incident. "It was not a big deal," Zhitnik insisted. "It was a stupid accident. It was my mistake. I was not kidnapped." When asked if he was beaten by thugs, he thundered, "Total bullshit! Nothing happened in L.A." On the other hand, he concedes: "I can't say extortion doesn't exist in the NHL. It exists."

Almost without exception the FBI has failed to bring extortion charges against gangsters shaking down NHL players. "We can't make a case unless somebody files a complaint," explains the FBI's John Epke, the head of the organized crime unit in Denver. But fearful ex–Eastern bloc hockey players, who often have the inherent distrust of the police that is a legacy of having grown up in a totalitarian state, are unwilling to go to the federal authorities. More significantly, like Tverdovsky, many of them still have vulnerable family members living in the former Soviet Union.

Even victims like Vancouver Canuck Alexander Mogilny are unwilling to acknowledge the presence of Russian organized crime in the NHL. Yet just a few years ago, Mogilny was abducted by two Russian goons who demanded that he deliver to them $150,000 in cash. As he drove to the bank, he picked up his car phone and called his agent, Mike Barnett, to ask what he should do. "Go to the FBI," urged Barnett. So he did: one of the extortionists fled the country; the other, thanks to Mogilny's testimony, became law enforcement's only successful conviction of a Russian NHL extortionist, and was subsequently deported. But today, when asked about extortion in the league, Mogilny says, "Why talk about it? It doesn't exist. There is no such thing." Oleg Tverdovsky has a similar response. "How can I say there is Russian organized crime in the NHL if I've not seen it? If you don't know, you don't know."

"It's their silence," says a law enforcement official, "that has allowed the Russians to become easy extortion victims" and made the FBI's attempts to convict the mobsters almost impossible.

Yet the corruption in the NHL goes much deeper than simply the extortion of individual players. Far from being victims, at least three of the league's top superstars have actively befriended members of the Russian mob, helping it to sink its roots further into North American soil: they are Slava Fetisov, who led the Detroit Red Wings to the Stanley Cup in 1997 and 1998; Valeri Kamensky, who did the same for the Colorado Avalanche in 1996; and the Florida Panthers' Pavel Bure, the four-time NHL All-Star nicknamed the "Russian Rocket" for his mind-boggling speed and deft stickhandling. "There are as many as ten other NHL players that have associations to Russian organized crime figures," says Reg King, a Royal Canadian Mounted Police agent who specializes in the Russian mob.

Detroit's Joe Louis Arena is a dilapidated, shambling facility abutting a river of green sludge. The defending champion Red Wings had just finished up an intense, two-hour practice, and the brooding, six-foot-one-inch, 215-

pound Slava Fetisov sat on a black swivel chair next to his locker, still dressed in his pads and sweating heavily.

At forty, he was the oldest player in the NHL, almost two decades older than some of the other Red Wings shuffling from the showers to their lockers. His forehead is deeply furrowed, and fissures run diagonally down his cheeks. It must have seemed like eons since the nine-time Soviet All-Star defenseman played in three Olympics, winning two gold medals and one silver. Many predicted 1998 would be his last season, and that he would return to Russia to run for political office. "I get lots of invitations to join [political] parties," Fetisov acknowledged. His friend, chess grandmaster Garry Kasparov, has said unequivocally that Fetisov is so popular, he "could be the future president of Russia."

However, Fetisov may need a bit of practice at handling tough questions from reporters. For he was ill-prepared when I stuck a tape recorder in front of him and asked what he knew about extortion in the NHL.

"I don't know," he replied curtly. "I have never heard of it."

"To your knowledge it doesn't exist?" I asked.

"I don't want to talk about it," he grunted, his dark eyes averting mine. "It's not related anyhow to me and to anybody else in this room. It's a made-up story, and I don't want to talk about it."

"Who would make it up?" I pressed.

"I don't know," he said, his anger mounting. "I have no idea."

Fetisov's teammates call him "the Godfather." The nearly universal homage that other Russian NHL players accord him reflects not only on his skill on the ice, his sage advice, but on the fact that he was one of the first Soviet players to come to play in the league. According to law enforcement, it is also an allusion to the fact that he has long been in business with some of the most feared gang-sters in the former Soviet Union.

"When Fetisov led the charge of Russian hockey players to North America and joined the New Jersey Devils, he was already mobbed-up," asserted a U.S. law enforcement source. In fact, the FBI says Fetisov's link to the mob goes back as far as the fall of the Berlin Wall. As a national sports icon, Fetisov was bound to attract high-level organized crime figures. But in 1989, according to a confidential FBI document, he got himself into a jam when he allegedly pur-chased a stolen Volvo in Sweden that he was supposed to bring back to Russia for Amiran Kvantrishvili, Otari's brother and co-head of a powerful Moscow-based crime family. Instead, Fetisov sold the car to another buyer for more money. Kvantrishvili in turn threatened Fetisov's father, which, the FBI believes, marked the beginning of Fetisov's increasingly complex ties to the mob.

His relationship with Kvantrishvili did not end when he left the country to play hockey in America for the New Jer-sey Devils. In 1992, Fetisov and Kvantrishvili were observed "engaged in serious conversation at a Russian dis-cotheque in Moscow during which Fetisov was seen ner-vously signing papers," states a classified FBI report. In addition, "he [Fetisov] began investing in various business enterprises in Moscow in 1993, and was believed to have paid protection money to Kvantrishvili."

Kvantrishvili was assassinated by rival mobsters that summer. But where Kvantrishvili left off, Vyacheslav Ivankov picked up, and Fetisov, according to a classified FBI report, became the *vor*'s "close associate." The year Ivankov arrived in America, he turned to Fetisov to fill a position in his global criminal empire. According to an FBI affidavit seeking a wiretap of his phones, Ivankov established a front company in New York called Slavic Inc. to conduct money laundering operations. But records filed with the New York Department of State show that on August 26, it was, in fact, Fetisov who signed the business incorporation papers, naming himself as president. It was notarized, and executed by two lawyers. Though Fetisov was the only named corporate officer, FBI documents assert that Slavic Inc. was really run by Ivankov—a fact that even the mobster's lawyer Barry Slotnick confirmed, although he insisted that the business was a legitimate import-export firm. In fact, according to the FBI, it was a giant Laundromat for dirty cash operating out of a storefront on Neptune Avenue in Brooklyn, as well as a front used to obtain fraudulent visas for mobsters and criminal associates. Illicit funds were passed through Slavic Inc.'s bank account to give it the veneer of legitimacy, "when in fact they weren't conducting any commerce whatsoever," said the FBI's Raymond Kerr. According to Russian and American intelligence sources, the millions flowing into Slavic Inc. had already passed through a number of front companies in Russia and Europe before winding their way to Brooklyn, where they fueled the Russian mob in America. On August 20, 1996, just a month and a half after Ivankov's extortion conviction, Fetisov signed the dissolution papers for the company, according to New York Department of State records.

Fetisov, of course, denied everything. He shifted uncomfortably in his seat, perhaps knowing Ivankov well enough not to get on his bad side. "Is it true that you were the president of Slavic Inc.?"

Fetisov turned away, visibly fighting to control his temper. "No," he said. "That's not true."

"But your signature, in your handwriting, is on the documents, naming you the president of the company."

"Are you trying to instigate something or what?" he asked.

"Is there a link between Slavic Inc., you, and Ivankov?"

"I've got nothing to do with this guy, this person, and with Slavic Inc. I have no relationship of any kind."

"But your name is on the incorporation papers."

"What incorporation?"

"The papers you filed with New York State."

"I don't want to talk about this right now," he said. "I don't want to talk about anything."

Fetisov's patience was wearing thin, so I tried another tack, asking him to explain his acquaintance with a New York art dealer and hockey fan named Felix Komorov—the man the FBI asserts in a wiretap affidavit and confidential documents is Ivankov's "right hand man in New York," "who was laundering money" for his group, while claiming to be second-in-command in the Brighton Beach area, in "control of all the extortionist activities of Russian émigré businessmen." Though Komorov vehemently denies the allegations, he has admitted that he has been in telephone contact with Ivankov both before and after the *vor* was imprisoned.

What he cannot deny, however, is his avid courtship of Russian hockey players. Fetisov and several other Russian hockey players attended a reception at Komorov's New York Russian World Art Gallery on Fifth Avenue, across from Central Park. Its walls were decorated with photographs of the jowly Russian shaking hands with a panoply of celebrities, including Al Pacino, Pierre Cardin, and New York City Mayor Rudolph Giuliani.* Komorov also received

---

*Komorov caused a stir when the *Washington Times* revealed that the alleged mobster was the key organizer for a September 1997 star-studded gala concert at Carnegie Hall in celebration of Moscow's 850th birthday. Moscow's mayor unsuccessfully lobbied Secretary of State Madeleine Albright to lift the State Department's travel ban on Joseph Kobzon so he could come to New York and sing at the festivities.

permission from the NHL to make each member of the 1997 world championship Detroit Red Wings a solid silver hockey puck, engraved with the player's name and the Stanley Cup logo, which he bestowed as gifts to the team.

"Some people like to give us presents," said Fetisov with an annoyed shrug. "Do we have to say no? Do we have to check his background or what? I don't know what you're talking about anyhow." Fetisov did admit, though, that he had "some business" with Komorov.

It is precisely such "business" connections with hockey players that worry law enforcement, for it is through them that people like Komorov can spread their influence, reaching into many levels of American society. Wall Street has been the Russian mob's prime target. Gavin Scotty, for instance, is a senior vice president at Paine Webber, and a onetime pro basketball player who handles large portfolios for a number of Russian NHL players. When he decided the time was ripe for the company to do some business in Ukraine and Russia in 1998, he invited in some of these clients to ask who the leading Russian business guru in New York was. They unanimously identified him as Felix Komorov.

As it happened, Scotty already knew Komorov. "A couple of my players had won the Stanley Cup so we've been invited to parties that he's thrown," Scotty said. "I thought he was a legitimate, nice guy." Scotty later met with Komorov at the Oyster Bar at Grand Central Station to inquire about potential business deals. The Russian had a number of ambitious plans, and was eager for Scotty to meet his associates in Kiev. After the meeting, Scotty was inclined to embark on some of the ventures Komorov proposed.

Then, by chance, he learned that his dining companion might in fact be a high-ranking member of the Russian mob. Scotty broke off contact. "I don't want to be in the middle of problems," he explained. "I've got a family, and I've got a big, big business, and I don't need this."

As the FBI's Kerr pointed out, the possibilities available to men like Komorov through friendships with hockey players are almost limitless: they can provide introductions to valuable business contacts, to high flyers on Wall Street, to their personal money managers, to league coaches, general managers, and agents. Kerr suggests one possible scenario: With the threat of violence, a mobster forces a player to surrender a kickback on his sports endorsements. From there, the mobster could get an entrée into the sponsoring advertising firm, by having the player introduce a "friend" who's ostensibly skilled at marketing. "[The friend's] name is 'Svetlana.' She's an old KGB hand. And she works for the mob. She dates a married executive at the firm. The liaison takes place at a hotel, and lots of pictures are taken. Then the mob tells the ad executive what it wants him to do. This is how it's done. This happens all the time. All the time. It's as old as the KGB. Older," the FBI man recounted with a chuckle.

In certain respects, Kerr says, the current level of corruption in the NHL is strikingly reminiscent of the old Jewish and Italian mobs' infiltration of American society through their control of the garment industry and labor in the 1930s and 1940s. The mobs' first step was to take over many of the unions, ranging from the truck drivers and longshoremen locals to the International Brotherhood of Teamsters. "Then the LCN bled millions and millions of dollars from the Teamsters' pension fund, and built hotels in Las Vegas with this money," explained Kerr. "That helped them get into the legitimate gambling business and the hotel business in Las Vegas." These legal and quasi-legal operations were much harder for law enforcement to crack, and the vast sums of money made from them were later invested into other mob-controlled businesses. The FBI fears the NHL could similarly become not only one of the Russian mob's biggest cash cows but also a stepping-stone into legitimate society and commerce.

Komorov, according to the FBI, is already involved in such schemes. But Fetisov refused to see the importance of the connection between Komorov's relationship with NHL players and the FBI's contention that Komorov is a high-ranking member of the Russian *Mafiya*. "I know that Komorov owns a nice little art studio, and he made presents for all the Red Wings players," I said to Fetisov. "And according to the FBI, he's *Mafiya*."

"Why do you have to put all these things together?" Fetisov asked. "They are not related anyhow."

"If you go to Brighton Beach," I said, "and mention the name Komorov, it's like saying John Gotti. Everybody knows who he is."

Fetisov continued to insist that he has no criminal dealings with Komorov or Ivankov whatsoever, and called such charges "false allegations." He was completely exasperated. "You're probably not allowed to ask these kinds of questions, right?" Fetisov asked incredulously. "Are you allowed to ask any questions you want?"

"Sure. Yes. This is America."

Fetisov realized there was only one escape: furious, he stood and ordered me to leave. "The interview," he said, "is over."

Had Fetisov been the only Russian NHL superstar to have befriended the *Mafiya*, law enforcement might not have such cause for alarm. But he is hardly alone. When Ivankov ordered his brother-in-law, and second-in-command, Vyacheslav Sliva, to move from Moscow to take over the Russian Jewish mob's Canadian operation, Sliva turned

for assistance to someone he considered an old friend—
Valeri Kamensky, the left-wing All-Star for the Quebec
Nordiques (which later moved to Denver to become the
Colorado Avalanche).

Though Sliva had lied to immigration officials about not
having a criminal past, and though he had been able to provide a forged government document backing up that claim,
the feared crime lord still needed the endorsement of a
respected citizen to help him through the visa process.

Kamensky obliged, asking the co-owner and president of
the team, Marcel Aubut, to write a letter on Sliva's behalf to
the Canadian embassy in Moscow. "Please issue a visitor's
visa to a friend of one of our players, Valeri Kamensky," wrote
Aubut. The document succeeded and Sliva was granted an
interview with Canadian immigration officials, at which he
described himself as Kamensky's longtime friend. "The only
reason why I'm coming to Canada," Sliva told the officials,
"is to visit Kamensky." In 1994, Sliva was awarded the visa.

"So Sliva comes over here on the strength of that invitation," says a top Canadian law enforcement official. "Let's
just say that their relationship was more than just having
dinner together. Sliva was interested in making sure that
Kamensky's career was going good and that he was looked
after, that he wouldn't have any problems. Then later down
the road, Kamensky would owe Sliva."

It didn't take long for Sliva, based in Toronto, to dominate Canada's thriving Russian Jewish mob. In the process,
however, he drew the scrutiny of the Royal Canadian
Mounted Police. "We covered Sliva like a blanket," says the
Canadian official. According to testimony by Canadian law
enforcement, Sliva was recorded talking to associates in
Russia and North America, making death threats, and discussing drug deals, extortion, and money laundering. Seven
of the taped conversations were with Ivankov in which the

gangsters talked about how to divvy up their proceeds. In conversations held between April 28 and May 5, 1994, they were overheard plotting to assassinate Igor Golembiovsky, the prominent Russian editor of the newspaper *Izvestia*, which had published an article on April 28 about Ivankov's connection to some unsavory elements in the KGB.*

But the Mounties say Sliva isn't the only Russian crime lord that Kamensky is chummy with. More than one hundred phone conversations were monitored between Kamensky and Vatchagan Petrossov, whom the FBI contended is an Armenian *vor v zakonye* and the head of the Russian mob in Denver. According to law enforcement officials, the men are "very close," and their friendship became even closer when the Nordiques moved to Denver.

Petrossov, asserts a classified FBI report, was allegedly Ivankov's "strategic advisor" and involved with him in "drug trafficking and extortion." Ivankov frequently traveled to Denver, where he stayed at Petrossov's home, even using his address to apply for a Colorado driver's license.

Denver may seem like an unlikely refuge for the Russian mob, but by one estimate the area boasts as many as sixty thousand Russian émigrés, many of them illegal. In addition, the relatively crime-free solitude of Denver offers a good cover for laundering money. In order to blend in, the Russian mobsters dress tastefully, drive Toyotas and an occasional late-model Mercedes, and live in fairly modest homes. They donate to charities and try to keep a low profile.

---

*Ultimately, Ivankov's treatment of irksome journalists turned deadly. Vladimir Listyev, the director of Russian public television and a man as beloved as Walter Cronkite in this country, had fearlessly spoken out against the mob's attempt to steal the lucrative advertising revenue from his top-rated show *Ostankino* and other newly privatized programming. In March 1995, Listyev was shot in the head near his Moscow apartment. The hit was allegedly the joint effort of several mob groups, including Ivankov and his acolyte Sliva.

Petrossov has described himself as a philanthropist and
a businessman, and an officer of a midtown Manhattan
company called PetroEnergy International, which he
claims develops new technology in oil production. However, PetroEnergy doesn't have any customers yet, and
prominent oil and gas research firms in New York and
Houston say they could find no information about Petrossov's purported company. The FBI, Customs, and the
NYPD are looking into the enterprise.

One Petrossov business that did exist was a restaurant
called the St. Petersburg, which he opened in the early
1990s in Glendale, a small, middle-class suburb of Denver.
Ivankov was apparently a partner. (A business card identifying Ivankov as the owner of the St. Petersburg was found
among his possessions when he was arrested in Brighton
Beach.) The FBI and the IRS suspected that Petrossov and
a Denver-based Russian partner constructed the restaurant
to launder money: the more than $2 million it cost to build
was wired into the personal bank accounts of both individuals at the First Interstate Bank in Denver in increments of
$200,000 and $300,000. "All construction was paid for in
cash, as were the land, their personal residences and cars,"
the FBI report says. "Russian emigres working on the project have been treated roughly, with payments to them
delayed."

The sprawling restaurant covered over 16,500 square
feet, featured a billiards room, and sported a state-of-the-art
stage for Vegas-style floor shows. Despite its size and ameni-
ties, it was almost always empty, even on weekends, said
federal law enforcement sources who surveilled the eatery.
"The restaurant does not seem to generate enough business
to pay the salaries of the employees brought from Russia to
serve and entertain," said the FBI report. Beefy Russian
wiseguys seemed to be its only customers. "I know Ivankov

was there," Moody says. "Two or three other thieves-in-law that visited the United States stopped there, too."

The source of the restaurant's financing, the feds discovered, was apparently Intercross International, a company in Moscow in which "'Thief-in-law' Petrossov is a director," according to a classified FBI report. Intercross's income was derived from deals Petrossov made importing cigarettes from R. J. Reynolds Tobacco Co. in the United States and manufacturing polyester goods for sale in Russia. Much of the cigarette trade in Russia is untaxed contraband dominated by the mob, and Petrossov was reported to have been able to stay in business by making payments to a people's deputy in the Russian government, says the FBI document. He also made contributions to political figures who allowed his shadowy company to operate unencumbered from a heavily guarded compound in Moscow.

It was no coincidence that the restaurant, which was partly owned by Petrossov's wife and renamed Maverick's Steak House in the mid-1990s, was Kamensky's favorite hangout. He was apparently so taken with it that he appeared on Denver television commercials as Maverick's pitchman. At one point, according to a well-placed law enforcement source, the Avalanche star was asked by the FBI if he knew Petrossov, or had any information about the extortion of Russian hockey players in the NHL. Kamensky denied all knowledge of both. "He lied through his teeth," says the source. (Kamensky, traded to the New York Rangers in 1999, never responded to requests for an interview.)

In June of 1997 the Mounties were able to prove that Kamensky's friend Sliva had forged the document averring his crime-free past — in fact, FBI records indicate that Sliva had spent ten years in the Gulag with Ivankov for extortion and torture. The Immigration Board, ruling that he posed a grave danger to Canada, deported the haggard-looking mobster via a jet bound for Moscow.

Unlike Sliva, Petrossov managed to sidestep an attempt in 1997 to deport him on visa fraud for failing to disclose his criminal past, which a confidential FBI document says included fifteen years in the Gulag for rape and inciting a riot. According to law enforcement sources, his lawyer convinced a judge not to give credence to the accusations of a corrupt communist regime, claiming that his client was set up by a prostitute, and that, moreover, his record was expunged by a Soviet court in 1989. Not surprisingly, one of Petrossov's character witnesses at the Denver deportation hearing was Felix Komorov, who was identified in court as president of Rolls-Royce of Moscow.*

---

*Petrossov almost didn't get into the United States in the first place. He was twice banned from obtaining a U.S. visa at the American embassy in Moscow, and put on a list of rejected applicants. V. B. Rushailo, chief of the MVD's organized crime section in Moscow, sent a letter to U.S. officials warning that Petrossov was considered a dangerous thief-in-law. So Petrossov traveled to Riga, Latvia, and applied for a visa with a clean passport, without mentioning his previous conviction, which is required under U.S. law, whether it has been expunged or not. A frustrated State Department source says Petrossov slipped through the American security net because the Riga embassy was using an outmoded computer system.

Like Ivankov, Petrossov's U.S. visa was sponsored by an American film company. Its name was International Home Cinema Inc. of Santa Monica, California. Its chairman, Rafigh Pooya, an Iranian, was working on a $500,000-budget, *Days of Our Lives*–style potboiler set in Baku, Azerbaijan. A filmmaker friend referred Pooya to Petrossov, then living in Moscow, who invested $50,000 in the production under the name of his company, Intercross International. As Pooya tells it, Petrossov contacted him one day asking to visit his investment. Pooya wrote a letter of recommendation to the U.S. embassy inviting Petrossov to be his guest. Petrossov, whom Pooya described as a "small man with a small round face," turned up with a "fat lawyer and an associate." Pooya said they weren't interested in screening rushes, but instead bragged about jetting around North America, visiting their other investments.

The FBI says Pooya's "company is known to have issued previous invitations which have been suspected of being fraudulent."

"Allegations, allegations," Pooya says indignantly.

Nevertheless, when Petrossov—Ivankov's cousin by marriage—last tried to enter Canada on unspecified business in 1996, "we kicked his ass across the border," beamed Glenn Hanna, a criminal intelligence officer of the RCMP's Eastern European Organized Crime Division. He added that a computer check identified Petrossov as a thief-in-law and a major Russian gangster.

Despite Petrossov's successful bid to remain in the United States, the FBI still considers him the leader of an increasingly active Russian mob in Denver. It has assigned one of its top agents—a veteran of the Oklahoma City bombing case—to reexamine the thief-in-law's extensive file line by line.

Petrossov's home is in leafy Glendale. One Friday afternoon in the winter of 1998, I decided to pay him a visit to ask about his relationship with Kamensky and Ivankov and extortion in the NHL. In a bit of a role reversal, I brought along an attorney built like a nose tackle, who is licensed to carry a concealed weapon and is black belt in Sambo, a form of Russian martial arts. Usually, it is a big Russian who knocks on a victim's door; so when the freshly shaven and heavily perfumed Petrossov opened the door wearing an expensive Italian knit shirt, slacks, and shoes, he seemed a little taken aback. I introduced myself.

"Friedman, you are a bad man, a liar!" he barked— apparently, my reputation had preceded me. He accused me of persecuting the Russian people with fabricated stories about mobsters. His tirade was interrupted only when his pink shar-pei, Amy, darted out of the house and into the street, agitating him even more. "Amy, come back," he pleaded to the pooch.

"It's not proper," he said. "You come without calling?"

"I'm sorry, Mr. Petrossov, but you have an unlisted number."

Not surprisingly, he refused to answer any specific questions about whether he is involved with organized crime, has done time for rape, or is friends with Kamensky and Ivankov (although he attended Ivankov's month-long extortion trial in Brooklyn, and defended him in an interview with the *New York Daily News*, calling him "a hero to the masses." He still visits Ivankov in prison, and is allegedly the Armenian *vor* who handed Ivankov the suitcase stuffed with $1.5 million in cash when he arrived at Kennedy Airport).

"Why are you afraid to answer my questions, Mr. Petrossov?" I asked. "Law enforcement says you are a *vor v zakonye.*"

"What is law enforcement?"

"They say that you are a godfather," I said, standing nose-to-nose and toe-to-toe with the dapper *vor*.

"I don't know what you mean!" He shouted. Shaking with rage, he finally threw me off his property. As a parting gesture, he slammed the front door so hard that it bounced back open, barely missing his precious little Amy.

Pavel Bure is as slick as ice. Despite his many ties to Russian mobsters, the twenty-seven-year-old four-time All-Star handles grilling like a veteran politician, claiming he has never heard of the Russian mob's extortion of hockey players.

"People have problems everywhere," said Bure with a shrug, as he sat, freshly showered and wearing a T-shirt and jeans, in the locker room of the spectacular Vancouver stadium that's home to the Canucks, where he was then playing. "But I never heard somebody who had, like, problems with the *Mafiya* or whatever. I don't know," he continued with a smirk, "what's *Mafiya*? It's the criminal, right?"

Bure, with his soft, blond good looks, isn't as innocent

as he pretends, for he has never denied his close friendship with forty-nine-year-old Anzor Kikalishvili, the native Georgian the U.S. government considers one of Moscow's top crime bosses. In addition, he has been seen in Moscow in the company of singer Joseph Kobzon who is, according to a classified FBI report, "the spiritual leader" of the Russian mob, and his stunning New York University–educated daughter. As early as 1993 the Vancouver Canucks had ordered Bure to stop his unseemly associations with Russian underworld figures, and though he agreed to the demand, he has in fact never honored it.

"I spoke to an agent who spent a lot of time in the former Soviet Union," recounted a source close to the congressional investigation of the Russian mob and the NHL. "He said, 'This guy Bure, you just wouldn't believe who he hangs out with over there. He's constantly doing the town with the mobsters.'"

In fact, Bure is also in business with them. He and Kikalishvili have recently reestablished the watchmaking concern of Bure's great-great-great-grandfather, which was famous for the beautiful timepieces it made for the czars. They are "very, very expensive," Bure said proudly. "I gave one to the mayor of Moscow." Boris Yeltsin was also a recipient of one of the watches.

In early 1998 it was widely reported in Russia that Kikalishvili had named Bure president of his "nonprofit" company, the Twenty First Century Association — a promotion from Bure's former title of vice president in charge of sports. Billboards throughout Moscow depict a beaming Bure and Kikalishvili promoting the Twenty First Century Association. While the FBI asserts this business is a *Mafiya* front that is worth at least $100 million in illicit funds, Kikalishvili insists it is a legitimate enterprise. The company has extensive interests in real estate, hotels, banks, and as many as ten casinos. According to FBI records, it also retains a combat brigade of fifty ex-athletes to protect it from other mob families and carry out criminal activities such as extortion and arms trafficking, including the sale of high-tech weapons to Iran.

Yet when I asked Bure if he is president of the Twenty First Century Association, he denied it. "How could I be the president if I play here in the U.S.?" he asked.

A few weeks later, in a telephone interview from his Moscow office, I asked Kikalishvili the same question.

"He was the vice president for sports and still helps," replied Kikalishvili, carefully choosing his words. "So of course the vice president, when the president leaves, should assume the role of president."

The relationship between the Russian Rocket and the Russian gangster dates back to Bure's childhood. "I knew him when he was a boy and played on a children's [hockey] team," Kikalishvili acknowledged. A sportsman himself, he eventually became head of the Russian Youth Sports League and, later, the Russian Olympic Committee.

Kikalishvili, forty-nine, initially impressed his fellow gangsters as a pompous buffoon: he claimed to be a descendant of an ancient Caucasus prince named Dadiani, he used a royal crest, and he featured his own lordly visage on a vintage wine he produced. Over time, however, Anzor "demonstrated new maturity," revealed a classified FBI report. During his sojourn in Miami in the mid-1990s, he was allegedly involved in the drug trade with South America, in bringing Eastern European prostitutes to the United States, buying tens of millions of dollars' worth of real estate to establish a beachhead, and in extortion with Tarzan, according to an FBI wiretap affidavit and law enforcement sources. "People treated him like a god when he was in America," says retired FBI

agent Robert Levinson, who specialized in Russian organized crime.

Kikalishvili, of course, denied all criminal allegations.
"In my whole life, I've never been in a police station, even
as a witness," he told me. "I've never stolen anything, not
even a pack of gum." He insists that he is merely a philan-
thropist, though few philanthropists are currently on the
State Department's watch list of organized crime figures.
But even international law enforcement's opinion of
Kikalishvili apparently isn't good enough for the Russian
Rocket.

"I have to see [the evidence] with my own eyes, you
know, to believe it," said Bure, who was traded to the
Florida Panthers in January 1999. "I know the guy. He's
really nice to me. So what am I supposed to say, 'You're not
my friend anymore'? I don't think it's fair and I think it's
rude. There's got to be a really big reason why I don't want
to be a friend with him. Like, if he does bad stuff, like . . .
drugs or arms, some big deal, you know?"

While ex–Eastern bloc players like Pavel Bure have
their own reasons to continue associating with the Russian
mob, the real question is why the NHL tolerates its presence.
Despite organized crime's frightening penetration into the
sport, the NHL, according to several sources, stood by idly,
even stonewalling the 1996 congressional investigation into
the situation. "We had subpoena power," says the committee's chief investigator, Michael Bopp. "We were a congressional committee, and still doors were just slammed in our
faces at every turn [by top league officials]."

Bopp first contacted the league's head of security, Dennis Cunningham, in the fall of 1995 for assistance. "He was
all excited," Bopp recalls. "He said, 'Oh yeah, this is a problem. Players have come to me and told me about extortion

attempts, actual extortion. I'm glad someone is looking into it. We're going to do everything we can to help you out.'"

Although Cunningham has claimed that he attempted to help with the congressional investigation, Bopp says that, "Slowly . . . over the next few months, [Cunningham's] demeanor changed 180 degrees, to the point where [he was saying], 'I don't know why you are looking into this. This isn't a problem.' The league just didn't want us poking around."

The FBI, likewise, has had little success in dealing with the NHL. "The teams won't let us talk to players about extortion," says a frustrated FBI official. "And we're here to protect them."

As a result, federal authorities have come to fear that the NHL is now so compromised by Russian gangsters that the integrity of the game itself may be in jeopardy and that the most dreaded word in sports might possibly infect professional hockey: "fix." "If you have a real high-powered scorer and you take him out of the game, it really helps out on the odds," says former top FBI official James Moody. "Gangsters play the odds. If they can cut down on the odds by taking out the prime scorer, or if the player takes himself out by purposely getting into foul trouble and is banished to the penalty box, then the potential to fix a game is there."

"Organized crime is in the gambling business," says another top FBI official. "If they can handicap the game with their players they will beat the spread. Do we know that Russian organized crime has tried to fix games in the past? What's the difference? That's exactly where they are going."

"That's the biggest concern," concurs Moody. "And I think as time goes on we're seeing more and more of that."

If the "fix" is in, the NHL isn't doing much to stop it. "I get really irritated with the National Hockey League," says another FBI agent in a large regional market with an array of pro sports teams. "Professional baseball, football, and basketball want us to be involved if we know of gambling, or dope, or anything that goes on with those leagues. But the National Hockey League, they don't care." Though the FBI office in New York has had some contact with the league, which has its headquarters there, the FBI man maintains, "I've never been asked to go talk to the National Hockey League [in my city], and as far as I know, none of our people has been asked to go to speak to any National Hockey League team."

After I wrote an investigative article documenting the Russian mob's infiltration of the NHL for *Details* magazine in May 1998, the league threatened to sue for libel and hired James Moody to look into the matter. Moody, who had left his position as the FBI's head of organized crime in 1996 to set up a private investigative agency, was asked to verify the claims of player extortion and mob collusion and provide an analysis. Moody had already worked occasionally for the NHL, having been responsible for providing the security for the Stanley Cup when the Detroit Red Wings' Russian players brought it to Moscow for a glittering celebration. To guarantee its safety, the cup was locked inside the KGB's notorious Lubyanka prison.

In the course of his investigation, Moody reinterviewed some of the article's off-the-record law enforcement sources, and tapped his considerable contacts in Russia. "Overall, the article was as fair and as accurate as it could possibly be," the FBI's John Epke told Moody.

Moody's probe unsettled him. "You look at some of the players like Slava Fetisov and . . . his association with Ivankov, and Kamensky's association with some of the thieves-in-law . . . [and] it is a cause for great concern." As for Bure's relationships with mob bosses, he says, "Anzor

Kikalishvili and Kobzon have been ID'd before Congress as members of organized crime and if you ask anyone in Russia they'll tell you the same thing." Moody sent his report to NHL headquarters, and the league could no longer plead ignorance, for it confirmed a disturbing portrait of the mob's insidious influence over the league. "Russian organized crime has a major foothold in the NHL," said a top bureau source, "and we've talked to them and they say it doesn't exist. . . . Then they hire one of the top experts in the world with the best sources in Moscow to prepare a report [which] said [the piece in *Details*] was letter perfect, and that the situation is actually quite worse. [Moody] has an unassailable reputation. . . . So now why wouldn't they cooperate with law enforcement or start their own investigation?"

Of course, the NHL has never made the Moody report public. Nor has Bure, Fetisov, Kamensky, or any other player associated with Russian mobsters been officially reprimanded, censured, or suspended. The league's corporate counsel has stated that he is not troubled by Fetisov's and Kamensky's alleged relationships with Russian crime bosses, and that Bure's friendship with Kikalishvilli was not at the point "where we thought it was problematic, either to the image or integrity of our sport." If it was, he said, "We would act on it." Meanwhile, Moody's confidential document is evidently gathering dust.

Since NHL commissioner Gary Bettman and head of security Dennis Cunningham both refused all requests for interviews, the reasons behind the NHL's apparent lack of concern for its players can only be surmised. A mixture of fear and greed seems the most obvious explanation. "Russian organized crime has a stranglehold over the league, [and] for the NHL to acknowledge it would be a PR disaster," said a top FBI official, noting that the league's top brass probably fear that its advertising revenue, its $600

million deal with Disney to broadcast hockey over ESPN
and ABC, and even its supply of raw Russian hockey players might vanish were it to challenge the Russian *Mafiya*.
"The league would see it as an existential threat."

Finally, hockey's critics say the league's moral standards
are simply lower than those of other major sports. For
example, the National Football League and baseball have
gone a long way to combat even the appearance of impro-
priety. New York Jets football legend Joe Namath was
forced by the commissioner of the NFL to sell his popular
Manhattan restaurant, which was frequented by mobsters,
or give up his career. New York Yankees owner George
Steinbrenner was banned from baseball's American League
for three years for having had a relationship with a gambler.
Baseball great Pete Rose was banished from the sport for
life for gambling on baseball.

Nevertheless, at the NHL, it is business as usual. Jittery
NHL scouts, scouring the far corners of the ex-Soviet
superpower for talent, are as vulnerable to mobsters as the
players they are trying to sign. It is not uncommon for gangsters to demand that scouts pay protection money to be
able to operate, international law enforcement sources say.
If they're lucky enough to sign a promising prospect, they
may also be asked to pay a percentage of the player's contract.

Meanwhile, the NHL is reportedly exploring the possibility of expanding the league to the ex–Soviet bloc at a
time when hockey there has perhaps never been more corrupt. In April 1998, the Russian Ice Hockey Federation's
president, Valentin Sych, was gunned down near his country home by an assassin with a Kalashnikov assault rifle.
Sych had been foolhardy enough to crusade against the
presence of organized crime in sports. Just before he was
killed, he charged that senior Russian hockey league offi-

cials are "the biggest thieves. All they're concerned with is lining their own pockets. Our hockey is now so corrupt that I don't see how we can ever clean it up." In the wake of Sych's murder, four hockey players were killed or grievously injured in the former Soviet bloc by assailants who demanded a piece of their salary. One, twenty-year-old Maxim Balmonchnykh, was stabbed while visiting his home in the industrial city of Lipetsk just after he had secured a multimillion-dollar contract with the Mighty Ducks of Anaheim, which is owned by Disney.

If the NHL plans to open franchises in the former Soviet Union, it will almost certainly have to negotiate with the *Mafiya*. Everyone who wishes to do business there, from Fortune 500 companies to adventurous entrepreneurs, "has to play the game to survive," says Joel Campanella, the New York cop who worked on the Brokhin case and is now a senior intelligence specialist for the U.S. Customs Service. As long as the former Soviet Union provides such a rich reservoir of talent, the NHL is likely to continue its de facto accommodation of the mob. And as long as everyone from the league's superstars to its own commissioner fails to speak out against it, the NHL will remain an irresistible opportunity for the world's most powerful and ruthless criminal cartel.

THE MONEY PLANE

On a hot, muggy afternoon in September 1992, two Hungarian police officials—a man and a woman—approached Alexander Konanikhine as he ate lunch with his wife at the Aquarian Hotel in Budapest. The lanky, twenty-three-year-old banker from Moscow kept a comfortable apartment in Budapest, where he often went for business. But a premonition had prompted him to check into the more secure luxury hotel. The policewoman, wearing a drab brown pants suit, ordered Konanikhine to accompany them to the Ministry of Security for questioning. They produced IDs, but Konanikhine could not read Hungarian.

"Do I have to go?" Konanikhine asked.

"No," said the woman. "We don't have official orders. But it will save a lot of trouble and paperwork if you come with us."

Konanikhine was driven to an ornate, five-story building in the center of downtown Budapest, several blocks from the security ministry. When the police ordered him inside, Konanikhine was suddenly terrified. He was the head of the All-Russian Exchange Bank, the largest commercial financial institution in the former Soviet Union. Ever mindful of the large number of Russian bankers who had been kidnapped and assassinated by mafiosi, he told his abductors that he had changed his mind and wanted to go back to the hotel.

"That's too bad," said the woman, a semiautomatic pistol protruding from her jacket. "We insist."

Konanikhine was led into a large room, and then a smaller inner sanctum where V. B. Adeev, the All-Russian Exchange Bank's chief of foreign investment, was standing inside the doorway. Adeev, twenty-five, was a massively built man with a Buddha belly. He was flanked by an even bigger Russian who was introduced as Sasha. "Most of the talking was done by Adeev," Konanikhine recalls. "The big guy didn't need to talk. Adeev wanted everything! My companies! All my money!"

Konanikhine, who was used to having his orders followed, and was irritated by Adeev's insolence, snapped, "You cannot tell me what to do!"

"You want me to kill you?" Adeev sneered, threatening to toss the young banker into a scalding bathtub and have Sasha work him over. Sasha lumbered toward him brandishing an electric iron, an incarnation of brute force.

"I don't want to die, Adeev," Konanikhine whispered.

"No pain. Just sign everything over."

"I was considered easy prey," Konanikhine, now thirty-three, recalls without a trace of emotion. "I was young and had a baby face. I didn't look dangerous. Many Russian businessmen have a very heavy look. They look like you don't want to fuck with them. That's the message and it was their protection."

The next few moments, he knew, would be dicey. He either played along, or Sasha would kill him. But he feared that as soon as he signed away his assets, he'd be killed anyway, and then they'd go after his wife. So Konanikhine stalled for time.

"I said, 'Fine. How do you want to do this?'"

"Well, just call your bank and transfer your money," Adeev instructed him. "I have a list of your accounts and business holdings."

Konanikhine convinced his captors that he needed his own letterhead stationery, a notary, and an attorney in order to complete the transfers without arousing the suspicion of his Swiss bankers. The process, he said, would take several days. He haughtily demanded to be taken back to his hotel so he could begin the paperwork.

"They were extremely dangerous, but very stupid," Konanikhine recounts. "I talked to them with a tone of authority. Russia and Eastern Europe are divided by social classes. They were from the subservient class used to taking orders from bosses." Konanikhine shook hands all around, and praised them for their fine organization. "Their social position in Russia was much less than mine, so it was like a general complimenting a private."

Konanikhine was driven back to the Aquarian, minus his passport and cash, which the group kept in order to prevent him from fleeing. Six guards were also posted in the hotel—one in the corridor near his room, the others in the lobby. Later that evening, Konanikhine calmly retrieved a second Russian passport with multiple business entries into the United States and some U.S. currency that he had earlier deposited in the hotel safe. He and his wife then somehow managed to slip out of the hotel by walking right out the revolving front door. Waiting for them was a friend with whom they had previously made dinner plans. "We jumped in our friend's car," Konanikhine remembered. "I told him to drive like crazy. He did. He was a businessman. He had the latest model of Volvo. The thugs tried to arrange a pursuit in a couple of Czech-made Scodas. They had no chance. We outran them in about one minute. We flew top speed to Bratislava, which is just two hours away from Budapest." There, Konanikhine and his wife boarded a plane bound for John F. Kennedy International Airport. "The next day we were walking in New York."

While Konanikhine, relieved to land safely on U.S. soil, was stepping off the plane at JFK, a not unrelated event was unfolding at a terminal nearby. At Gate No. 14, the usual assortment of passengers milled about waiting to board Delta Flight 30 nonstop to Moscow: American businessmen prospecting the new Russian capitalism, Russian entrepreneurs returning from investor hunting, expatriates going home to visit family, tourists yearning for a glimpse of the once-closed Soviet land. One passenger, though, was a courier, and knew something none of the other passengers was aware of: that the plane would be carrying one million fresh hundred-dollar bills in its belly.

At about 5:00 P.M. a cream-colored armored truck drove up to the red, white, and blue Boeing 767. While Delta workers casually went about tossing luggage into the hold, two armed guards began placing large white canvas bags on a conveyor belt. In the bags were stacks of uncirculated new $100 bills, all still in their Federal Reserve wrappers, dozens to a bag. And there were dozens of bags.

The plane departed JFK at 5:45 P.M. Throughout the nine-hour flight, the unarmed courier, who worked for the

Republic National Bank of New York, relaxed in the passenger cabin while the money sat "all by its lonesome" in the cargo hold, according to one law enforcement source. Upon arrival at Sheremetyevo airport at 10:55 A.M. Moscow time, the money was transported by a fleet of armored trucks to Russian banks, which purchased the $100 bills on behalf of clients, who typically paid for it with wire transfers from London bank accounts.

Rather remarkably, no one ever tried to hijack Delta Flight 30, even though it left JFK at the same time five days a week—rarely carrying less than $100 million and sometimes more than $1 billion. Since January 1992, federal authorities estimate more than $80 billion—all in uncirculated $100 bills, hundreds of tons of cash—was shipped to Russia. That amount far exceeds the total value of all the Russian rubles in circulation. The huge shipments of money remained safe only partly because of security; another reason was that anybody who might have been inclined to pull off such a heist was also well aware who is buying all those $100 bills.

"If you rip off Russian banks, you rip off the Russian mob," says one Mafia source here in the United States. "And no one's got big enough balls or a small enough brain to do that."

The Russian mob, according to numerous well-placed law enforcement sources, has been using an unimpeded supply of freshly minted Federal Reserve notes to finance its international crime syndicate. Ironically, the cash is supplied to dirty banks in Russia with the full blessing of the Federal Reserve in an attempt to prop up the ruble and preserve Russia's fragile free market economy. American C-notes have become the unofficial currency of Russia, and, of course, can get things done there that rubles cannot; but the hundreds are also being used to fuel the

Russian mob's flourishing dollar-based global drug trade, as well as to buy the requisite villas in Monaco and Cannes. The Russian *Mafiya* has also used laundered funds to set up operations abroad, including its American offshoot in Brooklyn's Brighton Beach, and has begun investing in legitimate businesses across Europe and in the United States.

In his speech to the United Nations in January 1995, President Bill Clinton declared money laundering a threat to national security. "Criminal enterprises are moving vast sums of ill-gotten gains through the international financial system with absolute impunity," he said, signing a presidential directive ordering the attorney general and the Treasury to identify individuals and organizations involved in global financial crime and seize their assets here and abroad.

When the Soviet Union collapsed in 1991, so did the entire government-controlled banking system. Replacing the government banks were private institutions chartered and supposedly regulated by the new Russian Central Bank. But as Major General Alex Gromov of the Russian tax police told a 1994 international conference on Russian organized crime, the "application" to charter a new bank typically consisted of making a $100,000 bribe to a banking official. "A grossly underregulated banking sector sprang up virtually overnight," says Harvard economist Jeffrey Sachs. "Now you have two thousand banks, many of which are deeply undercapitalized, and therefore everything is possible."

No one saw the possibilities more clearly than the mob. On July 2, 1993, two chartered jets touched down in Yerevan, the capital of the Republic of Armenia, and disgorged a panoply of wiseguys from the United States,

Germany, Turkey, Italy, and South America. They had been summoned by Rafik Svo, the gangster equivalent of an international diplomat, who had tried to broker the peace accord between Elson and Nayfeld. Svo was determined to bring order and mutual prosperity to the Thieves' World by ending destructive turf wars and forging alliances between the Sicilian Mafia, the Brighton Beach *Organizatsiya*, and Colombian drug lords, all of which sent emissaries. At the meeting it was decided that the Russian banking system, new and vulnerable, would be used to launder funds, make favorable loans to "friends," and supplant Zurich as a haven for dirty money. The big joke at the Armenian conclave was, "Why rob a bank when you can own one?"

While initially the mob used Russian banks just to park their money, they soon began to "buy banks, to find out who had big deposits so they knew who to kidnap," said Jack Blum, a Washington lawyer who directed congressional investigations into money laundering and who broke open the Bank of Credit and Commerce banking scandal. Then, in collusion with politicians, government bureaucrats, black marketeers, and the KGB, the mob used the banks to facilitate the huge post-perestroika looting of the former Soviet state. Profits from the sale of stolen raw materials, of weapons snatched out of military arsenals, and of assets stripped by insiders from newly "privatized" industries were all spirited out of the country into off-shore companies and bank accounts. U.S. officials privately complain that tens of millions of dollars in aid have gone into Russian banks, never to be seen again. In fact, within just two years after the fall of communism, untold billions' worth of rubles, gold, and other material assets had already disappeared from the former U.S.S.R.

"Many of these Russians do not consider their activities to be criminal," said a CIA official. "For them, it is just 'business.' Their sense of right and wrong is nonexistent." Crime was the only growth industry in Russia, and the country had become, in the words of one former CIA director, a "kleptocracy."

Of course, that illicit money was not applied toward capitalizing legitimate businesses. Almost all of it was used by the *Mafiya* to fund its international criminal activities, from extortion to drug trafficking to arms dealing. Mob-controlled Russian banks took in huge deposits of narco-dollars from South America, converting them to rubles, then back into dollars through European and U.S. banks. Increasingly, they have purchased European companies with histories of legitimate banking activity, and then used them as a conduit to pass illicit funds into the international banking system. More ominously, they have acquired hidden control of banks in Austria, Germany, France, Switzerland, and England, according to U.S. law enforcement sources. In fact, in only eight years, the Russian banking system has already become one of the world's leading money laundering centers, replacing Panama as the favored dirty-currency exchange of the Colombian cartels and the Italian Mafia.

"Almost all Russian banks are corrupt," Major General Alex Gromov explained at the international conference, which was co-sponsored by the Financial Crimes Enforcement Network (FINCEN), which tracks money laundering for the U.S. Treasury. A 1994 classified CIA report identified ten of the largest Russian banks as mobbed-up fronts. And in a 1995 meeting in Moscow with State Department envoy Jonathan Winer, Viktor Melnikov, the Central Bank's director for foreign exchange control, "expressed great concern about the state of the Russian banking system, citing estimates that anywhere from 50 to 80 percent of Russian banks were under the control of organized crime," according to a State Department cable. FINCEN director Stanley Morris put it more bluntly: "Russia's banking system is a cesspool."

The *Mafiya*'s takeover of Russian banking has been shockingly easy. Since there are no regulatory controls over proprietorship, even felons are permitted to own banks. What's more, there are no money laundering laws, regulatory agencies, or depositor insurance. The Russian Central Bank is notoriously lax in exercising control over the nation's nascent financial system—a point some Russian central banking officials readily concede.

"It's very difficult to tell from the outside what a transaction [with a Russian bank] really means," says the State Department's Wincr. "There are not a lot of public documents. You can't go to an SEC to look at a balance sheet for a Russian firm the way you can in the United States. You can't go to a bank regulator and [find out] what kinds of loans have been made, what the underlying source of capital is, or any other number of key issues, let alone who their customers are.

"These are issues which the Russian Association of Bankers is concerned about, because they are not unrelated to the murder of the bankers."

More than sixty Russian bankers have been killed by mobsters since 1994—one for simply having refused to make a loan. In a particularly grisly incident, Oleg Kantor, president of Moscow's Yugorsky Bank and a gas and oil mogul, was found outside a luxury hotel on July 20, 1995, with a huge hunting knife plunged into his chest in what police called a contract killing connected to his bank's business with a mobbed-up aluminum company. Kantor had been stabbed seventeen times, his throat was slit, and his chest slashed vertically in half. Many more bankers have been threatened. The deputy superintendent of the New York State Banking Department, Robert H. McCormick, has heard stories of Russian bank examiners being chased away from doing their jobs by a hail of gunfire.

"It's very frightening," says Dan Gelber, the former minority chief counsel of the Senate Subcommittee on Investigations. "What [do] you do with a bank that from top down is not honest? I mean, it almost creates a situation where there is no remedy."

Russian banker Alexander Konanikhine was confident that America would provide a safe haven from the cruel forces that had dispossessed him. If he could make a mint in the motherland, why not in the U.S.A., where cunning could also turn dreams into fabulous fortunes?

Still, the loss of Konanikhine's bank in Russia was a severe blow to the financial prodigy. He had grown accustomed to the lavish perks of Klondike capitalism. By 1992, he had controlled a Russian banking and real estate colossus with some 100 companies; his personal net worth was more than $300 million. The anchor of the whiz kid's financial empire was the All-Russian Exchange Bank, the first commercial bank to be granted a government license to operate a hard currency foreign exchange. It was also permitted to issue unusual certificates of deposit in the form of specially minted sterling silver doubloons, bearing the aquiline profile of Konanikhine's wife. "You can't imagine what kind of wealth was produced," Konanikhine boasted. "By the time I was twenty-three, there wasn't a single hard currency in which I was not a millionaire. I was one of the richest entrepreneurs in Russia."

Along with a score of other fabulously wealthy young

capitalist princes, Konanikhine had helped to finance Boris Yeltsin's successful 1991 presidential campaign. The election victory was followed by a failed coup by hard-liners, in which Yeltsin, like Lenin at Finland Station, rallied the masses from atop a tank. Fearing the return of totalitarianism and the end of an era that gave them the unfettered license to make money, Konanikhine, along with the other new capitalists, increased their support for the new president.

A grateful Yeltsin treated Konanikhine as a favored son, inviting him to join his delegation during his first official state visit to America. In addition, Yeltsin bestowed upon him a sprawling state residence that once housed Mikhail Gorbachev, as well as the former compound of Soviet World War II hero Marshal Zhukov, who led the Red Army into Hitler's Berlin. Konanikhine also built his own showy dacha in a densely wooded area not far from Moscow with eight bedrooms, a private gym, a swimming pool, and a twelve-car garage—which hardly accommodated his fleet of sixty automobiles. The banker says he was protected around the clock by a praetorian guard of some 250 veteran KGB security men.

To protect his companies, Konanikhine claims he hired four KGB officials, including Adeev, placing them in top management positions. Later, he asserts, he discovered that the men were secretly running a multimillion-dollar money laundering ring through the All-Russian Exchange Bank. It was his attempt to fire them, he explains, that resulted in the kidnapping in Budapest, the home base for the Red *Mafiya*'s powerful crime lord Semion Mogilevich, whom the FBI believed had joined forces with the KGB men to chase Konanikhine out of his banking kingdom.

But Konanikhine couldn't easily abandon all that he had

worked for in Russia. After arriving in the United States, he initiated a furious letter-writing campaign to President Yeltsin and the Russian press, bitterly complaining about his abduction and the *Mafiya*'s seizure of his assets. He named names and demanded a police investigation.

His strategy backfired when Adeev filed a criminal complaint with federal prosecutors in Russia, charging that Konanikhine had embezzled $3.1 million from the All-Russian Exchange Bank. "[Konanikhine] has a persecution complex," Adeev told *Kommersant*, a respected daily business newspaper in Moscow. "[He thinks] I am following him and that I want to kill [him]. But in all my affairs I follow the principles of economic expediency. And it tells me that this is not to our advantage to kill Konanikhine until the time when the bank gets the $3 million back. But as for me, I would not give a single dollar for the life of this man." Adeev's charges prompted Deputy Prime Minister Anatoly Kulikov to declare before the Duma that Konanikhine had actually embezzled an astounding $300 million from the bank, and a warrant was issued for his arrest.

A few months after settling in America, Konanikhine went to work for Menatep Bank, one of the largest banks in Russia. According to a 1995 classified CIA report, Menatep was "controlled by one of the most powerful crime clans in Moscow," and that it had set up "an illegal banking operation in Washington." Konanikhine's boss, Mikhail Khodorovsky, was one of the titans of the Russian business world. The thirty-five-year-old tough-talking chairman of Menatep was worth some $2.5 billion, and enjoyed a spot on the Forbes 200 list of billionaires. Through Menatep, Khodorovsky controlled tens of billions of dollars of Russian assets, among them Yukos Oil, the country's second biggest oil company, as well as vast mineral, media, and capital assets—all won, the CIA claimed, by trawling the murky shallows of the Russian underworld, a claim Khodorovsky vehemently denies.

Konanikhine and Khodorovsky had first met in Moscow where they were rival bank moguls. "I had a lot of respect for him," Konanikhine admitted. "He had a lot of respect for me. I wound up here in the U.S. with not much to do, and he said: 'Why don't you help me turn Menatep into Russia's first international bank? Russian banks don't have much of a presence in foreign countries. They are very domestic.' We made a lot of research, and I started implementing it."

Konanikhine received a $1 million employment contract from Menatep, which he claims named him the company's vice president. He soon resumed his lavish lifestyle, quickly acquiring a $315,000 condo in the Watergate Complex with a view of the White House, homes in Antigua and Aspen, a Mercedes 600SL, and a BMW.

High on the Russian bankers' list of objectives, says Konanikhine, was to persuade the Federal Reserve to grant Menatep a license to open branch offices in New York and Washington, which would enable it to accept American deposits and make loans. Branch offices in the United States, with its iron-clad financial system and the respect it had earned in the international community, would immediately lend credibility and prestige to any bank, greatly facilitating its business anywhere in the world. Attorneys hired by Konanikhine made their case to the Fed, and were turned down immediately. Menatep subsequently took out full-page ads in the *New York Times* and the *Wall Street Journal*, hoping to counter its unsavory image. The Russian banking giant also paid $66,000 to PBS's New York affiliate, WNET, to have its name and corporate logo appear in fifteen-second spots before and after *The MacNeil/Lehrer NewsHour,* which ran six times a week for almost a year.

After finding that opening a branch bank in the United States would be problematic, Konanikhine tried to help Menatep set up "false-flag" banks in Austria, England, and Uruguay. "The bank in Uruguay was supposed to become the financial bridge between South America and Eastern Europe," Konanikhine explained.

In was in the Caribbean, however, that Konanikhine had his greatest success. In July 1994, Konanikhine and Khodorovsky discreetly founded an Internet bank in Antigua. The European Union Bank (EUB) was created, according to the CIA, with a $1 million investment from Menatep. The initial company filings in Antigua listed EUB as a subsidiary of Menatep and Konanikhine as the bank's sole shareholder. The Bank of England later informed the Federal Reserve that Konanikhine had been in Antigua in 1995, "where he called on government officials to request their cooperation in keeping Menatep's ownership of European Union Bank confidential," according to a U.S. banking document. EUB's prospects were helped by the fact that Clare Roberts, who became Antigua's attorney general, registered it and was a member of its board. To lend EUB an air of international respectability, Lord Benjamin Murkoff, a member of the British House of Lords, was brought on board as founding chairman. (Murkoff bailed out when the Bank of England told him there was something "dodgy" about EUB.)

It was no accident that EUB was set up in Antigua, the center for dirty money in the Caribbean. Despite its tiny population of 66,000, the island has more than fifty banks, at least eleven of which are owned by Russian organized crime, according to the State Department's Jonathan Winer. The country's officials receive enormous bribes from gangsters willing to pay to operate quietly there. "Antiguan officials promise they're going to clean it up, and as soon as I step on the plane and fly back to Washington, they open another mobbed-up bank," the State Department's Winer complained. In March 1997, the State Department called Antigua the "most vulnerable East Caribbean island to money laundering" and a "key transit zone" for drugs smuggled into the United States.

Touted as the world's first Internet bank, EUB thrived for a few glorious years. It offered fabulous rates on CDs, money wiring services, and credit cards, and quickly became, assert law enforcement sources, one of world's premier money laundering facilities—a kind of crooked bankers' Stargate, where gangsters using secret-coded accounts could hurtle funds around the globe in nanoseconds. Its elegantly designed Web site promised super-secrecy so that its cybercustomers could conduct any number of transactions, such as laundering funds from fictitious companies, over the Internet. The Russian and Colombian cartels allegedly washed millions through the bank before U.S. law enforcement officials caught on. More embarrassing still, although EUB's office was located above a noisy bar in Antigua, its computers were operated by Russian techies out of Konanikhine's advertising agency located in Washington, D.C.'s, courtly Willard Hotel, just blocks from the White House. If a crime was being committed, therefore, it was under U.S. jurisdiction. But by the time the FBI woke up to the alleged money laundering operation, it had been shut down and the computers, the master server codes, and records had been shipped to Canada.

According to INS documents filed in Virginia, Khodorovsky responded to a Federal Reserve inquiry about

Konanikhine's and Menatep's banking activities by admitting in a letter that Konanikhine was authorized "to carry out a study of American and offshore markets" for Menatep. Menatep's lawyers, however, professed minimal involvement in establishing EUB, further stipulating in a letter to U.S. banking regulators that while Khodorovsky intended to serve on EUB's board, he and Menatep severed their ties to Konanikhine shortly after EUB was chartered. For his part, Konanikhine claims to have sold his shares of the bank before it was shut down and went bad, though he refused to say to whom.

According to Canadian law enforcement officials, however, it was Vitali Papsouev, an eighth-grade dropout and the son of a janitor, who bought the holding company. He happens to be one of Toronto's top Russian organized crime figures, according to the RCMP.

Whatever the truth of the matter, EUB was merely a cog in the Russian mob's money laundering colossus. Congressman Jim Leach, who heads the House Banking Committee, has asserted that billions of dollars may have been laundered out of Russia since 1995, and that dozens of Western banks have been used as conduits for this money. "Any time that dirty money can find its way into the U.S. financial system, it poses a risk to us," said Jerry Rowe, the IRS's chief officer of narcotics and money laundering.

The Russian mob's monstrous growth has been aided considerably by its ability to quickly and easily launder its dirty criminal proceeds into clean—and now supposedly counterfeit-proof—U.S. hundreds. It is this money that has allowed the Russian dons to swagger into Miami and ratchet up prices on the luxury housing market by paying for million-dollar properties with minty new $100 bills, or to set up shell companies in Brighton Beach to sponsor U.S. visas for Russian gangsters, or to hire sophisticated money managers and lawyers in Los Angeles and Denver to invest in import-export companies. This money "can, in fact, give criminals an opportunity to operate in a legitimate arena," said Rowe, "whether it be in the political arena or buying up businesses. I mean, we could end up with those companies in some way supporting political candidates that they think will help them in one way or another."

In banking, reputation is everything. So when agents of the Criminal Investigation Bureau of the New York State Banking Department learned in 1993 that Republic National Bank was selling tens of billions of dollars' worth of federal currency to as many as fifty corrupt Russian banks, they became particularly alarmed. "This posed a question to us: if there are legitimate reasons—and there very well may be—for this money to be going over to Russia, why is it being sent to entities which have been determined, rightfully or wrongly, and I believe rightfully, to be controlled by organized crime?" said a source close to the Banking Department's investigation. "It just didn't make sense to me. The analogy I always use is that it would be like sending money to [John Gotti's] Bergin Hunt and Fish Social Club. Why are we doing that?"

New York State banking officials were so concerned by these findings, the source said, that they urged federal agencies to probe Republic's banknote trade with Russia. But "right down the line" from the FBI to the CIA, "basically, the response that we were getting was, 'Yeah, it looks like we've got a potential problem here, but you know what? It's not our problem.'

"To us, it was like a sore on Cindy Crawford's face! I mean, it was there. And I said, 'Geez, isn't someone curious about how that sore got there?'"

If American law enforcement was slow on the uptake, the Russians certainly knew what was going on. At the September 1994 conference in the United States, a Russian general was asked why Russian banks were buying billions of dollars in U.S. currency. According to a participant at the meeting, he chuckled, and said, "'Oh, that's money laundering.' Then he went, 'Hey, we're being ripped off in our country; the money is coming over here, being cleaned, and being brought back [into the United States].'"

State Department officials explain that money laundering works something like this: Russian assets, such as oil, are stolen by underworld figures or corrupt plant managers and sold on the spot market in Rotterdam. The proceeds are wired through front companies on the Continent and deposited in London banks. Gangsters place an order for, say, $40 million in U.S. currency through a bank in Moscow. The bank wires Republic, placing a purchase order for the cash. Republic buys the currency from the New York Federal Reserve. Simultaneously, Republic receives a wire transfer for the same account from the London bank. Republic pockets a commission and flies the cash from New York to Moscow. It is then used by mobsters to buy narcotics or villas, or run political campaigns.

As far as Republic is concerned, if there was a problem with a customer, it was up to the banks in London or Moscow to warn it. According to a provision of the 1992 Annunzio-Wylie Anti–Money Laundering Act, American banks are required only to make sure that they're not knowingly doing direct business with criminals or their agents. "All that's incumbent upon the American bank is to see if the other bank is a duly constituted bank, recognized by the central bank of that country," said the New York State Banking Department source. "To me, looking at it as someone who has been in law enforcement all my life, do I think maybe we might have some willful blindness here, or blinking, or looking the other way? I think so. Can I prove it? No. Republic's guilty of willful blindness, though not in technical violation of any existing law. . . . It may be overly simplistic, but I'll put it like this: if you identify bad guys, and you're sending money to bad guys, I mean, to me that's not good!"

"That money is used to support organized crime; it's used to support black market operations," agreed an official at the federal Comptroller of the Currency office, which regulates Republic. "In my personal opinion, this is an absolute abomination. It should not exist. Yet it appears that at least part of the federal government sees nothing wrong with it."

One part of the government that has chosen not to address the problem is the U.S. Treasury, which stands to gain $99.96 from any $100 bill that leaves the country and never returns. The Federal Reserve is similarly, blissfully ignorant. "What do we know of Republic's customers?" said New York Fed spokesman Peter Bakatansky. "We don't. It's their responsibility to know who they are sending it to."

For the record, the Republic National Bank, which made millions from the currency sales, insisted it certainly was not knowingly selling $100 bills to mobsters. "That's my responsibility, to make sure we don't sell to the banks that have organized crime ties," said Richard Annicharico, one of Republic's compliance officials. "That's the hardest thing to find. In fact, if you know of any, let me know.

"I've run out of places to check," continued Annicharico, a retired IRS agent. "Someone tells me [the banks are corrupt] and gives me substantial reason why—you know, anything, really—we don't sell to them. I mean, anybody who tells us not to, we'll stop them tomorrow."

Asked about a classified CIA report that named ten major Russian banks—among them many Republic clients—that are run by organized crime, Annicharico replied, "We looked at that, and we stopped doing business with some of those banks as a result of that." In fact, Annicharico asserted, Republic would completely shut down the dollar trade if federal officials ever showed it hard evidence that its client banks in Russia are corrupt. "Believe me, I wish they would," he said. "But you have a large faction of the U.S. government that thinks this is great! You have some of the law enforcement people who are negative on it. So you have a dual thing."

Annicharico acknowledged that a federal money laundering task force had contacted him about Republic's currency trade with Russia. "The task force told me that they think Russian organized crime is involved in money laundering. But so what?" he said. "Who? What? Who? No one's been prosecuted. What's the crime? Tell me—I'll stop. I always tell them, 'Tell me which banks, and we'll stop.' I can't find them. I'm not being facetious."

Despite the number of investigations, high-level meetings, and international conferences that seem to involve Republic, Annicharico insisted the bank has never been officially accused of selling money to a mobbed-up bank. "No. I never heard that," he said. "But the innuendo is there because we sell to [Russia]. But so what?"

In the wake of all the attention Republic was attracting concerning its dollar trade with Russia, Anne T. Vitale, senior vice president and deputy counsel of Republic National Bank and a former assistant U.S. attorney, was assigned by Republic to investigate whether selling cash to banks in the former Soviet Union was potentially illegal. She turned to the FBI, to see if they would "give her a letter that everything Republic was doing was clean," according to a former government official. The FBI refused, stating that while Republic's sale of dollars to Russian banks is legal, it "doesn't pass the smell test."

Many law enforcement officials were not surprised that it is Republic that became the focus of concern regarding these controversial banking practices. "Republic has had a checkered past," said a New York State Banking Department source. "They've been a subject of suspicion over the years. . . . People have sort of grinned when they heard Republic's name linked to mobbed-up banks in Russia." Buddy Parker, an assistant U.S. attorney in Atlanta who has prosecuted major money laundering cases, said: "Well, let's say Republic always had some very interesting customers who find the government looking at them, more so than maybe other banks. I know that a number of customers of Republic Bank have been targets, some of which have been prosecuted, some of which haven't. . . ."

As for Republic's dollar trade with mobbed-up banks, former U.S. commissioner of customs William von Raab said with characteristic bluntness, "That's the smell that was always coming off Republic."

Proclaimed by *Institutional Investor* to be "perhaps the most successful banking entrepreneur of the postwar era," Republic's owner, Edmond Safra, built up a $50 billion global empire while amassing a personal fortune exceeding $2 billion. A Lebanese-born Orthodox Jew descended from generations of Syrian traders, Safra was also a financial prodigy. By the age of twenty-one he had founded Banco Safra in Brazil, which became a magnet for Jewish-flight capital from the volatile Middle East and later South America. In 1966, he founded Republic National Bank in New York with a scant $11 million in capital and a single branch in a Manhattan brownstone.

Republic quickly became known on the street as a bank that would send an armored car to pick up large sums from its customers with no questions asked. In the 1980s, Republic became the Russian bootleggers' bank of choice, and its suspect client accounts were subpoenaed by federal officials. Although Marat Balagula and dozens of other Russians were subsequently convicted of gasoline bootlegging, by then, hundreds of millions of dollars of illicit bootleg money was already flowing through the U.S. banking system, having been washed through a welter of shell companies.

The bank grew rapidly and became the twentieth largest in the United States, with assets of $50.4 billion and some seventy branches in New York, California, and Florida. An arm of Safra's Geneva-based Trade Development Bank (TDB), Republic had a net income for the nine months ending September 30, 1998, of $143 million, though it lost a staggering $190.7 million on Russian securities trading.

Safra specialized in niches that most other banks eschew, such as trading gold and banknotes. Though Republic's commission on banknote sales was not publicly divulged, "it's always profitable," Safra once told *Institutional Investor*. According to Charles Peabody, a banking analyst at UBS Securities, this kind of trade became "increasingly significant" to Republic's revenue stream. "It's a volume business, and it ties into the relationships they have with the central banks of the world . . . and I think Republic does have good relationships with the central banks of the world, probably built up through their gold-trading operation." Republic controlled more than 95 percent of banknote sales to Russia.

In the mid-1980s, Safra became the victim of a smear campaign orchestrated by American Express, which had bought Republic's Swiss parent, TDB, for $520 million in 1983. (Safra regained control of TDB five years later.) American Express hired a convicted felon to spread false stories in the international press depicting Safra as an unscrupulous operator involved in everything from the Iran-contra scandal to money laundering. Safra successfully sued two newspapers in France for libel and eventually won a public apology from American Express and $8 million, which he donated to four charities, including the International Red Cross and the Anti-Defamation League. Though Safra was stung by the accusations, they helped to inoculate his bank against subsequent money laundering allegations that were the result of legitimate law enforcement inquiries, as well as to scare away reporters.

Ironically, at around the same time American Express was disseminating these malicious falsehoods, the DEA, Customs, and the Swiss police had begun investigating Safra's banks in Switzerland and New York for laundering Colombian and Turkish drug money. "I can say on the record that the sense I got from the Customs agent with respect to Republic was that they were concerned about its activities," said William von Raab, the U.S. commissioner of customs from 1981 to 1989. (Despised by the banking industry for his outspokenness, von Raab had accused bankers at a 1982 conference in Miami of knowingly washing cartel drug money, shouting, "I am ashamed of all of you. You and your banks are engaging in sleaze!" A few years later, the crusading von Raab helped draft America's first money laundering law.)

Investigators had first been led to look into Republic's business through a bizarre set of circumstances. On Thanksgiving Day 1987, two Armenian brothers arranged to fly from Los Angeles to Zurich on KLM, having checked their baggage through to Zurich on Pan Am. "The Pan Am people were panicky about a bomb," Greg Passic, then a DEA supervisor and now with FINCEN, revealed. "The bomb squad put the suitcase in one of those blast containers, and exploded it, and $2.2 million went flying out of the thing."

The suitcases were addressed to the Magharian brothers, who were major currency traders. They had been depositing drug money into Shakarchi Trading company of Zurich, which in turn had allegedly been wiring it, as well as the funds of many other drug dealers, into account number 606347712 at Republic. According to *Newsday*, the account was "the junction of two major narcotics-money-laundering investigations spanning four continents." Customs agents were convinced that Republic was complicit. "The agents were really, really down on Republic," a top-level Customs source says. "I think they just felt it was a rotten bank."

A classified DEA investigative report prepared by a field agent in Bern, Switzerland, and approved by the DEA's Passic, dated January 16, 1988, described the link between Shakarchi, Safra, and Republic: "Shakarchi Trading company of Zurich, Switzerland, operates as a currency exchange company and is utilized by some of the world's largest trafficking organizations to launder the proceeds of their drug-trafficking activities. Its director, Mohammed Shakarchi, has been closely associated with the heads of these criminal organizations and assists those criminal organizations.

"Shakarchi Trading maintains accounts at the Republic National Bank of New York, a bank which has surfaced in several previous money laundering investigations.

"While he was alive, Mahomoud Shakarchi (Mohammed's father) maintained a close relationship with Edmond Safra, owner of the Safra Bank and founder of the Trade

Development Bank as well as owner of approximately 38 percent of the stock in Republic National Bank of New York. All of those banks surfaced in Mahomoud Sharkachi's alleged drug laundering activities."

In March 1989, the Magharians were indicted in Los Angeles for money laundering; two years later, Shakarchi's records were subpoenaed by Swiss and American police, who also confiscated Shakarchi's account at Republic, through which more than $800 million had passed over a five-year period. Neither Republic nor Safra nor Shakarchi was indicted, though Shakarchi later told Israeli journalist Rachel Ehrenfeld that he was convinced that the DEA was going after him to get him to testify against Safra.

The case against Shakarchi was quietly dropped in 1990, after the U.S. attorney for the Eastern District in New York concluded that there wasn't enough evidence to prove the money in the Republic account consisted of drug proceeds, said Robert Cozzolina, deputy special agent in charge of the U.S. Customs Service in Manhattan. Ehrenfeld, who investigated the case, alleged in her 1992 book *Evil Money* that a corrupt U.S. government official purposely inserted errors in the subpoena so that Shakarchi's attorneys could easily quash it and stop the investigation. To this day, Passic says he believes Shakarchi Trading was knowingly doing business with drug traffickers. Customs agents who have investigated Safra preferred not to talk about him because of his power. "If you go after somebody like Safra, you had better dot every i and cross every t," asserted one of the Customs agents who worked the Shakarchi case.

Although Republic had become a convenient fulcrum to help U.S. policymakers deal with Russia, by supporting its economy with the sale of badly needed dollars, many officials in both law enforcement and the Treasury Department privately worried that their dollar trade was funding the mob and not a needy ally. Officially, the Treasury and the Fed back the sale of U.S. dollars to Russian banks, arguing that market forces and geopolitics—and not the priorities of law enforcement—should drive the trade. At a high-level meeting of Fed and Treasury officials convened in Washington in 1995, specifically to discuss the huge dollar sales by Republic to Russia, Fed officials defended the practice, insisting that, other than through direct loans, it was the best way to bulk up the sagging ruble and help Russia enter the global free market, according to one participant.

When one official at the meeting suggested that Republic might, in fact, be doing business with banks controlled by organized crime, another vigorously defended the institution, saying that it did a tremendous amount of due diligence to make sure that Russian banks were legitimately operated.

"And that in itself is a big laugh," said the participant. "There is no possible way for anybody to conduct due diligence on a Russian bank. There were people there from the Fed who have no common sense at all."

The dissent in the government reaches all the way to the Comptroller of the Currency's office. When one senior official there was asked about Republic's dollar trade, he replied, "What I understand is that they are aiding in organized crime activities out of the former Soviet Union through their so-called correspondent bank relationships."

Indeed, an interagency federal task force on economic crime made a preliminary finding that Republic's dollar trade with Russia was consistent with money laundering, according to the Comptroller of the Currency source and another investigator with knowledge of Republic's activi-

ties. Drafts of working papers prepared by task force ana-
lysts stated this finding, but the charges were "tempered
substantially" in the final drafts that went to senior policy-
makers, said the official.

Although the early versions of the drafts did not explic-
itly use the term money laundering, "they indicate that the
volume of new money being transferred out of Republic
Bank into Russia is beyond that which is needed to support
the normal use of U.S. dollars in the former Soviet Union,
and that a further study needs to be made as to the actual
use of those funds," said the Comptroller of the Currency
official. But then the individuals who are in charge of
researching all that state that this is, in fact, used to support the black market and organized crime. But that does
not appear [in] the final report that is submitted to the
policy-makers."

So far the most vigorous government action that has
been taken regarding mobbed-up Russian banks has come at
the state level in New York. "We frankly have had a number
of expressions of interest from Russian banking institutions," said Robert H. McCormick. However, McCormick
said, "There is a whole potpourri of problems connected
with the Russian banks, [including] money laundering activity and underworld connections. So we generally discour-
age Russian banks from applying for branch or agency
licenses." Because of strict state and federal licensing standards, only a few Russian banks have applied for even representative office status in New York, which would allow
them to conduct public relations work, but not operate as
banks; other Russian banks backed off, after learning they
would have to submit to a rigorous investigation by the
state and the Fed's board of governors. "We have to be concerned about the competence of the people running the
bank, their experience, their background," said McCormick,

"and sometimes when we check that very briefly, the news is not good."*

In 1992, Stolichny Bank, then one of Russia's five largest private financial institutions and a major recipient of cash from Republic, met with New York's banking officials to inquire about obtaining a charter. After being discouraged, it never followed up with an application. Stolichny has been identified in a classified CIA report as a front for organized crime; the respected Austrian newsweekly *Wirtschafts Woche* has cited police records that alleged Stolichny's owner, Alexander Smolensky, was an international drug dealer in the top echelon of the Russian *Mafiya*. Two other allegedly mob-linked banks that bought cash from Republic—Inkombank and Promstroybank—also submitted New York applications. Promstroybank's license to open a representative office was approved by the State Banking Department in June 1995, and later by the Fed. Inkombank's April 24, 1995, application failed to pass either agency, and in October 1998 its license was revoked

---

*As for Republic, just as it was being acquired in September 1999 by HSBC Holdings PLC of London for $10.3 billion, U.S. federal prosecutors and banking regulators launched an investigation into its securities unit for massive fraud, centering on allegations that the head of the unit vastly inflated the value of an investment fund in which Japanese investors had placed more than $1 billion. The federal government charged in the indictment that the unit's head, Martin Armstrong, siphoned more than $500 million of investors' money in a giant Ponzi scheme in an apparent attempt to hide enormous trading losses. Republic's stock tanked in response, sparking rumors that the deal with HSBC might fall through. Although Republic cooperated with the investigation, it was legally liable for the lost funds. In November 1999, Safra accepted $450 million less than was made in the first offer for his controlling stake in the company. "Safra also agreed to be personally liable for up to an additional $180 million in costs related to the investigation beyond an already agreed and undisclosed sum," according to the *New York Times*.

On December 3, 1999, Safra was asphixiated by a thick, smoky fire in his Monte Carlo apartment complex set by a male nurse. The attack came during the final stages of the purchase of Republic Bank by HSBC.

by the Central Bank of Russia for its inability to honor its loan obligations. The bank collapsed amid allegations that Russian underworld figures looted accounts and used the banks to launder dirty money. "Why is it that there are so few Russian banks that operate in New York?" asked the Banking Department source. "The primary reason is that none of them are trusted."

But Russian mobsters have found a way around regulators. Instead of trying to bring Russian banks to the United States, they are buying stakes in privately held banks across the nation. Officials in California, for instance, are investigating the Russian mob's penetration of the state's privately held banks. As long as their investment remains under 10 percent, the mobsters do not have to file financial disclosure statements to the state or federal government. In some cases, several Russians acting in concert have allegedly bought sizable shares of California banks.

Although combating money laundering may have been stated to be a top priority of the Clinton administration, it's virtually impossible to stop. There are about 700,000 wire transfers a day, totaling $2 trillion. Some $300 million of that—less than one sixtieth of one percent—represents laundered funds, which are hidden by the huge volume of legitimate transfers, said a September 1995 report by the Office of Technology Assessment. The report concluded that no existing technology is capable of identifying all but the most obvious trade anomalies. "There is no way you can program the system to say, 'I want you out of these 700,000 transfers to look for [dirty] banks,'" said Rayburn Hesse, a State Department senior policy adviser who chairs a federal task force on money laundering. "The result is that we have an international banking system that knows no horizons. It operates around the clock. Our laws, however, know horizons called national boundaries." By 1999, law enforcement officials estimated that between $500 billion and $1.5 trillion (or 5 percent of the world's gross product) was being laundered every year.

No one in government with even rudimentary knowledge about Russian organized crime doubts that it has penetrated the international banking system. Many insist that selling dollars to mobbed-up Russian banks is morally indefensible, regardless of whether the trade is sanctioned by the Federal Reserve. Equally, they believe that if the dollars are bought with wired funds derived from asset-stripping, narcotics, stolen U.S. aid, or the black market sale of arms or nuclear materials, then the transaction should be considered money laundering. "Even though you can't fault Republic as to the current interpretation of the law, it doesn't necessarily mean that it's legal," said a Treasury source.

"It just means that some of the questions that you ask [are] ahead of where we have gotten," adds the State Department's Winer. "We are grappling with it. We are trying to put it together. But all of this has happened very quickly, and it's taking us some time to get adequate answers."

As part of that effort, the Treasury has helped the Russian Central Bank draft money laundering laws. But the legislation has stalled the Russian parliament, which has dozens of convicted criminals among its members.

Meanwhile, Russia's lawlessness has become so rampant that it has virtually capsized the country's banking system. In November 1998, Andrei Kozlov, the Russian Central Bank's deputy chairman, announced that mobbed-up banks had stolen Western government loans and aid, contributing to the meltdown of Russia's economy in August 1998, and leading to the insolvency of about one half of Russia's remaining 1,500 commercial banks. Menatep, for one, became insolvent and lost its license. Audit Chamber, a Russian government budgetary watchdog, and the Prosecutor General's office charged that Central Bank officials had made off with as much as $9 billion loaned to Russia by the World Bank and the International Monetary Fund. The looting had allegedly begun as early as 1992, but Central Bank officials and well-connected investors used the financial crisis of 1998 as an opportunity to seize even more funds, once they knew the ruble was about to be devalued. Amid the accusations, Central Bank chief Sergei Dubinin resigned. While denying any wrongdoing, he tried to quash the investigation, which is looking into allegations that he personally had stashed huge amounts of cash in Cypriot accounts. In September 1998, former deputy prime minister Anatoly Chubais admitted to the *Kommersant Daily* that he "conned" the International Monetary Fund out of more than $20 billion when he lied about the true state of Russia's ailing economy.

Meanwhile, Alexander Konanikhine's story continues to unfold. In June 1996, dozens of FBI and INS agents, accompanied by two ill-mannered Russian prosecutors, barged into Konanikhine's condo at the Watergate to arrest him and his wife for visa fraud. At a press conference shortly thereafter, the government announced that it had captured a dangerous international fugitive, who had bilked his bank in Russia out of $300 million. "We lived in the Watergate for three years," Konanikhine told me. "The building is full of Secret Service men, who protect all the politicians like Bob Dole who live there. It is the least likely place in the world for an international fugitive to hide. From my balcony, I can see the White House roof. It would be a hell of a place to start shooting. I was one of the few businessmen who tried to confront the *Mafiya* even before

it was a serious problem. Then I'm declared an international money launderer, an international fugitive. If you
want to find a crook, all you have to do is knock on any door
of the Watergate. I hate the fact that the *Mafiya* is in control of my country."

Konanikhine was placed into an INS jail in Winchester,
Virginia, without bail; his wife was released on her own rec-
ognizance, pending the ruling on their deportation hearing
by an INS judge. The couple applied for political asylum,
arguing that Russian bankers as a social class were being persecuted by the Russian mob.

Federal authorities argued during Konanikhine's INS
case that the mob had used the All-Russian Exchange Bank
to launder billions of dollars, and that despite Konanikhine's vehement denials, it was implausible that he didn't
knowingly participate in the scheme—especially given how
brilliant, meticulous, and controlling he is.

They further argued that, from the moment he arrived
in America, he laundered money for the Russian *Mafiya*
through EUB. The evidence for that, wrote the federal
prosecutor in the government's closing argument against
Konanikhine, was "clear, compelling and uncontroverted."
Indeed, three of Konanikhine's own expert witnesses testified that, in all likelihood, he is a skilled money launderer.
No less of a money laundering expert than Jack Blum said
that EUB "was a criminal fraud," and that it was highly
probable that Konanikhine was aware of the *Mafiya*'s ties
to the institution. Seen in this light, said the prosecutor, the
conflict between Konanikhine and his mobbed-up KGB
comrades and ex–business partners in Moscow was nothing
more than a falling out among thieves.

Miraculously, Konanikhine won his case for asylum on
appeal, becoming the first Russian since the end of the Cold
War to do so. He also succeeded in persuading the judge

that the INS and the Russian prosecutors had fabricated evidence against him as part of a quid pro quo that the FBI had entered into for help on the Ivankov case. In fact, the Russians threatened to close the FBI's office in Moscow unless the bureau handed Konanikhine over, according to memos sent from the FBI's field office in Moscow to Washington. The Justice Department's Office of Professional Responsibility is looking into the charges of misconduct by the INS and the FBI. Konanikhine, however, is now under investigation by the feds—for money laundering, a charge he denies. The Justice Department is also appealing the INS judge's decision to grant him asylum.

Yet the banking wizard is still bullish about his future in America. Grinning over a fruit plate at the Waldorf-Astoria hotel in Manhattan in 1999, he boasted that his new advertising firm was doing landmark business. "In a year," Konanikhine crowed, "I'll be a billionaire again."

THE WORLD'S MOST
DANGEROUS GANGSTER

Outside the small town of Ricany, near Prague, are two picturesque villas, an improbable setting for one of the most dreaded mob families in the world to savagely murder its victims. The mob's young enforcers, trained by veterans of the Afghanistan war, are infamous for their brutality. Their quarry, usually businessmen who have balked at extortion demands, are stabbed, tortured, and mutilated before being butchered. The carnage is so hideous that it has succeeded in frightening even the competing crime groups in the area.

The torture chambers are run by what international police officials call the Red *Mafiya*, a notorious Russian mob group that in only six years has become a nefarious global crime cartel.

The enigmatic leader of the Red *Mafiya* is a fifty-four-year-old Ukrainian-born Jew named Semion Mogilevich.

Known as "the Brainy Don," he holds an economics degree
from the University of Lvov. But hundreds of pages of classified FBI, British, and Israeli intelligence documents, as
well as statements by a key criminal associate and dozens of
law enforcement sources in the U.S. and abroad, describe
him as a malevolent figure who has become a grave threat to
the stability of Israel, Eastern Europe, and North America.

"He's the most powerful mobster in the world," crowed
Monya Elson, who is listed in the classified documents as
one of Mogilevich's closest associates and partners in prostitution and money laundering rings. "You can't imagine
what kind of power this guy has. He has more power than
Yeltsin."

When Elson was forced to flee Brighton Beach, it was
Mogilevich who spirited him out of the country and set him
up in a massive money laundering scheme in Fano, Italy. "If
I tell on Mogilevich, Interpol will give me $20 million,"
boasted Elson, who as of March 2000 was still awaiting
trial. "I lived with him. I'm his partner, don't forget. We are
very, very close friends. I don't mean close, I mean very,
very close. He's my best friend." Nevertheless, the irrepressible Elson ultimately confirmed some of the details
about Mogilevich contained in the classified FBI, British,
and Israeli reports, which extensively detail the full array of
Mogilevich's criminal activities: he traffics in nuclear materials, drugs, prostitutes, precious gems, and stolen art. His
contract hit squads operate freely in the United States and
Europe. He controls everything that goes in and out of
Moscow's Sheremetyevo International Airport, which is a
"smugglers' paradise," according to Elson.

There is apparently no deal that the godfather of the
Red *Mafiya* considers beneath consideration. An FBI informant told the bureau that one of Mogilevich's chief lieutenants in Los Angeles met two Russians from New York

City with Genovese crime family ties to broker a scheme to dump American toxic waste in Russia. Mogilevich's man from L.A. said the Red *Mafiya* would dispose of the material in the Chernobyl region, "probably through payoffs to the decontamination authorities there," stated a classified FBI report.

Mogilevich represents a novel and especially fearsome variety of Russian gangster, the prototype don of the new millennium. He has created a global communications network through secure satellite telephones, cellular clone phones, encrypted fax machines, e-mail systems, and state-of-the-art computers, all of which are conducted by a host of Ph.D.'s he employs. Relaxed travel restrictions and the greatly increased volume of international trade have enabled Mogilevich to extend his operations throughout the world, setting up a welter of legal and illegal companies that have helped him to penetrate international banking systems and stock exchanges, where he has planted top aides. He is protected by a web of relationships with high-ranking officials of international security services, high-flying financiers, and politicians. His licit and illicit concerns are administered by loyal white-collar managers and dozens of "soldiers," who "take care of all his business so that he himself keeps his hands clean and has no criminal record," says a classified Israeli intelligence report. He has built a highly structured criminal organization in the mode of a "classic" American Mafia family in which blood ties bind central figures: many of the organization's three hundred core members are his relatives, mistresses, and in-laws. The organization has a defined chain of command, with selected individuals within the group appointed to manage specific criminal activities, such as weapons trafficking or prostitution, while others are responsible for particular geographical regions. His strong leadership qualities, his acute

financial skills, his talented associates, and his political connections have effectively made the Brainy Don impervious
to prosecution.

Mogilevich, who is bald, weighs nearly three hundred
pounds, and favors florid shirts and luminous pinky rings,
was first exposed to the world at large in a profile I wrote
that appeared in *The Village Voice* on May 26, 1998. He
became internationally notorious, however, when federal
authorities accused him of perpetrating the biggest
money laundering scheme in U.S. history, washing an
astonishing $7 billion through the venerable Bank of New
York. In the media storm that followed, Mogilevich
denied the allegations, telling a Hungarian news magazine
that he just couldn't understand why he was being
accused of such heinous crimes, since he is, after all,
nothing more than a humble grain merchant. The only
money he ever laundered, he quipped, was a five-dollar
bill that he forgot to retrieve from his shirt pocket before
it went to the cleaners.

Little is known about Semion Mogilevich's early years.
He was born in Kiev and his mother was a podiatrist and his
father the manager of a large state-owned printing company. Legend has it that as a young man, he ran a small fruit
stand in Moscow, despite the Soviet Union's strict laws
against private enterprise. Soviet authorities first learned of
his criminal activities in the early 1970s, when he was a
member of the *Lyubertskaya* crime group, which operated
in the Moscow suburb of the same name. He was involved
in petty theft and counterfeiting, and was later convicted
for illegal currency speculation in Ukraine, for which he
spent eighteen months in prison. A few years later, he was
again arrested for dealing currency on the black market, and
received a four-year prison term.

But Mogilevich made his first millions fleecing fellow Jews. In the mid-1980s, when tens of thousands of Jewish refugees were hurriedly emigrating to Israel and America, Mogilevich made deals to cheaply buy their assets—rubles, furniture, and art—with the promise of exchanging the goods for fair market value and sending refugees the proceeds in hard currency. Instead, he simply made the sales and kept the considerable profits.

In early 1990, Mogilevich fled Moscow, as did many other dons, to avoid the gangland wars that were then roiling the capital. With his top henchmen he settled in Israel, where they received citizenship. In Israel, which does not extradite its citizens, Mogilevich kept a low profile, preferring to maintain the Jewish state as a place where he could move without restriction, rest, or find refuge in times of trouble, according to an Israeli intelligence report. Yet he "succeeded in building a bridgehead in Israel" and took "advantage of his Israeli citizenship and Jewishness, that allows him to travel freely in and out of that country," says the report.

Keeping a low profile did not, however, preclude "developing significant and influential [political and business] ties," according to the report. He forged contacts with Russian and Israeli criminals, and maintained control of several businesses through proxies, such as an international kosher catering service, a tourism company, and a real estate firm. "Since 1991 he has opened bank accounts in Israel in the names of various companies, and has attended gatherings in Israel with other known criminals," revealed the Israeli report. In addition, an Israeli bank, with branches in Moscow, Cyprus, and Tel Aviv, was "allegedly owned by Mogilevich, who is reportedly laundering money for Colombian and Russian Organized Crime groups," according to a classified FBI document. Mogilevich also unsuccessfully tried to gain control of the giant kosher distillery Carmel Mizrachi, according to Israeli intelligence.

Mogilevich, however, became disenchanted with living in Israel. "There are too many Jews in Israel," he told the *National Post* of Canada. "Too much arguing. Everybody is talking all the time and their voices are so loud." In 1991, Mogilevich married Katalin Papp, a Hungarian national, a union that allowed him to legally reside in Budapest, where he moved and began to build the foundations of his global criminal empire. He bought a string of nightclubs called the Black and White Clubs—with locations in Prague, Budapest, Riga, and Kiev—that became one of the world's foremost centers of prostitution. Mogilevich primarily used German and Russian women in these venues, providing cover jobs for them as well as bodyguards. In 1992, he cemented his ties to other Russian and Eurasian organized crime groups by selling partnerships in the prostitution business to the *Solntsevskaya* and Ivankov organizations. Monya Elson was also a partner, according to his own admission and classified FBI documents. The Black and White Club in Budapest became the hub of Mogilevich's worldwide operations, and he added a casino in Moscow and nightclubs in Eastern Europe as a way to account for the excessively high cash inflow from his criminal activities.

Mogilevich also fortified his organization by coordinating activities with non-Russian crime groups such as the Japanese Yakuza and the Italian Camorra. His mutually beneficial relationship with the Camorra, arguably the cleverest, most cunning, and most violent of the four Mafia families in Italy, gave him much cachet in the underworld. In one oft-repeated swindle, the Italians passed counterfeit American hundred-dollar bills (which had been made from bleached one-dollar bills) to the wily Russians, who passed the fake currency from their bases in dozens of countries. In turn, Mogilevich provided the Camorra with large quantities of synthetic narcotics along with expert money laundering services to wash the profits. The close ties between Mogilevich and Italian Camorra strongman Salvatore DeFalco particulary unsettled law enforcement authorities as they watched the Italian and the Eurasian crime bosses venture into new frontiers. The Italian authorities surveilled Camorra members operating in the Czech Republic in concert with Mogilevich, where they primarily trafficked in weapons. Meanwhile, Mogilevich made staggering sums smuggling huge amounts of cocaine and heroin into Russia from the United States and Canada. "The profits were then introduced into the banking system and moved across the world via the UK," states a confidential British intelligence report. Mogilevich even bought a bankrupt airline in the Central Asian former Soviet republic of Georgia for millions of dollars in cash so that he could ship heroin out of the Golden Triangle into Europe. Some of the drugs were to be allegedly smuggled into England by sea, says an Israeli intelligence report.

Mogilevich's organization was augmented dramatically with the creation of layer upon layer of sham companies that spanned every conceivable business. He had already established two such businesses in Alderney, one of the Channel Islands, which are well known as tax havens. One, Arbat International, was a petroleum import-export company, of which Mogilevich owned 50 percent. His friend Ivankov held a quarter share of the company. Mogilevich's other partners in Arbat—who jointly had a 25 percent share—were *Solntsevskaya* crime lords Sergei Mikhailov and Viktor Averin.

The other, a holding company called Arigon Ltd., became the heart of his criminal empire. Initially, it had seven investors; each owned approximately 14 percent of the stock, which cost one pound sterling. The Budapest branch of Arigon was allegedly managed by the wife of *Solntsevskaya* kingpin Sergei Mikhailov, according to Israeli intelligence.

Mogilevich was particularly intrigued by art fraud, and in early 1993 reached an agreement with the leaders of the *Solntsevskaya* crime family to invest huge sums of money in a joint venture: acquiring a jewelry business in Moscow and Budapest. According to classified FBI documents, the company was to serve as a front for the acquisition of jewelry, antiques, and art that the *Solntsevskaya* mob had stolen from churches and museums in Russia, including the Hermitage in St. Petersburg. The gangsters also robbed the homes of art collectors and even broke into synagogues in Germany and Eastern Europe to steal rare religious books and Torahs.

In another joint venture with the *Solntsevskaya* gang, Mogilevich purchased a large jewelry factory in Budapest where Russian antiques, such as Fabergé eggs, were sent for "restoration." Mogilevich's men shipped the genuine Fabergé eggs to an unwitting Sotheby's auction house in London for sale, and then sent counterfeits as well as other "restored" objects back to their original owners in Moscow.

Mogilevich also acquired a giant vodka plant in Russia and a plant for manufacturing hard liquor in Hungary, which he used to become a major smuggler of alcohol, claims a secret Israeli intelligence report. In 1995 alone, he smuggled 643,000 gallons of vodka out of Hungary. On May 5, 1995, twelve railroad cars filled with Mogilevich's vodka were seized by Hungarian authorities as he tried to slip the hooch past customs without paying duty.

More ominously, Mogilevich set his sights on the arms

industry. He had already sold $20 million worth of pilfered Warsaw Pact weapons, including ground-to-air missiles and twelve armored troop carriers, to Iran, according to the classified Israeli and FBI documents, and a top-level U.S. Customs official. However, to the even greater consternation of international law enforcement officials, Mogilevich began to legally purchase virtually the entire Hungarian armaments industry, jeopardizing regional security, NATO, and the war against terrorism. The companies he bought include:

• Magnex 2000, a giant magnet manufacturer in Budapest. *Solntsevskaya* crime boss Sergei Mikhailov allegedly served as its deputy director, asserts Israeli intelligence.

• Army Co-op, a mortar and antiaircraft gun factory. Army Co-op was established in 1991 by two Hungarian nationals, both in the local arms industry, who were looking for a partner. Mogilevich bought 95 percent of Army Co-op through Arigon Ltd., which also deals extensively with Ukraine, selling oil products to the Ukrainian railway administration.

• Digep General Machine Works, an artillery shell, mortar, and fire equipment manufacturer. Mogilevich financed the company with a $3.8 million loan from the London branch of Banque Française De L'orean. The loan was secured by the Mogilevich-controlled company Balchug, which manufactures and sells office furniture.

In 1994, Mogilevich purchased a license permitting him to buy and sell weapons through Army Co-op and other Hungarian arms companies, which established him as a legitimate armaments manufacturer. A Mogilevich company participated in at least one arms exhibition in the United States, where it displayed mortars modified by Israel.

Like mob bosses everywhere, Mogilevich would have been unable to sustain the growth of his empire without police and political confederates. In Europe and Russia, the "corruption of police and public officials has been part of the Semion Mogilevich Organization's modus operandi," says a classified FBI document. In Hungary, two former policemen serve as security coordinators for the Red *Mafiya*'s formidable combat brigades. "When his back is up against the wall, he's got a very effective body-guard force that keeps him alive," says former FBI agent Robert Levinson. Mogilevich's lieutenants are trained in intelligence operations and countersurveillance, and provide warnings of impending police actions against the organization. Law officers in Hungary and elsewhere keep him apprised of police efforts to penetrate his organization.

"He also ingratiates himself with the police by providing information on other [Russian crime] groups' activities, thus appearing to be a cooperative good citizen," a classified FBI report asserts.

In fact, Mogilevich has used precisely that ploy to compromise other European intelligence services. On April 28, 1998, the German national television network ZDF reported that the BND (the German intelligence agency) had entered into a secret contract with Mogilevich to supply information on rival Russian mob groups. The charges were made by several sources, including Pierre Delilez, a highly regarded Belgian police investigator who specializes in Russian organized crime. If the television report is accurate, one possible motive for BND's deal, believes a U.S. law enforcement expert on the Russian mob, is that the Germans faced an intelligence gap after having "pulled their people out of Moscow in 1998 because they didn't like the level of cooperation they were getting from the

Russian authorities on the Russian mob." Because of the deal with the BND, police in Belgium, Germany, and Austria have complained that it is now impossible to investigate the Brainy Don.

Mogilevich also developed substantial and well-concealed political connections, particularly in Israel, according to reports by Israeli intelligence, which notes the mysterious and unexplained disappearance of Mogilevich's Ministry of Interior file. In Brussels, Mogilevich's man Anatoly Katric, a Ukrainian-born Israeli citizen who spent much of his time entertaining international diplomats for the Red *Mafiya*, approached Philip Rosenberg, the head of the far-right, anit-immigrant National Front Party, which held 5 percent of the seats in the Brussels parliament. Katric offered Rosenberg 3 billion Belgian francs to obtain Mogilevich Belgian citizenship. Rosenberg allegedly agreed, but was indicted on corruption charges and fled to Papaya, Thailand, before the deal could be consummated. Investigators found suspected bribe money in a Swiss bank account, which Katric ultimately admitted to the Belgian police came from Mogilevich.

In France, Mogilevich approached Alferd Cahen, a recently retired high-ranking Belgian diplomat who had been ambassador to the Belgian Congo and France. Cahen had just been named secretary of the North Atlantic Treaty Association, the lobby group for NATO in Paris. Mogilevich, banned from entering France, wanted Cahen to arrange a meeting with French intelligence so he could propose passing political and gangland information to them in exchange for surreptitious access to the country. Cahen agreed to make the introductions, and both sides were apparently satisfied with the results, said Pierre Delilez. A disturbed Delilez had warned French intelligence against working with the mobster, for, "The more that these agencies use Mogilevich's services, the more trouble it will be to prosecute him." Cahen himself wasn't prosecuted, as there was no proof that money had changed hands, although investigators later found $180,000 in a bank account belonging to Cahen's son, which they suspected came from Mogilevich.

Extending his operations from his base in Budapest, Mogilevich had, in just a few years, forged a far-flung criminal empire with thousands of employees and an unprecedented reach from Great Britain to New Zealand. He had taken over all the black markets from the former Soviet republics through the Czech Republic, cornered the legal and illegal weapons market, and trafficked tons of drugs and precious stones, said a December 1994 British intelligence report.

Mogilevich has also sent contract hit teams throughout the world, including the United States, where the assassins arrive from Russia under tourist visas arranged by Vladimir Berkovich, the owner of the Palm Terrace restaurant, a watering hole for Russian gangsters in Los Angeles. Berkovich also supplied the mobsters with weapons and arranged for their return to Russia, according to a classified FBI document. (Berkovich said the government's charges are "total bullshit.")*

------

*Although Vladimir Berkovich has no criminal record in the United States, his son, Oleg, was convicted in Los Angeles of solicitation to commit murder on October 11, 1989. He was sentenced to four years. Oleg's business card identified his employer as Magnex Ltd., a company owned by Mogilevich in Budapest. Oleg's uncle, the colorful Lazar Berkovich, arrived in New York after having survived a shoot-out in 1978 with Italian gangsters, says his brother Vladimir. The FBI says Lazar was head of Russian criminal activities in Italy, involved in the trafficking of antique relics, homicide, and robbery prior to escaping from Italian authorities and coming to the United States with the help of Mogilevich to recuperate from wounds suffered in his clash with the Italian Mafia.

* * *

Mogilevich's spectacular invasion of the North American financial markets began in 1993. That year, a company called YBM Magnex International in Newtown, Pennsylvania, was infused with some $30 million from Arigon Ltd. By then, the Brainy Don had already set up dozens of shell companies in the United States to launder proceeds obtained from criminal activities. Typically, many of the "businesses" were located in the residences of organization members. Numerous wire transfers of funds from Arigon Ltd. and other Mogilevich accounts overseas were transferred to these entities in amounts ranging from under $10,000 to more than $1 million.

But Mogilevich had particularly grand plans for YBM, which was merged with Magnex 2000, his Hungarian company that sold industrial magnets and military hardware. He appointed his brilliant, trusted, childhood friend and adviser Igor Fisherman as YBM's chief operating officer. Fisherman, who lived in Budapest, served as the coordinator of Mogilevich's criminal activities in Ukraine, Russia, the United States, the United Kingdom, the Czech Republic, and Hungary, according to FBI documents. A trained mathematician, Fisherman had once been a consultant to Chase Manhattan Bank in New York City.

Mogilevich and Fisherman discovered a fact that Canadian financial criminals had long known—the poorly regulated Canadian stock exchange was a convenient entry point into the North American markets, one where the mob's substantial funds could be hidden under the umbrella of a publicly held company. Mogilevich chose Jacob Bogatin, a fifty-one-year-old professor of physical metallurgy, to prepare a public stock offering for YBM. Born in Saratov, Russia, Bogatin, YBM's group vice president, and the company's largest initial shareholder, had served on the board of Arbat and Magnex in Budapest.*

Under the watchful eye of Mogilevich and Fisherman, Jacob Bogatin traveled to northern Canada in 1995 to initiate the YBM plot by creating a legal shell company on the Alberta Stock Exchange. Christened Pratecs Technologies Inc., the company was a blind pool, or a business without assets. Blind pools are given eighteen months to come up with a major acquisition to capitalize themselves, otherwise they are delisted. Pratecs then began the process of acquiring YBM, which had already purchased Mogilevich's Channel Island holding companies, Arigon and Arabat. Pratecs subsequently issued 10 million shares of the company at 20 cents each, and prepared the YBM transaction for completion.

But on June 19, 1995, just a few months before the transaction to acquire YBM was to close, the Alberta Stock Exchange halted trading in Pratecs's stock. The company cryptically explained the suspension as a response to "allegations made in London, England, against two individual shareholders of YBM," whom they identified as a pair of British companies and their lawyers. "The companies are in

---

*Jacob Bogatin was certainly no stranger to the mob. His brother, David, is a top Russian crime figure in America, who once fought in North Vietnam for the Soviets in an antiaircraft unit, and is now serving an eight-year term in a New York State prison for a multimillion-dollar gasoline tax fraud scheme. Just prior to trial, David Bogatin had jumped bail, fleeing to Poland, where he set up the country's first commercial banks, which moved vast sums of money controlled by Russian wiseguys. He lived like royalty in a five-star Viennese hotel, surrounded by 125 Polish parachutists, some of them bedecked in shiny gold uniforms. Eventually, he was apprehended and returned to the United States. David Bogatin's European businesses were taken over by Sergei Mikhailov, who later sold them. (Before he fled the United States, he turned over his mortgages for five pricey Trump Tower apartments to a Genovese associate. The mortgages were liquidated and the funds were moved through a Mafia-controlled bank in Manhattan's Chelsea.)

no way related to YBM or its subsidiary, Arigon," an obscurely written press release stated.

In truth, both Canadian regulators and Bogatin himself were aware that British intelligence had spent three years investigating Mogilevich's racketeering empire, traveling across the globe to gain knowledge of its structure, according to British intelligence documents and sources on the Alberta Stock Exchange. The Canadian authorities were told that YBM and Pratecs were not only controlled by Mogilevich, but that the probable intention of obtaining Pratecs a listing on the exchange was to have a vehicle to launder dirty money, manipulate stock shares, and bilk legitimate investors.

By the summer of 1995, British intelligence was ready to strike against Mogilevich and his network of companies in Great Britain, which they suspected as fronts for drug trafficking, stolen goods, and money laundering. In an action code-named Operation Sword, British police raided Arigon's offices in London, as well as the offices of its attorney, Adrian Churchward, who was arrested and interrogated. Documents found in Churchward's office showed that over a three-year period the lawyer had used clients' accounts to launder more than $50 million in criminal proceeds on behalf of Mogilevich. The funds, laundered through the Royal Bank of Scotland with the help of a solicitor, "originated from a variety of dubious sources in the former Soviet Union," says a British intelligence report, which describes the money as "largely the proceeds of Russian organized crime in Eastern Europe from the Mogilevich and *Solntsevskaya* organization."

The High Court of Justice in London issued orders freezing the assets of Arigon and several of its shareholders, including Churchward and his wife, Galina, Mogilevich's onetime paramour. She had an eleven-year-old son with

Mogilevich who was being educated at a private school at
Kent.

But the criminal cases against Mogilevich, Churchward,
and others had to be dropped after Russian prosecutors
deliberately refused to turn over evidence, according to
British intelligence. Mogilevich didn't escape unscathed,
however, for he was banned from entering the U.K. His
British businesses were shut down, his solicitor's reputation
was ruined, Churchward was disbarred, and the Royal Bank
of Scotland was subjected to a high-level internal inquiry by
the Special Investigation Unit of the Bank of England.

The British affair was not the only incident that nearly
thwarted Bogatin's attempt to gain a foothold in Alberta. In
May 31, 1995, Czech police stormed a summit meeting of
Eurasian mob chieftains at the U Holubu restaurant in
Prague, which Mogilevich had bought in 1991 to use as a
prime money laundering center, according to FBI and
Israeli intelligence reports. The gangsters were meeting on
the occasion of Sergei Mikhailov's birthday to discuss carv-
ing up criminal jurisdictions and to iron out turf disputes
between Mogilevich and Mikhailov's *Solntsevskaya* organization. After years of cooperation, the men had come to
despise each other. Mikhailov had tried to shake down
Mogilevich for $3.5 million. There had been shouting
matches, and then bombing attacks.

On the eve of the conclave, an unidentified Russian
delivered an anonymous letter to the chief of police in
Budapest, stating that Mogilevich was to be assassinated at
the celebration. "Mogilevich knew he was dealing with
some very, very treacherous people," said former FBI agent
Robert Levinson. "They'd kill him in an instant."

After receiving the tip, the Czech prosecutor dispatched hundreds of cops to the restaurant, where they
arrested, photographed, and fingerprinted two hundred

partying mobsters. Their diaries, journals, and other documents were confiscated for photocopying. Anticipating a bloody shoot-out, the Czechs had parked two large refrigeration vans outside the restaurant to store the bodies. But the mobsters surrendered quietly, and following their release from custody they returned to their homes in Germany, Hungary, Russia, and Israel.

Mogilevich himself was conspicuously absent from the celebration. "Mogilevich may have [sent in the] tip himself as a protective measure, or, having arrived late, noted the police presence and fled," stated a classified FBI report. Whatever the case, five individuals were declared persona non grata by the Czech Republic following the police raid, including Mogilevich, Viktor Averin, and Sergei Mikhailov.

Although Canadian intelligence had been aware of both the Czech and British incidents, stock market regulators had only to inspect the rogues gallery that made up YBM's initial shareholders list to guess at its true nature. According to the author's analysis of the disclosure documents, Mogilevich and his confederates owned up to 90 percent of the shares. Among the major stockholders were the Brainy Don himself, his fifty-two-year-old Ukrainian-born ex-wife, Tatiana, and their twenty-eight-year-old daughter Mila, a blue-eyed blonde, who lived on Wilshire Boulevard in Los Angeles, as well as Mogilevich's ex-mistress Galina Grigorieva.*

---

*Another key stockholder was Mogilevich associate Alexei Viktorovich Alexandrov, aka "the Plumber." His nickname stemmed from his deft handling of "leaks" and planting disinformation for Mogilevich's organization. He was also Mogilevich's contact with the Hungarian National Police, and the source of derogatory information on Mogilevich's competitors. Based in Prague, the Plumber was also responsible for procuring Russian women for Mogilevich's sex market. Like many of Mogilevich's colleagues, he is well educated, holding degrees in economics and engineering, as a classified FBI document reveals. The FBI also reports that he has an address in Los Angeles. Alexandrov, a director of Arigon Ltd., was one of the five who were declared persona non grata after the incident at the U Holubu nightclub.

Despite the events of the previous months, on July 25, 1995, Pratecs publicly announced that it had received a clean bill of health. Canadian regulators in Alberta later acknowledged that, without any actual court convictions, they lacked the hard proof necessary to keep the company off the exchange. And so "after a six-week halt in Pratecs' shares," wrote the *Vancouver Sun*, "the Alberta Stock Exchange allowed Pratecs to merge with YBM, a move that allowed the company to transform itself from a shell whose only asset was its stock exchange listing into a manufacturing firm with plants in Hungary, Kentucky and ultimately a listing on the Toronto Stock Exchange in 1996."

Touted by Bay Street underwriters, YBM quickly became the darling of the Toronto Stock Exchange, eventually being included in the prestigious TSE 300 Index, the Standard & Poor's 500 Index of Canada. The company's glossy brochures boasted about big international deals and amazing new technologies. Almost overnight, it became nearly a billion-dollar-cap company. To enhance its image, YBM soon dropped many of the Russians from the board of directors, and added, among others, the powerhouse lawyer David Peterson, the former premier of Ontario.

While YBM's stock thrived, the Bay Street financial world continued to ignore the warning signs in the company's operations. A November 1995 confidential report by Britain's National Crime Squad concluded that Mogilevich had been transferring funds from Britain to Hungary, and from there to the United States and then on to Canada through YBM. Circulated throughout the top rungs of regulatory and financial circles by word of mouth, the report also asserted that Mogilevich was using the Canadian stock exchange listing "primarily to legitimise the criminal organisation by the floating on the stock exchange of a corporation which consists of the UK and USA companies whose existing assets and stocks have been artificially inflated by the introduction of the proceeds of crime," including drug and arms trafficking and prostitution.

A spokesman for one of YBM's major underwriters, First Marathon, later admitted that it had heard rumors about the company's ties to the Russian mob, but its concerns were allayed after auditors Deloitte & Touche initially reported the business to be financially sound. Unlike the bulls on Bay Street, the FBI was more skeptical. YBM—whose home office remained in Newtown—listed a paltry projected gross sales of $8,573 on its 1993 U.S. tax returns. In 1995, at the time of the acquisition of YBM by Pratecs, it claimed net sales of $32.5 million, net income of $3.3 million, and stockholder equity of $17.5 million. Surveillance of a YBM facility in Pennsylvania by the FBI revealed that it occupied a small section of a former school building. The space, the bureau concluded, was not capable of supporting either the 165 employees or the $20 million in sales YBM claimed in its glossy published report.

Although by August 1996 YBM's board was aware that the firm was being investigated by the U.S. Attorney's Office in Philadelphia, as minutes of a confidential YBM board meeting confirm, the company never informed its investors of the fact. During that same period, Bogatin was even promoting the company to the New York Stock Exchange, and the company was waiting approval for a listing on Nasdaq.

Investors also had no way of knowing that YBM's prestigious auditor, Deloitte & Touche, had issued a highly critical report, declaring that it had found irregularities and possible criminal fraud in the company's 1997 annual report. It noted that "one or more illegal acts may have occurred which may have a material impact on [YBM's] 1997 financial statements." Among other problems, auditors discovered that $15.7 million in magnet sales to the Middle East and North America had been fabricated. Deloitte & Touche resigned when YBM failed to follow its recommendation to hire an outside forensic auditor to conduct a sweeping reevaluation of the company's books and business methods. Several of YBM's directors, meanwhile, sold millions of dollars of their shares in YBM stock after they received the report from Deloitte & Touche, but well before it was made publicly available.

The beginning of the end finally came on May 13, 1998, when at 10:15 A.M., U.S. Attorney Robert Courtney, head of the Organized Crime Task Force in Philadelphia, led some five dozen agents in a joint FBI, IRS, INS, Customs, and State Department raid on YBM's offices in Newtown. Fax machines, computer hard drives, Rolodexes, bank statements, and shipping invoices were seized and loaded onto trucks. Citing the company's alleged ties to Russian organized crime, the law enforcement agencies asserted that YBM was a vast money laundering machine for Mogilevich. Just twenty-three minutes after the raid, trading in YBM's stock on the TSE 300 Index was suspended by Canadian authorities, but not before a quarter of its value had been wiped out.

In the months that followed the raid, a succession of bizarre revelations besmirched what was left of the company's tattered reputation. The *Financial Times* of London reported that a "revolutionary" scientific process YBM claimed it had invented for desulfurizing oil, and which accounted for 20 percent of its revenues in 1997, didn't even exist, according to the top earth scientists interviewed by the prestigious newspaper.

On September 22, 1998, irate institutional investors finally staged a coup after court documents filed in Alberta revealed that more than $20 million in cash was missing from YBM's accounts. Five directors, including Fisherman, were fired. On November 23, Bogatin received a "target letter" from the Justice Department stating it had gathered sufficient evidence to indict him for money laundering. He resigned two days later.

The new board's forensic investigators discovered what international police had strongly suspected all along—that Mogilevich had been directly involved in the affairs of YBM, siphoning money from the accounts of its subsidiaries, as well as using the company as a vast money laundering machine—with money passing through various front companies and banks in Moscow, the Cayman Islands, Lithuania, Hungary, and a Chemical Bank branch in Buffalo, New York. YBM received $270,000 from Benex, a shell company allegedly controlled by an associate of Mogilevich. Investigators later claimed that Mogilevich, using Benex, had laundered huge sums through the Bank of New York. When YBM's newly installed board sent Pinkerton men to visit the company's plant in Budapest, they were turned away by brutish guards brandishing Berettas and Uzis. The board couldn't even get a key to one of the foreign plants. In all, not only were tens of millions of dollars of reported YBM sales bogus, but customers and even entire product lines turned out to have been fabricated.

Finally, in late December 1998, the board announced that it expected YBM would be indicted and that it had no viable criminal defense. YBM was placed into receivership by an Alberta court. The government accused the company of fraudulently inflating the value of its securities by creating the appearance of record sales and revenues, while failing to disclose that it was run by a Hungarian-based mob boss. On June 7, 1999, YBM pleaded guilty to one count of mail fraud and one count of securities fraud. It was fined $3 million and agreed to make restitution to the thousands of

defrauded shareholders. The company admitted that its
principals played a shell game for regulators and investors,
setting up paper companies to hide its actual control. The
U.S. Attorney's Office has allegedly filed three sealed
indictments against company insiders, one of which has the
Brainy Don's name on it. Belatedly perhaps, in November
1999, ten of YBM's former board members, including
David Peterson, were charged by Canada's leading securities commission with violating the Ontario Securities Act
for allegedly failing to disclose to investors that the company was being investigated by U.S. authorities for its ties
to Russian organized crime. They deny the charges.

In the end, more than half a billion dollars in YBM's
market capitalization simply vanished. Perhaps billions
more was made by mobsters manipulating the stock's price,
buying and selling blocks of shares on inside information.
During its dramatic run on the Toronto Stock Exchange,
YBM raised over $100 million in hard Western currency,
and laundered hundreds of millions of dollars more. The
casualties included many average investors, as well as
groups like the Ontario Teacher's Pension Fund, which was
left holding $32 million of worthless shares. "It's now clear
that YBM's only successful business [was] the laundering of
criminal proceeds," said shareholders in one of many class
action suits filed against YBM's former board of directors,
Deloitte & Touche, and several law firms.

"This is the most significant and serious case of stock fraud
that I've investigated in eighteen years," said Adrian du Plessis,
a respected analyst for StockWatch in Vancouver, and a private
forensic stock investigator. "It represents a level of corruption
of the marketplace that is unprecedented in its nature."

The sensational size, sophistication, and sheer boldness
of the YBM scam, however, should not obscure a fact that
has continued to disturb many in law enforcement: namely,

that it was hardly a unique event. "This is just one case," says former FBI official James Moody, "but there are others just like it throughout the world."

How accurate that assessment was was strikingly demonstrated when, two years after the YBM scandal broke, Mogilevich found himself in the middle of the biggest money laundering case in U.S. history. It had been discovered that, through a series of front companies spanning Russia, Europe, and the United States, he and others, primarily Russian businessmen evading local taxes, had laundered billions through the esteemed Bank of New York. The massive scale of the operation, combined with the fact that it had occurred on U.S. soil, was a startling embarrassment to U.S. law enforcement and the government. (While the bank has not been charged with any wrongdoing, some investigators believe that the money laundering could not have taken place unless senior bank officials were bought off or otherwise involved. Indeed, in February 2000, Lucy Edwards, a former vice president of the bank's Eastern European division, and her husband, Peter Berlin, pleaded guilty to money laundering charges. Indictments of other bank officials are expected.)

Actually, Mogilevich had been making a mockery of law enforcement for a very long time. Although as early as the mid-1990s he had been publicly identified in congressional hearings as one of the top Russian mobsters in the world, prompting the U.S. State Department to bar him from obtaining a visa, the prohibition never stopped him from continually entering America under aliases on temporary traveler's visas issued in Tel Aviv. Between December 1, 1995, and December 7, 1995, for instance, Mogilevich traveled to Toronto, Philadelphia, Miami, and back to Philadelphia. Well after the YBM affair had become headline news, the brazen don boasted to a Hungarian magazine that he traveled to Los Angeles in late 1998 to surprise his granddaughter on her birthday. In January 2000, Mogilevich slipped into Boston to conduct business, say top European and U.S. law enforcement officials.

Although he is also barred from entering seven European countries, Mogilevich travels extensively around the world in order to manage his business affairs. He has almost as many passports as he has aliases, which have included Semion Mogilevich, Senior Mogilevich, Semion Mogeilegtin, Semion Mobllerltsh, Seva Magelansky. Other members of his organization travel just as freely, often using forged passports of superior quality. Some of them are couriers who transfer large sums of cash from country to country, according to Israeli intelligence files.

Mogilevich still controls a variety of criminal activities from one American coast to the other. And while he has been careful not to defile his own hands with the blood of his gangland victims, he has not refrained from associating with known killers while in America, prime among them Elson and Ivankov, whom he regularly visited on one of his numerous fraudulent passports.

The Bank of New York scandal was not without its repercussions for Mogilevich, however. Perhaps most seriously, the man who had relied on his underlings to take responsibility for his crimes had lost his anonymity, one of his most valuable assets. In addition, the FBI—which ironically had built an international training academy just a short cab ride from Mogilevich's Budapest headquarters in 1994—put intense pressure on the Hungarians to crack down on his operations there, and his homes and offices were raided by the Hungarian tax police. His presence in Budapest was costing too much blood, in any case; there had been more than 170 mob-related bombings in Budapest between 1994 and 1999, many of them directed at or initiated by Mogilevich.

Although Mogilevich has apparently abandoned Budapest as his base of operations, his global empire is still largely intact, and the Brainy Don spends much of his time flying between Moscow and Tel Aviv on his private jet. Mogilevich claims to feel secure in the Jewish homeland notwithstanding his feelings about his clamorous country-men. When asked in September 1999 by a Hungarian reporter to respond to charges that he was a major Russian crime czar, he laughed, dismissing the accusation as the mad "ravings of the FBI." That same month, he successfully won a libel case brought against a Hungarian television sta-tion that broadcast a report about his criminal activities. When asked why he didn't likewise sue the American media for similar stories, he replied that he wasn't really a rich man, and that, in any case, he joked darkly, he had just paid a hit man $100,000 to kill American reporter Robert I. Friedman.

Later that month, he complained to ABC News, "I have no business now. Who would do business with me?" he asked dejectedly as his underlings provided security, their faces hidden from the cameras. "I've lost my spark. Maybe I should tear my shirt off and prove my innocence, but I don't even care anymore. . . . There is a saying in Russia, 'if you tell a rabbit over and over that he is a pig, he'll oink.' Everybody says I'm a criminal. I'm used to it. And the pub-lic is, too."

When questioned how the charges that he was a crimi-nal had surfaced, he attributed them to a plot by the jour-nalist Friedman and the American Justice Department. A few days after the TV interview, say reliable sources, he was trying to obtain a permanent residence permit in Spain so that he could operate his "humble grain business" from that country's beautiful Costa del Sol and Barcelona.

GLOBAL CONQUEST

When the international press, bankers, and law enforcement officials professed outrage at the announcement that Red *Mafiya* boss Semion Mogilevich was allegedly behind the laundering of as much as $7 billion through accounts at the Bank of New York, it recalled the scene in *Casablanca* when the corrupt but worldly wise Vichy prefect masterfully played by Claude Rains told Humphrey Bogart's Rick that he was "Shocked, just shocked!" that gambling was going on in Rick's cabaret.

In fact, intelligence officials and government leaders had known since the early 1990s the true state of affairs in the former Soviet Union. The CIA alone claims to have published more than a hundred reports since 1998 for the American foreign policy establishment documenting crime and corruption in Russia—a society where everything from submarines for the likes of Tarzan to fissionable material for

Mogilevich was for sale. The agency reported that the Russian mob and its cronies in government and big business have looted the country into a condition resembling medieval beggary: the economy has declined every year since 1991. More than 40 percent of the country's peasants are living in abject poverty, suffering through Russia's third Great Depression this century. In the unforgiving fields, peasants are killing each other over potatoes. Social indices have plummeted. Workers' minuscule paychecks come late or not at all. Horrific terrorist bombings, apparently the responsibility of rebellious Islamic republics, about which the authorities can seem to do nothing, are causing a further erosion of the public's trust of the government.

At the same time on Moscow streets are more Mercedes per capita than any place on earth, and the number one concern of the city's nouveau riche is how to avoid paying taxes and hide their fortunes offshore. They revel away nights in gaudy sex clubs and expensive restaurants, gorging themselves on South American jumbo shrimp washed down with vodka and cocaine. Disputes are settled with bursts of submachine gunfire. It is a classic fin de siècle society erected on a seemingly limitless supply of dirty money.

No post-Soviet institution has been immune from corruption, and even investigators have been investigated, often for good reason. Vladislav Selivanov, head of the Interior Ministry's Organized Crime Division, admitted in a July 1998 press conference that a probe of the Federal Security Service, the successor to the old Soviet KGB, resulted in several criminal prosecutions and the dismantling of the service's organized crime unit on the grounds that it had ties to the Russian mob. A few months later, during a bizarre news conference in Moscow, a group of mid-ranking FSB agents wearing sunglasses and ski masks declared that their once-vaunted agency harbored thugs, extortionists, and *Mafiya* hit men.

To make matters worse, the country's few political reformers have been sacked or killed. The Duma is a den of thieves, as was Yeltsin's inner circle. The same has even been alleged of Yeltsin and his family, who have purportedly taken a million dollars' worth of kickbacks from a Swiss contractor that renovated the Kremlin. But corruption and influence-peddling are a national plague in Russia as old as the czars. No one in Russia can purchase anything of value without a cash-laden handshake.

Astonishingly, both the Bush and the Clinton administrations have unwittingly helped foster the Russian mob and the untrammeled corruption of post–Soviet Union Russia. When the CIA was asked in 1992 by Kroll and Associates, working on behalf of the Russian government, to help locate $20 billion that was hidden offshore by the KGB and the mob, the Bush national security policy team declined to cooperate. The Bush group rationalized, according to Fritz Ermath, a top CIA Soviet policy analyst writing in *The National Interest,* "that capital flight is capital flight. It doesn't matter who has the money or how it was acquired even if by theft; so long as it is private, it will return to do good things if there was a market."

Of course, that never happened, yet it did not prevent the Clinton administration from handing billions in aid to Russia without any accountability. With the vigorous support of the United States another $20 billion of International Monetary Fund loans has been deposited directly into Russia's Central Bank since 1992. However well intentioned, the Clinton adminstration simply has no way to deliver "economic aid that will give benefits directly to the people," as Brent Scowcroft, Bush's national security adviser, has asserted. The chastened Russian Central Bank, admitting that it lacked any mechanism to monitor aid money once it was deposited, initiated an investigation to determine if the funds were stolen, and if so, whether they were part of the monies passed by Mogilevich and others through the Bank of New York.

Until the Bank of New York fiasco, the top rungs of the U.S. foreign policy establishment refused to acknowledge the Russian government's staggering corruption. In 1995, the CIA sent Vice President Al Gore, who had developed a "special" relationship with then Russian prime minister Viktor Chernomyrdin, a thick dossier containing conclusive evidence of his widespread corruption. Gore's friend had become a multibillionaire after he took over Gazprom, the giant natural gas monopoly, with holdings in banking, media, and other properties. The CIA said it cost $1 million merely to gain entry into Chernomyrdin's office to discuss a business deal. It was also alleged, though Chernomyrdin denied it, that he was among the oligarchs who had been stealing the country's resources after the fall of communism.

Gore angrily returned the report, scribbling a barnyard epithet across the file, according to the *New York Times*, and declared that he did not want to see further damning reports about Russian officials. It is unlikely, then, that he read the classified FBI file claiming that two colonels in the Russian Presidential Security Service had traveled to Hungary in 1995 to pay Mogilevich for information on the upcoming Russian political campaign, which was then allegedly passed on to Chernomyrdin. "The corruptive influence of the Mogilevich organization apparently extends to the Russian security system," asserts the FBI report.

"The bottom line is that Clinton and Gore had lots of warning about Russian corruption under Yeltsin's banner of reform," wrote political columnist David Ignatious in the *Washington Post.* "And the question continues to be: Why didn't the administration do more to stop it?"

The most charitable explanation, which now seems tragically ironic, is that they truly believed they were helping the ex–Soviet Union make a meaningful transition to democracy and a free market economy.

"The American political establishment didn't want to hear about Russia's corruption," says Jack Blum. "They believe they're looking at nascent capitalism, and they are flat-ass crazy. A bunch of thugs run the country. They have stolen everything that isn't bolted down, moved it offshore, and then globalized their criminal business."

It was only a matter of time before the Russian mob tried to buy its way into the American political system that has contributed to it so generously, if inadvertently. In New York, for instance, they almost succeeded. The invitations had been mailed, the menu prepared, and everything had been arranged down to the last detail for a $300 per couple, black-tie fund-raiser for then Governor Mario Cuomo on October 10, 1994, at Rasputin—the garish nightclub then owned by Monya Elson and the Zilber brothers. But on the eve of the event, the Cuomo campaign canceled. Officially, the explanation was a scheduling conflict; discreetly and quite unofficially, federal investigators had warned the Cuomo campaign that Rasputin was a bastion of the Russian *Mafiya.*

A few months before the Cuomo fund-raiser occurred, there was a similar misjudgment, and one that represented a serious lapse in national security. Grigori Loutchansky, a Latvian-born convicted felon and president of the Austrian-based NORDEX, a multinational trading company, had been implicated in everything from major money launder-

ing to smuggling nuclear components. House Speaker Newt
Gingrich once said that U.S. government officials believed
Loutchansky had shipped Scud missile warheads to Iraq
from North Korea. The ubiquitous Loutchansky was also a
former business associate of both Chernomyrdin and
Semion Mogilevich, according to the CIA and other Western intelligence officials. Yet somehow this enormously
wealthy underworld rogue was invited to a private Democratic National Committee fund-raising dinner for Clinton
in 1993. During coffee, Clinton turned to the mobster to
ask a favor: would he pass a message along to the Ukrainian
government requesting it to reduce its nuclear stockpile?
Clinton then posed for a photograph with the grinning
hood, which Loutchansky later liberally passed out among
his cronies, greatly enhancing his stature among corrupt
government officials and the criminal underworld. When
the photo of the men shaking hands was eventually published in a Russian newspaper, the CIA analyzed it to see if
it was a fake. When they discovered it was genuine, agency
officials were aghast. "Loutchansky had one thing in mind:
legitimization," a congressional investigator probing Russian
organized crime explained. "He wanted U.S. citizenship
and he wanted to buy a U.S. bank."

In July 1995, the DNC invited the mobster to a
$25,000-a-plate fund-raising dinner for Clinton at the Hay
Adams Hotel in Washington. At the last minute, the security services provided information on Loutchansky and the
State Department denied him a visa, which he had
obtained in Israel. He was subsequently banned from entering the United States, Canada, Hong Kong, and England.

The mobsters were not easily dissuaded, however. In
September 1995, not long after the Loutchansky ban, his
partner at NORDEX, Ukrainian mob boss Vadim Rabinovich, attended a Clinton-Gore fund-raiser at the Shera-

ton Bel Harbor Hotel in Miami. Rabinovich came as a guest of Bennett S. LeBow, the chairman of Brooke Group Ltd., parent of Liggett, a cigarette manufacturing company. (LeBow refused to comment.)

Rabinovich, who by his own account once served an eight-year jail term in Ukraine for theft of state goods, should not have even been in the United States, let alone attending a gala for the president, for he was on a State Department Watch List that bans aliens from entering the United States to commit crimes. Nevertheless, he, too, cleverly managed an all-important photo op, squeezing in between a smiling Clinton and Gore. That picture, too, appeared in the Eastern European press, greatly adding to the mobster's reputation.

The Republicans have not been immune to the Russian mob's advances, either. In March 1994, Vahtang Ubiriya, one of Mogilevich's top criminal lieutenants, was photographed by the FBI at a tony Republican party fund-raiser in Dallas, says a confidential FBI report. Ubiriya, a high-ranking official in the Ukrainian railway administration, has a prior conviction for bribery in that country. A friend of Mogilevich for some twenty-five years, he has been involved with him in extortion, fraud, and illegal currency operations there.

This was not Mogilevich's only attempt to manipulate the U.S. political system. After the INS and the State Department denied visas to YBM employees arriving from Budapest and Ukraine, Jacob Bogatin contacted the FBI office in Philadelphia for an explanation. Rebuffed, Bogatin — who had donated $2,250 to the National Republican Committee and an additional $500 to the National Republican Congressional Committee, a soft money account, between April 1996 and April 1998 — called upon Pennsylvania Republican congressman Jim Greenwood for help obtaining the visas. "I remember when they came to visit me and they brought all those brochures, and I remember how impressed I was that such a high-tech enterprise was there in the Newtown industrial park," Congressman Greenwood recalled. "And I remember thinking, 'Gee, I wonder how they had escaped my attention.' Normally when there is a particularly interesting high-tech industry in your district you become aware of it and often take a tour."

Greenwood's staffers petitioned the State Department on Bogatin's behalf, requesting a reason for the denial of the visas. After it was "nonresponsive, I then made personal calls to the State Department to get to the bottom of it, and I was essentially told that what I ought to do is talk to the FBI," said Greenwood. "We arranged for FBI representatives to come to my office in Washington." Greenwood recalled that the agents told him in confidence that Russian godfather Semion Mogilevich was running YBM and that it was under investigation for money laundering among other crimes. They also said that Bogatin "had to know" what was going on. "It took a hell of a lot of gall if Bogatin was aware of this and [yet he] sat with a U.S. congressman, demanding that our government [allow] their employees back into the country," Greenwood angrily declared.

By the dawn of the new millennium Russian mobsters were lavishing millions of dollars in contributions on Democratic and Republican politicians. In New York City, commodities mogul and alleged wiseguy Semyon (Sam) Kislin has been one of mayor Rudy Giuliani's top campaign supporters. Kislin, various relatives, and his companies, raised or donated a total of $64,950 to Giuliani's mayoral campaigns in 1993 and 1997. A Ukrainian immigrant well known among the Russian Jewish community in South Brooklyn, Kislin has also made generous donations to

Democratic Senator Charles Schumer as well as other state politicians.

According to a confidential December 1994 FBI report and underworld sources, Kislin is a member of the Ivankov organization. These sources say that Kislin's New York commodities firm has been involved in laundering millions of dollars, and co-sponsored a U.S. visa for a man named Anton Malevsky, who is a contract killer and head of one of Russia's most bloodthirsty *Mafiya* families.

Kislin's donations to charities and politicians bore fruit in 1996 when he was appointed to be a member of New York City's Economic Board of Development Corporation. On December 2, 1999, Giuliani reappointed Kislin to the board, stating in a letter that his "service is deeply appreciated." Kislin has denied any ties to the Russian mob, insisting at a December 1999 press conference that "I have done nothing evil."

Although the Russian *Mafiya*'s invasion of American politics is still in its infancy, it already poses a huge threat to U.S. national security interests abroad. The mob dominates Russia, and has Eastern Europe in a bear hug. It is also turning Western Europe into its financial satrapy, and the Caribbean and Latin America have quickly become sandy playpens for coke and weapons deals with Colombian drug lords. There are few nations where the Russian mob does not hold some influence, making efforts to combat it ever more difficult.

A striking example is Switzerland, where the *Mafiya* has been drawn by the country's world-renowned, highly secretive banking system. "There are three stages of Russian *Mafiya* penetration," Jean Ziegler, a university professor in Switzerland has explained. "When the Soviet Union broke up, Switzerland was the laundering place for immense fortunes. Then *Mafiya* leaders started sending their children to expensive private schools here. Now we are in the third stage, where some of the *Mafiya* dons are transferring their operational headquarters to Switzerland—and that is very dangerous." More than six hundred Russian dons have moved to Switzerland, and, according to Swiss court documents, more than $60 billion of Russian mob money has been laundered through its banks.

In one of Switzerland's first strikes against a major Russian gangster, Sergei Mikhailov was arrested in October 1996 in Geneva for money laundering and for his leadership of the *Solntsevskaya* crime family. Headquartered in Moscow, the *Solntsevskaya* mob openly operated out of a stylish commercial office building at Leninsky Prospekt, where it controlled much of the city's gambling, casino, and banking business, as well as prostitution, drugs, the city's used car trade, and the Vnukovo airport, the city's principal cargo terminal. It also owned real estate from Malaysia to Monaco, setting up a labyrinth of fictitious international firms and offshore accounts to launder money received from the sale of narcotics, arms, and extortion. At the time he was apprehended, Mikhailov was living in a quaint château outside Geneva, where he drove around in a blue Rolls-Royce, maintained a $15,000-a-month clothing budget, and doted on his wife and two children. He traveled on a Costa Rican diplomatic passport and had been appointed that country's honorary consul to Moscow.

Inside Mikhailov's lavish home, police found sophisticated Israeli military devices that allowed him to eavesdrop on secret Swiss police radio communications and to tap telephones. They also discovered a trove of documents listing front companies he allegedly used to launder money from drugs and arms sales. Investigators learned that Mikhailov had invested millions of his laundered dollars in

America: he had bought a Brighton Beach disco called Nightflight, which he owned with Ivankov. He acquired another club in Los Angeles. He also purchased a car dealership in Houston with a local who agreed to send red Jeep Cherokees to him in Geneva so he could give them as gifts to friends. The Texan had no idea of the danger to which he was exposing himself when he began to pocket Mikhailov's money, and though the furious gangster sent a hit man to Houston, the killer was captured by the police.

Investigators learned that apart from the tranquil Geneva suburbs, Mikhailov's favorite hangout was Miami. After his men committed murders in Europe and Russia, they would check into the Fontainebleau Hotel "where they would stay by the beach and wait for the heat to cool off," according to retired FBI agent Robert Levinson. But before hitting the soft white sand, the mobsters liked to stop at a nearby Sports Authority, where they bought snazzy jogging outfits to preen for South Beach's glamorous models.

Although Mikhailov insisted, typically, that he was a simple businessman, he is a career criminal with an excellent strategic mind. Born on February 7, 1958, in Moscow, the onetime waiter was first convicted in the Soviet Union in 1984 of theft and perjury, according to a classified Russian document. He was later investigated for murdering a casino owner and a banker. In 1989 he was arrested for extortion, but the victim found it judicious to recant.

The Swiss authorities were confident that they had an excellent case against the mobster, but on the eve of Mikhailov's Swiss trial, a Dutch father and son who had engaged in some questionable business dealings with Mikhailov in Moscow were executed gangland-style. The father was stabbed in the eye and bled to death; his son was gunned down. Soon afterward, Moscow's chief of police sought political asylum in Switzerland, claiming he was threatened by Mikhailov's men. The press was targeted, too. Veteran Russian mob reporter Alain Lallemand of *Le Soir* in Brussels was threatened after he wrote a series about Mikhailov that apparently displeased the mobster. Lallemand was warned by several intelligence services that Mikhailov had scheduled his assassination, and the reporter and his family went underground for a month. The police captured an ex-Belgian gendarme in Brussels who was about to carry out the contract.

Despite these intimidation tactics, the trial went forward, with a total of ninety witnesses being issued protective vests and placed under close guard. The key witness against Mikhailov was Robert Levinson, the ex-FBI agent based in Miami who specialized in the Russian *Mafiya*. Some foreign intelligence agents, however, were dismayed when they saw his briefing book, which seemed to primarily consist of warmed-over FBI gossip. Why hadn't the bureau dispatched active agents with more current material that would hold up as evidence? asked Pierre Delilez. "They are always telling the European intelligence agencies to share. They share nothing." Lallemand, however, insists that the FBI's material was excellent, though the best of it never made it into evidence.

Meanwhile, Mikhailov had succeeded in securing a high-profile paid expert witness for his defense: former U.S. Attorney General Ramsey Clark. Clark has become something of a heretic for having taken on a series of unpopular cases like representing a German SS guard who the U.S. government said massacred Jews during World War II and then illegally gained citizenship.

Clark was first approached by a young Russian lawyer representing Mikhailov, who thought an American with his prestigious legal pedigree would be of great help to his client. Clark politely declined, but Mikhailov's men persevered over the next several months. A group even came to his downtown Manhattan office and asked him to slam the FBI with a "slap suit" that would keep their evidence out of Swiss court. Clark informed them that they didn't have a legal theory that would stand up in an American courtroom.

Finally, Mikhailov's lawyers convinced Clark to look at Levinson's FBI briefing book and some documents that they had obtained in discovery. After reading the material, Clark changed his mind. The FBI reports reminded him of the kind of malicious, untested gossip the bureau had used when it wanted to bring down civil rights leaders. "It was American criminal imperialism," he stated.

Even though the burden of proof was on Mikhailov — under Swiss law, he had to prove that he was *not* the head of a mob family — Clark skillfully helped dismantle Levinson's testimony, not only showing its inconsistencies, but arguing effectively that the bulk of it was built on rumor, hearsay, and derived from unverifiable anonymous sources. Levinson could neither read nor write Russian, Clark declared, but more importantly, the ex-FBI man's intelligence files — or information culled from them — would almost certainly never be allowed into evidence in a U.S. court of law.

Yet Clark's defense alone could not have vindicated the mobster. At least as damaging to the Swiss authorities' case was the fact that several Russian prosecutors working with the Swiss were suddenly and inexplicably fired, after which the Russian government reneged on its previous promises to send crucial documents to Geneva.

Mikhailov, who had been held in a Swiss prison for two years, was acquitted in December 1998. "My heart is full of gratitude," he announced at an airport press conference. "I love you." He was then quietly deported to Moscow aboard an Aeroflot jet. The acquittal was a devastating blow to both Swiss and international law enforcement who had been battling the Russian mob, and it was followed by the usual round of fingerpointing. "The next time we try a major Russian mob boss, we are going to need a watertight case," said Pierre Delilez, who believes that the FBI intentionally fumbled the case, perhaps in order to be able to use Mikhailov as an intelligence agent. James Moody, meanwhile, blamed Levinson for a poor performance. In truth, it was Mikhailov's power, money, and international connections that had succeeded in winning his release and enabling him to continue his glorious criminal career.

The Swiss, meanwhile, are still struggling with the intractable problem of the Russian mob. Ziegler says the only way to derail their inexorable advance is to ban Russian banks from operating in Switzerland, since most of them are controlled by gangsters. Some Swiss banks have already adopted a blanket policy of not accepting any Russian clients. On September 3, 1999, Swiss authorities announced that they had frozen fifty-nine bank accounts, and asked Swiss banks to provide information on the two dozen Russians who held them. Yet in a country where it is not illegal to bribe a public official, the Swiss skirmish against the Russian mob smacks of the Marx Brothers going to war against a mythical kingdom in *Duck Soup*.

Of all the nations where the Russian mob has established a presence, none has been more deeply compromised than the State of Israel, America's staunchest ally in the volatile Middle East. More than 800,000 Russian Jews have made *aliyah* or settled in Israel since the first massive wave of immigration in the 1970s. The Russians took advantage of Israel's most sacred law—the Right of Return, which guarantees Jews the right to return to their ancestral homeland, where they would receive citizenship and live as free men and women outside the odious yoke of anti-Semitism. "The Russians are a blessing," said Israel's top political columnist Nachum Barnea, who stands in public awe of their brilliant intellectual gifts in a variety of fields.

But just as in Brighton Beach, Russian immigration to Israel has brought a more unwelcome element—the *vor v zakonye* and their criminal minions. Ten percent of Israel's five million Jews are now Russian, and 10 percent of the Russian population "is criminal," according to NYPD notes of a briefing in Manhattan by Israeli police intelligence official Brigadier General Dan Ohad.

"There is not a major Russian organized crime figure who we are tracking who does not also carry an Israeli passport," says senior State Department official Jonathan Winer. He put the number at seventy-five, among whom are Mogilevich, Loutchansky, Rabinovich, and Kobzon.

Many of the mobsters who have Israeli citizenship, such as Eduard Ivankov and Sergei Mikhailov, are not even Jewish. In the mid-1990s, an Israeli police sting—code-named Operation Romance—netted, among others, a high-ranking Interior Ministry official who was taking payoffs from Mikhailov and convicted KGB spy Shabtai Kalmanovitch to issue passports to dozens of Russian gangsters, according to Brigadier General Hezi Leder, the Israeli police attaché in Washington, and classified FBI documents. (Kalmanovitch, after serving time in an Israeli prison for treason, became one of Moscow's most notorious mobsters and frequently returns to Israel.)

Russia's criminal aristocracy covets Israeli citizenship "because they know Israel is a safe haven for them," said Leder. "We do not extradite citizens."

"The Russians then use the safe haven to travel around the world and rape and pillage," added Moody.

The country has also remained attractive to gangsters because "Israel is good for money laundering," explained Leder. Under Israeli law, banks can accept large cash deposits with no questions asked. In one instance, a corrupt ex–deputy prime minister of Ukraine smuggled $300 million of illicit cash into Israel in several suitcases, and deposited it into a bank, as Israeli Minister of National Security Moshe Shahal told a gathering of intelligence heads in June 1996. "I've watched Russian mobsters exchange suitcases full of cash out in the open at the Dan Hotel's swimming pool," laughed an American underworld crime figure. "Israel is a country that encourages people to come and invest money," said Leder. "There is no mechanism to check the origin of the money."

Israeli police officials estimate that Russian mobsters have poured more than $4 billion of dirty money into Israel's economy, though some estimates range as high as $20 billion. They have purchased factories, insurance companies, and a bank. They tried to buy the now defunct, pro–Labor Party *Davar* daily newspaper, and the pro-Likud *Maariv*, the nation's second largest newspaper. They have even put together a *koopa*, or a pool of money, for bribes and other forms of mutual support. One of Leder's greatest fears is that the Russians will compromise Israel's security by buying companies that work for the military-industrial complex. The mobsters, in fact, attempted to purchase a gas and oil company that maintains strategic reserves for Israel's military. "They could go to the stock market and buy a company that's running communications in the military sector," he complains.

Insinuating themselves throughout the country, Russian dons have bought large parcels of impoverished development towns, taking over everything from local charities to the town hall. For instance, Gregory Lerner, a major Russian crime boss who arrived in Israel with huge amounts of money, allegedly owns everything from fashionable restaurants to parts of several port city waterfronts.

"Do you know what Gregory Lerner did in Ashkelon?" Leder asked me during an interview in New York. "His mother was three times in the hospital there. He bought new medical equipment and dedicated it to his mother! It's the way the mobsters wash their name." They do so, he explains, in order to build up grassroots support and openly influence politicians—or even run for elective office. Leder worries that one day three or four Russian gangsters who have bought their legitimacy will win Knesset seats, take over a key committee, and be in an ideal position to stop an important piece of anti-crime legislation, such as a proposed bill to criminalize money laundering.

One of Leder's worst fears came true when Russian gangsters handpicked several candidates to run for local and national offices, according to the minutes of a classified Israeli cabinet meeting held by the Committee of the Controller in June 1996. And in May 1997, Israeli police launched a probe into allegations that Lerner attempted to bribe former Prime Minister Shimon Peres, among other Knesset members and cabinet ministers. The investigation was inconclusive, however, and no charges were filed.*

One politician already ensnared in the web of organized crime is Russian-born Natan Sharansky, the head of the

---

*Succumbing to persistent pressure from the Russian government, the Israeli police finally arrested Lerner in May 1997 as he was about to board a flight to the United States. He was charged with attempted bribery, defrauding four Russian banks of $106 million, and attempting to set up a bank in Israel to launder money for the Russian *Mafiya*. Lerner pleaded guilty to bank fraud and bribing government officials on March 22, 1998, after having fiercely maintained for months that he was a victim of an Israeli government plot to discredit Russian émigré entrepreneurs.

Russian Yisrael Ba-Aliya and minister of the interior in the government of Prime Minister Ehud Barak. Because of his resistance to the Soviet regime and his strong and open identification with Judaism, he suffered a long, brutal confinement in the Gulag before international pressure led to his release. In Israel, the charismatic dissident was lionized by the Jewish people, and he became a power broker for the large and growing Russian émigré community, whom he helped integrate into a rigid society that sometimes seemed jealous of the talented new Russians.

However, Sharansky has publicly admitted that his party has accepted campaign contributions from NORDEX president Grigori Loutchansky. Officials from the U.S. Congress, the State Department, and the CIA pleaded with Sharansky to sever his ties to Loutchansky. "We told Sharansky to stop taking money from Loutchansky," says Winer. "We told him about [Loutchansky's] MO: bribery, influence peddling, that he was a bridge between foreign governments and traditional organized crime."

Sharansky simply refused, arguing that he needed the money to resettle the tidal wave of Russian émigrés. "When we warned Sharansky," says the congressional investigator, "to stop taking money from Loutchansky, he said, 'But where am I going to put them,'" referring to the huge influx of Russian Jewish refugees. "'How am I going to feed them? Find them jobs?'" He figures Loutchansky is just another source of income.

"Sharansky is very shrewd," the congressional investigator continued. "He knows better. It was a cynical [decision]. He did take money. Then he asked, 'Why shouldn't I?' The CIA warned him that Loutchansky was trying to buy influence through him and his party for [the] Russian Organized Crime/Russian government combine. We told

Sharansky that Loutchansky is a major crook." (Sharansky declined to comment.)

Ignoring all the warnings, Sharansky introduced Loutchansky to Benjamin Netanyahu prior to Israel's 1996 national elections. The Israeli press reported that Netanyahu received $1.5 million in campaign contributions from Loutchansky, a charge the prime minister hotly denied. "The Likud is corrupt, and Bibi [Netanyahu] is disgusting," says Winer. "He's had meetings with Loutchansky and Kobzon—criminals promoting their own interests."

Kobzon's influence in Israel may exceed that of even Loutchansky and Mogilevich. "Kobzon has big [political] connections in Israel," says Leder. For instance, in January 1996, Kobzon was detained upon his arrival at Israel's Ben Gurion International Airport "because of his ties to the Russian *Mafiya*," Labor Party Knesset member Moshe Shahal said in his cramped Knesset office in Jerusalem. Shahal, at the time the country's security minister, intended to send the mobster back to Russia, but then the phones started ringing in the chambers of high government ministries. Kobzon's friends in Israel petitioned the minister of the interior, the minister of transportation, and Foreign Minister Shimon Peres, who finally ordered the airport police to free Kobzon and let him enter the country. Peres, who was being pressed by the Russian ambassador, told Shahal that he relented to avoid a messy incident with the Russian government. (The following year, Kobzon flew to Israel in his private jet to pick up Marat Balagula's eldest daughter, who lives in Netanya, to bring her back to Moscow to celebrate his sixtieth birthday.)

With two decades of unimpeded growth, the Russian *Mafiya* has succeeded in turning Israel into its very own "mini-state," in which it operates with virtual impunity.

Although many in international law enforcement believe that Israel is by now so compromised that its future as a nation is imperiled, its government, inexplicably, has done almost nothing to combat the problem. In June 1996 Leder, then chief of Israeli police intelligence, prepared a three-page classified intelligence assessment that concluded: "Russian organized groups [had] become a strategic threat" to Israel's existence. He documented how they were infiltrating the nation's business, financial, and political communities. Shahal used the report to brief Prime Minister Yitzhak Rabin, Shin Bet, Israel's FBI, and Mossad, and provided his own recommendations on how to uproot the Russian mob. Before Rabin had a chance to act on the plan, he was assassinated by a right-wing Jewish religious zealot in Tel Aviv following a peace rally. Shimon Peres subsequently set up an intra-agency intelligence committee on the Russian mob after reading Leder's report, but did little else. Leder's report was shelved by Netanyahu, according to Shahal.

"Israel is going to have to do something," says James Moody. "They could lose their whole country. The mob is a bigger threat than the Arabs."

Leder agrees: "We know how to deal with terrorist organizations. We know how to deal with external threats. This is a social threat. We as a society don't know how to handle it. It's an enemy among us."

Why should Americans be concerned about the global explosion of Russian organized crime and the concomitant corruption in Russia? The simple answer is that the nuclear-capable behemoth is on the verge of a political and economic meltdown. "The Russian [people] are deeply humiliated," Brent Scowcroft, Bush's national security adviser, has said. "They have lost their superpower status and they are turning against the U.S. and against the West." In historical terms, the closest analogy to the financial situation in Russia is the Versailles Treaty at the end of World War I, when the Western allies demanded reparations from the Germans. Huge amounts of capital were forced out of Germany, so impoverishing the nation that it helped set the stage for Hitler. "That is the only parallel we have of a vast change in a society, accompanied by massive decapitalization—and look at the consequences," said Jack Blum, who is consulting with the House Banking Committee in its investigation of Russian money laundering. "Russia is three times our size and has nuclear weapons. Why should we care? Excuse me. Common sense says you have to care mightily."

It should also by now be abundantly clear that the Russian *Mafiya* is made up of multipurpose, entrepreneurial master criminals. "Once funded, once flush, with the billions of dollars they ripped off, these boys are in business doing every shape, manner, and form of crime globally," Blum continued. "So it was Russians who were doing the gasoline daisy chains in New York, New Jersey, and Long Island, in which billions of dollars in excise tax was ripped off; it's Russians who are screwing around with Colombians, figuring out how to deliver weapons to them. Should Americans not care about that? That's going on right here.

"If nothing else, Americans should worry that they'll drive up the price of real estate in the Hamptons," Blum said with a sarcastic laugh.

"The Hamptons are filling up with Russians," Mike Morrison, a criminal investigator with the IRS told me. "When we ask them where they got the money to purchase their house or business, they produce a document from Uncle Vanya in St. Petersburg who says it's a gift. There is nothing we can do."

Meanwhile, Russian mobsters move easily in and out of the United States on visas "that they get in Israel to dance through our clearance process," says Blum. Or they obtain visas as employees of shell corporations like YBM, or as friends of NHL hockey players, or as "film consultants," as Ivankov did. "So should we worry about that?" asks Blum. "Of course!"

America's vast wealth will always be an irresistible target for the Russian *Mafiya*, and their most sophisticated scams are likely to cause the most damage: their devious financial machinations on Wall Street, their money laundering, their infiltration of prestigious institutions like the NHL. Should we worry about that? In a few years, predicts James Moody, the Russian mob will be bigger than La Cosa Nostra in America. And perhaps GE, and Microsoft, too.

GOD BLESS AMERICA

It's a warm summer day. Bobby Sommer looks like a shell-shocked grunt in a World War II movie. A detective in the 61st Precinct in Brighton Beach, he is clearly on the verge of surrendering to a force that has him outgunned, outfinanced, and outwitted. A Russian crime group bought the building directly across the street from his station house, and the gangsters have been photographing detectives as they saunter in with their snitches. It took the police about a year to wise up. Sommer is sometimes followed by Russian thugs at the end of a shift. "I'm tailing them, and they are tailing me," says the fifty-something cop, who wears cheap leather boots and a worn expression.

Sommer's gray metal desk is cluttered with case files. More than half are Russian mob–related. Arrayed across the criminal debris are glossy photos of dismembered Russian crime victims. "If you cut off the head, and the arms and feet are missing, too, you can't get a positive identification on the torso. It's brilliant," he says dejectedly.

"You can't work a homicide in Brighton Beach," Sommer continues, gloom settling in his face like the pall of smoke after a heavy battle. "The Russians don't talk. Someone could get whacked in a club in front of a hundred diners, and nobody would see anything. So they will kill with impunity."

Russian organized crime incubated in Brighton Beach for twenty years before the city and federal government tried to stop it, he says angrily. By then, it had merged with even more powerful organized crime syndicates that prospered in Russia after perestroika. Sommer says he barely has a budget to pay for snitches. How is he supposed to stop a Byzantine global crime menace?

"Why are we being victimized by noncitizens who can run to Israel or Russia and can't be extradited? The Russian gangsters have told me that they've come here to suck our country dry. My uncle died on the beaches of Normandy defending this country. How did the Russian mob become so entrenched? They are into Social Security, Medicare, and Medicaid fraud. Why is it that every ambulance service in Brooklyn is run by the Russian mob? Why are so many of their doctors practicing without a license? They have invaded Wall Street from boiler-room operations to brokerage houses. Nothing is too small for them to steal. Even the guys with the multimillion-dollar Medicare scam still have to have their food stamps. The first generation are all thieves. Maybe the second generation will become a little more American."

A few blocks away, in one of the tidy Art Deco apartment buildings that line the seaward side of Brighton Beach Avenue in Brooklyn, a big Russian is sprawled on his back on a leather workout bench. A masseur kneads his lumpy body. The living room, where he spends hours every day, is decorated like the interior of a coffin, with wallpaper painted to resemble gathered gray satin. He watches a thirty-two-inch color TV in a mirror.

"The police steal the drugs and kill everybody," he says, while a Russian-language movie blares in the background. "I've seen it before."

The Russian has an enormous chest and huge belly, but his legs are spindles. The masseur helps him sit up. Two large craters are sunk deep into his fleshy white back. They were made by dumdum bullets that shattered his spine.

The Russian was once an imposing figure, standing over six foot four — a man who favored floor-length black leather jackets with ermine collars. He was wearing his favorite jacket, a .45 concealed inside, when an assassin on a motorcycle shot him on a Brooklyn street corner in full view of a busload of schoolchildren several years ago. A onetime heroin and arms trafficker, he says that an ex–business partner commissioned the hit to settle a score. Before the ambush, he had been one of the top gangsters in Brighton Beach. Even after the shooting, he was working, running an extortion ring at Kennedy Airport from his wheelchair. He "taxes" Russians $1,000 to retrieve their shipped goods from Aeroflot.

Lifted onto his bed by his son and the masseur, the Russian sighs, appearing more like a young Buddy Hackett than a notorious criminal. "Look what they did to me," he says softly. "Look how everybody has to step over me. They ruined my life."

Yet talking about the Russian *Mafiya* reinvigorates him. "The Russians are stronger than the Italians," he says assuredly. He doesn't mean tougher — yet. He means wealthier. "Saudi Arabia is small potatoes," he boasts. "The

U.S. goes into Moscow with $100 million of aid, and the mob walks out with $105 million. They have so much money it would take years to count it with a computer."

The big Russian brags about the way the mob's tentacles have spread around the world in a few short years. "For Russians, enough is never enough. If a Russian makes $20 million, he wants $40 million. They never know when to stop. There is a saying in Russia: 'The house is burning and the clock is ticking.' It means you have to keep making money every minute.

"Even Russian racketeers and crooks want their children to be doctors and lawyers. But some of the kids have learned that they can make more money by being crooks," he says somberly. "Young Russian kids with MBAs are getting jobs on Wall Street. They are setting up all kinds of scams. They'll hurt a lot of people. There'll be a lot of suicides.

"In this country, it's so easy to make money," the Russian says. "I love this country. I would die for it."

INDEX

ABC-TV, 200, 261
Abelis, Leonid, 137–138
Adams, Cindy, 92
Adeev, V. B., 204–205, 213, 214
Agron, Evsei, 20, 23–42, 45, 79, 82
Alberta Stock Exchange, 250–252, 254
Albright, Madeleine, 183n
Alexandrov, Alexei Viktoriovich (the Plumber), 253n
All-Russian Exchange Bank, 204, 212–214, 234
Almeida, Juan, 152–153, 155–159, 163, 165–166, 168
Aloi, Benny, 94
American Express, 224–225
American League, 200
Andropov, Yuri, 76
Annicharico, Richard, 221–222
Antigua, 216–217
Arbat International, 243, 250
Arigon Ltd., 243–245, 249–251, 253n
Armstrong, Martin, 230n
Army Co-op, 245
art fraud, 244
Atiolkin, Viktor, 116
Atkom, 126
Aubut, Marcel, 187
Audit Chamber (Russia), 233
Austria, 126, 210, 216, 247
Averin, Viktor, 128, 243, 253
Azatian, Moucheg (Misha), 134
Azimov, Tofik, 126

Babushka (Miami restaurant), 161, 162, 165
Bagdasaryan, Rafik (Svo), 105–106, 209
Bakatansky, Peter, 221
Balagula, Aksana, 52, 133
Balagula, Alexandra, 44, 45, 66
Balagula, Jakov, 43
Balagula, Leon, 45
Balagula, Marat, 16–18, 41–48, 51–67, 83, 121, 224, 281
Balagula, Zinaida, 43
Balchug, 245
Balmonchnykh, Maxim, 201
Banco Safra, 223
Bank Chara, 134–135, 138

banking, xviii, 122–123, 203–235, 239. See also money laundering
Bank of Credit and Commerce, 209
Bank of England, 216, 252
Bank of New York, xix, 117, 131–132, 168, 240, 257, 259, 260, 263, 266
Banque Française De L'orean, 245
Barnea, Nachum, 277
Barnett, Mike, 177, 178
Belgium, 247
Benex, 257
Berger, Roger, xix, 79–80, 94
Berkovich, Lazar, 248n
Berkovich, Oleg, 248n
Berkovich, Vladimir, 248
Berlin, Peter, 259
Bettman, Gary, 199
Bialik (poet), 6
Bibb, Harold, 62–64
Biggs, Tonia, 35
bioterrorism, xviii–xix
Birbragher, Fernando, 152–153, 156–157
Black, Roy, 166
Black and White Clubs (Hungary), 242
Blinkin, Larissa, 34
Blitzer, Wolf, 58
Blum, Jack, 209, 234, 267, 283, 284
BND (German intelligence agency), 246–247
Bogatin, David, 250n
Bogatin, Jacob, 249–252, 254, 257, 269–270
Bojangles (fast-food chain), 34
Bophuthatswana, 59
Bopp, Michael, 196–197
Bor, Alexander (Timoka), 153
Bratsky Krug (Circle of Brothers), 117, 123
Breindel, Eric, 76–77, 82
Brezhnev, Leonid, xiv, 12, 115
Brighton Beach (Brooklyn, N.Y.), xii, xiv, 15–21, 218. See also Organizatsiya
Brokhin, Tanya, 75, 77
Brokhin, Yuri, 18–20, 75–83
Brown, Pam, 162–163, 167
Bulgaria, 82
Bure, Pavel, 179, 193–196, 198–199
Byrne, John, 48, 49

Cafe Arabat (Brooklyn), 102
Cahen, Alferd, 247–248
Cali cartel, 122, 153
California, xix, 219, 231
Camorra crime family, 242–243
Campanella, Joel, 35, 78, 79, 81,
    83–84, 201
Canada, 111, 127–128, 192, 217, 218
  Mogilevich's activities, 249–254,
    256–258
  Sliva's operations, 128, 133,
    186–188, 190–191
Capone, Al, 4, 29
Cardenelli, Louis, 14–15, 107, 117
Cardin, Pierre, 183
Carey, Hugh, 50
Carey, Martin, 50
Carmel Mizrachi (kosher distillery),
    242
Casso, Anthony (Gas Pipe), 55
Castellano, Paul, 34
Castro, Fidel, xix, 13
Cayman Islands, 257
Cefarello, Ralph, 107
Central Intelligence Agency (CIA), xiii,
    55–56, 156n, 263–266, 268,
    280–281
  and Russian banking and money
    laundering, 210, 214–216, 230
Channel Islands, 243
Chechen Mafiya, 114, 117
Chemical Bank, 257
Chernenko, Konstantin, 111
Chernomyrdin, Viktor, 266, 268
Chubais, Anatoly, 233
Churchward, Adrian, 251–252
Churchward, Galina, 251–252
CIA. See Central Intelligence Agency
cigarette bootlegging, 81n, 162
Clark, Ramsey, 274–275
Clinton, Bill, 208, 266, 268, 269
Clouns International, 60
Colombian drug cartels, 122, 152–153,
    271
  money laundering, 209, 210, 217,
    225, 241
  weapons trafficking, xii, 143,
    155–158, 163–164, 166–168, 283
Colombo crime family, 50, 54
Committee to Protect Journalists, xvi,
    xx
Committee to Reelect the President, 31
Comptroller of the Currency, U.S.,
    221, 228–229
contract assassins, 238, 248
Cosa Nostra. See Mafia
Costa Rica, xviii
Cotter, Patrick J., 85
Courtney, Robert, 256
Cozzolina, Robert, 227

C-24 squad, 89
Cunningham, Dennis, 196–197, 199
Cuomo, Mario, 50, 267
Customs Bureau, U.S., 95, 156n, 189,
    225, 226, 227, 245, 256
Czech Republic, 237, 243, 249,
    252–253

Dayne, Taylor, 17
DEA. See Drug Enforcement Agency
DeFalco, Salvatore, 243
Delilez, Pierre, 246, 247–248, 274, 276
Deloitte and Touche, 255–256, 258
Democratic National Committee, 268
Denver (Colo.), xix, 122, 188–190,
    192, 219
Dershowitz, Alan, 62
Details magazine, 198
Detroit Red Wings, 179–180, 184, 198
Digep General Machine Works, 245
DiPietro, James, 30, 79, 120
DiPietro, Sylvia, 92
Disney Company, 200
Doria, Ronald, 135
Dougherty, Edward, 91–92
Drubin, Barry, 74–75, 77–83
Drug Enforcement Agency, 95, 101, 131
  money laundering cases, 225,
    226–227
  Roizes and, 147, 160–162, 168
  Tarzan (Fainberg) and, xii, 143, 152,
    156, 157, 163–167
drug trafficking, xviii, 20–21, 35, 57,
    100–101, 225, 243
  Ivankov's activities, 122, 124–125,
    129
  Tarzan's (Fainberg) operations, 143,
    151–153, 167–168
  See also Colombian drug cartels
Dubinin, Sergei, 233
Dunes Hotel (Las Vegas), 32–33
du Plessis, Adrian, 258

Eaton, Brent, 151, 153, 164–165, 167
Economic Board of Development
    Corporation (N.Y.C.), 271
Economist, The (magazine), 81n
Edwards, Lucy, 259
Ehrenfeld, Rachel, 227
Eisenberg, Robert, 48, 49
El Caribe Country Club (Brooklyn), 24,
    36, 41
Elson, Abraham, 11
Elson, Marina, 4, 106–107
Elson, Monya, 3–21, 27, 75, 97–100,
    149, 162, 267
  Mogilevich and, 160, 238, 242, 260
  Nayfeld wars, 100–108, 120, 209
Energy Department, U.S., 156n
England, 60, 210, 216

Mogilevich's operations, 238, 242, 248–252, 254
Epke, John, 178, 198
Ermath, Fritz, 265
Escobar, Pablo, 153, 156, 157, 158, 163
ESPN (cable channel), 200
European Union Bank (EUB), 216–218, 234
extortion, xviii, 24–25, 36, 128, 136–138, 154
of hockey players, 176, 177–179, 196–197
Ezra, Joe, 51–52, 62

Faina (Tarzan Fainberg's common-law wife), 155
Fainberg, Alex, 152
Fainberg, Ludwig (Tarzan), xii, 122, 141–169, 195, 263
Fainberg, Maria Raichel, 146, 147, 149
Fasano, Robert, 61–62
Fat Felix. *See* Komorov, Felix
Federal Bureau of Investigation (FBI), 61, 71, 153, 189
and author death threats, xi–xiii, xv–xvi, xx
Bank of New York case, 131–132
Brokhin murder investigation, 77, 80–81
Denver mob operations, 188–190
Dunes Hotel investigation, 32–33
hockey-*Mafiya* ties, 175–179, 181–182, 185–186, 188, 194–195, 197–198
Ivankov and, 122, 123, 126, 127, 132–133, 134, 136, 139, 235, 271
Mikhailov case, 274, 275, 276
Mogilevich's activities, 238, 241, 244, 245, 246, 248, 249, 252, 253, 255, 256, 260, 266, 269, 270
money laundering operations, 217, 222–223, 233
Puerto Rico mob meeting, 130–131
Russian anti-*Mafiya* efforts and, 86–88, 94–95
Russian arms trafficking, 156n
Russian mobsters' manipulation of, 55–56
Russian mob threat downplay, 84–90
See also Russian Organized Crime Squad
Federal Reserve, 207, 215–218, 221, 228, 230, 232
Federal Security Services, 264–265
Federal Witness Protection Program, xvi, 138
Fedorov, Sergei, 177
Fernandez, Diana, 150
Fetisov, Slava, 130, 179–186, 198, 199
Fickenauer, James, 95

Financial Crimes Enforcement Network (FINCEN), 210
financial markets, xix, 34, 46, 239, 249–259, 284
Financial Times (London newspaper), 256
First Interstate Bank, 189
First Marathon, 255
Fisherman, Igor, 249, 250, 257
France, 210, 247–248
Franzese, Michael, 50, 51, 54
Freeh, Louis, xvii, 94
Furnari, Christopher (Christie Tick), 53, 54

Galizia, Joe, 43
Gambino crime family, 90, 147, 159
gambling, 197–198, 200
gasoline bootlegging, 46–56, 71–73, 90–94, 224, 283
Gavin, William A., 89
Gazprom, 266
Gelber, Dan, 212
Genovese crime family, 147, 239, 250n
Agron and, 28–30, 31
Balagula and, 53–54, 57, 59–60
Zilber brothers and, 70–73, 91, 120
Georgia (republic), 156n, 243
German Federal Police, 84, 159
Germany, 23, 84, 210, 246–247, 283
Getty Oil, 48–49
Gigante, Vincent, 138
Gilman, Benjamin, 61
Ginzberg, Vladimir, 120, 151, 162
Giuliani, Rudolph, 32, 183, 270, 271
Glugech, Valeri (Globus), 124–125
Goetz, Bernhard, 62
Goldberg, Boris, 34–38
Goldstein, Artie, 93
Golembiovsky, Igor, 188
Gorbachev, Mikhail, 44, 116, 213
Gore, Al, 266, 269
Gotti, John, 53, 72, 85
Gotti, John, Jr., xviii
Gravano, Sammy (the Bull), 4
Green, Pinky, 32
Greenwald, Ronald, 28, 30–32, 58–62
Greenwood, Jim, 269–270
Gregory, Richard, 159
Grigorieva, Galina, 253
Grinenko, Peter, 77, 80–81
Grishin, Vladimir, 116
Gromov, Alex, 208, 210
Guarnacchia, Francesco, 57n
Guccione, Bob, 35

Hamadei, Mohammed Ali, 64
Hanna, Glenn, 192
Harden, Blaine, xx

Health, Education, and Welfare Department, U.S., 32
Helitaxi, 166
Hesse, Rayburn, 231–232
hockey, Russian mob influence on, xix, 173–201, 284
Hoffa, Jimmy, 32–33
Hoover, J. Edgar, 86
Houston (Tex.), 122, 273
HSBC Holdings PLC, 230n
Hungarian National Police, 253n
Hungary, 203–205, 213, 242, 244–246, 249, 257, 260
Hynes, Joe, 81n

Ignatious, David, 267
Immigration and Naturalization Service, 121, 131, 217, 233–235, 256, 269
Inkombank, 230–231
Institutional Investor (magazine), 223, 224
insurance fraud, xix, 26
Intercross International, 190, 191n
Internal Revenue Service, 46–47, 71, 131, 189, 256
International Brotherhood of Teamsters, 33, 185
International Home Cinema Inc., 191
International Monetary Fund, 233, 265
Interpol, 60, 64, 238
Iorizzo, Lawrence, 49–50
Iran, 116, 156n, 195, 245
Iraq, 268
IRS. *See* Internal Revenue Service
Israel, 13, 14, 44, 123–124, 143
    Kalmanovitch's activities, 58, 59, 61, 123–124
    mob influence in, 123–124, 167, 276–282
    Mogilevich and, 238, 239, 241–242, 244, 245, 247, 252, 260
Italian Mafia. *See* Mafia (Italian)
Ivan (ex-Brighton Beach resident), 26–27
Ivan (Russian mobster), 82–83
Ivankov, Eduard, 123, 126, 277
Ivankov, Vyacheslav Kirillovich
    author death threats and, xv–xvi, xx–xxi, 312
    hockey players and, 181–183, 186, 187–188, 198
    Mogilevich and, 242, 243, 260
    Petrossov and, 189–190, 192, 193
    in Russia, 108–111, 113–117
    in United States, 119–139, 141, 153, 235, 271, 273, 284

Jackson, Henry (Scoop), 13
Jacmo (drug dealer), 36
Jermyn, Ray, 43, 53, 54, 55–56

jewel theft and smuggling, xix, 19–20, 57, 90, 100, 122
Josephson, Marvin, 28
Justice Department, U.S., 84, 95, 208, 235, 257, 261

Kalmanovitch, Shabtai, 58–61, 98, 277
Kamensky, Valeri, 179, 187, 188, 190, 192, 193, 198, 199
Kamikaze Club (Moscow), 158
Kantor, Oleg, 211–212
Kaplan, Robert, 127–128
Kasparov, Garry, 180
Katric, Anatoly, 247
Keenan, John, 168
Kerr, Raymond C., 89, 139, 182, 185
KGB
    espionage, 58, 64–65, 82
    looting of Soviet assets, 111–112, 150, 209
    money laundering by, 213, 234, 265
    Soviet jail emptying, xiv, 13, 23
Khodorovsky, Mikhail, 214–215, 216, 217–218
Kikalishvili, Anzor, 130
    Bure ties, 194–196, 198–199
    Tarzan (Fainberg) and, 154, 157, 163, 165
King, Reg, 179
Kislin, Semyon (Sam), 270–271
Kissinger, Henry, 13
Kobzon, Joseph, 70, 115–116, 128–131, 183n, 194, 199, 277, 281
Kommersant (Moscow newspaper), 214, 233
Komorov, Felix, xii, 123, 183–186, 191
Konanikhine, Alexander, 203–206, 212–218, 233–235
Korkov, Gennadiy (the Mongol), 109, 110
Kozlov, Andrei, 232
Kroll and Associates, 265
Kruglov, Sergei (the Beard), 104, 106
Kulikov, Anatoly, 214
Kvantrishvilli, Amiran, 181
Kvantrishvilli, Otari, 114–115, 116, 125, 130

Lallemand, Alain, xi, 274
Lansky, Meyer, xix, 38, 151
Laskin, Efim, 57, 64, 146
Las Vegas (Nev.), 32–33, 185
Lautenberg, Frank, 116
Leach, Jim, 218
LeBow, Bennett S., 269
Leder, Hezi, 277, 278, 279, 281, 282
Lehman, William, 151
Lerner, Gregory, 278–279
Lev, Leonard, 121, 122, 133, 137, 138

Levinson, Robert, 196, 246, 252, 273, 274, 275, 276
Liat (company), 59
Liebowitz, Leo, 48–49
liquor smuggling, 244
Listyev, Vladimir, 188n
Lithuania, 257
Long Island Motor Fuel Task Force, 49
López, Byron, 166
Los Angeles (Calif.), xix, 219
Loutchansky, Grigori, 267–268, 277, 280–281
Lubrani, Uri, 60
Lyubertskaya crime family, 135, 136, 240
Lucchese crime family, 53, 54, 55
Luchins, David, 76–77
Luciano, Lucky, 29, 38
Lynn, Amber, 142
Lyubarsky, Vyacheslav, 18

M&S International, 100
Mafia (Italian), xvii, 85, 86, 185–186, 248n
  Balagula and, 46, 53–55, 57, 59–60
  Camorra family, 242–243
  Colombo family, 50, 54
  Gambino family, 90, 147, 159
  gasoline bootlegging, 53–54, 71–73, 90–94
  Genovese family. *See* Genovese crime family
  Las Vegas interests, 32–33
  Lucchese family, 53, 54, 55
  money laundering, 209, 210
  Roizes and, 168
Mafiya (Russian), 287–288
  arms dealing. *See* weapons trafficking
  author death threats, xi–xiii, xv–xvi, xx–xxi, 261
  banking activities, xviii, 203–235
  global network, 14–15, 57, 120, 127–128, 133–134, 263–284
  hockey influence, 174–201
  post-Soviet rise of, 112–113
  scope of operations, xvii–xix
  U.S. politics and, 50, 267–271
  See also Organizatsiya; Red *Mafiya*
Magharian brothers, 226, 227
Magnex 2000, 245, 249, 250
Magnex Ltd., 248n
Malakhov, Vladimir, 177
Malevsky, Anton, 271
Mangano, Venero (Benny Eggs), 29
Mangope, Lucas, 59
Maverick's Steak House (Colo.), 190
Mazursky, Paul, 17
McCall, Michael, xi–xii, xv–xvi
McCormick, Robert H., 212, 229–230
McGovern, George, 31
McKenna, Jeremiah, 50

McMahon, Joseph, 164–166
McShane, Michael, 165
Medellín drug cartel, 158
Medicaid/Medicare fraud, xix, 26, 286
Melnikov, Viktor, 210–211
Menatep Bank, 214–216, 218, 232–233
Merrill Lynch, 60, 61
Metro-Dade Police Department, 164
Metropole (N.Y. nightclub), 79
Miami (Florida), xii, xix, 122, 141–143, 149–155, 159–168, 218, 273
Miami Beach Police Department, 149–150
Mikhailov, Sergei, 128, 243, 244, 245, 250n, 252, 253, 272–276, 277
Misha (St. Petersburg, Russia, crime lord), 164
Mogilevich, Mila, 253
Mogilevich, Semion (the Brainy Don), xiii, 117, 124, 160, 213, 237–264, 266, 268–270, 277, 281
Mogilevich, Tatiana, 253
Mogilny, Alexander, 177, 178–179
Momoh, Joseph, 57, 58
money laundering, 82, 153, 203–235, 284
  Bank of New York case, xix, 117, 131–132, 168, 240, 257, 259, 260, 263, 266
  Denver operations, 188–189
  hockey player involvement, 181–182
  in Israel, 278
  Ivankov's operations, 122, 126, 127, 271
  Konanikhine case, 203–206, 212–218, 233–235
  Mogilevich's activities, 238, 241, 243, 249, 251, 256–260
  Republic National Bank and, 207, 219, 220–230, 232
  Swiss banks and, 271–272, 276
Moody, James, 85–89, 95, 115, 132, 190, 197, 198–199, 259, 276, 277, 282, 284
Morelli, Anthony (Fat Tony), 72, 73, 91–92, 94
Morris, Stanley, 211
Morrison, Mike, 283
Moschella, William, 24, 77, 80
Moscow on the Hudson (film), 17
Mossad, 58, 282
Moynihan, Daniel Patrick, 76–77
Murkoff, Benjamin, 216
MVD. *See* Russian Ministry of Internal Affairs

Namath, Joe, 200
Nasdaq, 255
National (Brooklyn restaurant), 17, 82, 97

National Association of Securities
Dealers, 135
National Football League, 200
National Hockey League, xix, 174, 175,
177–180, 184–186, 190, 196–201,
284
National Republican Committee, 269
National Republican Congressional
Committee, 269
NATO, 245
Nayfeld, Benjamin, 24, 25, 36, 46, 62
Nayfeld, Boris (Biba), 24, 25–26, 36,
38, 41, 46, 100–108, 160, 209
Nelli (singer), 161, 162
Netanyahu, Benjamin, 281, 282
Newsday, 58n, 226
New York City, xix, 271. *See also*
Brighton Beach
New York Daily News, 193
New Yorker (magazine), 17, 58n
New York Police Department, 74, 84,
189, 277
Brokhin murder investigation, 74–75,
77–83
cops on mob payroll, 73, 79–80
New York Post, 92
New York State Banking Department,
219, 220–221, 223, 229–230
New York State Organized Crime Task
Force, 80
New York Stock Exchange, 255
New York Times, xiii, xx–xxi, 64, 71,
81n, 132, 215, 230n, 266
NHL. *See* National Hockey League
Nightflight (Brooklyn disco), 273
Nikiforov, Viktor (Kalina), 125
Nixon, Richard, 13, 31–32
Noriega, Manuel, 153
Novoye Russkoye Slovo (newspaper),
129
nuclear weapons, xviii–xix, 156n
NYPD. *See* New York Police
Department

Odessa (Black Sea port), 7, 16, 109
Odessa (Brooklyn restaurant), 16–18,
41, 46, 55, 121, 149
Office of Technology Assessment, U.S.,
231
Ohad, Dan, 277
Olga (hair salon owner), 25–26
Ontario Teacher's Pension Fund, 258
Operation Odessa, 159–160
Operation Red Daisy, 73, 87, 90–94, 95
Operation Romance, 277
Operation Sword, 251
Organizatsiya, 15, 209, 285–287
Agron as don, 20, 23–42, 45, 79, 82
Balagula's operations, 16–18, 41–48,
51–67, 83, 121, 224, 281

Elson-Nayfeld wars, 100–108, 120,
209
Goldberg gang, 34–38
Ivankov's activities, 114–139,
181–183, 186, 187–190, 192, 193,
198, 235, 242, 243, 260, 271, 273,
284
law enforcement agencies and,
55–56, 79–80, 83–85
Tarzan's (Fainberg) activities, xii, 122,
141–169, 195, 263
Zilber brothers as dons, 70–73,
90–91, 99, 119–120, 267

Pacino, Al, 183
Pagano, Daniel, 72, 73
Pagano, Joseph, 72
Paine Webber, 184
Palmer, Richard, 112, 163
Palm Terrace (L.A. restaurant), 248
Panama, 121, 210
Pantanella, Renato, 57n
Papp, Katalin, 242
Papsouev, Vitali, 218
Paradise Club (Brooklyn), 133
Parker, Buddy, 223
Passic, Greg, 226, 227
Paul (piano player), 161–162
Peabody, Charles, 224
People's Courts, 9, 18, 108
Peres, Shimon, 279, 281, 282
Peterson, David, 254, 258
PetroEnergy International, 189
Petrossov, Vatchagan, 122, 188–193
pickpockets, 12
Platenum Energy, 54
Plehve, Vyacheslav von, 6
plutonium, 156n
Poland, 100–101, 250n
police corruption
Hungary, 246
New York, 73, 79–80
Russia, 113–114, 246
Pollard, Jonathan, 58
Pooya, Rafigh, 191n
Porky's (Miami strip club), 122,
141–142, 150, 151, 154, 165
Potts, Larry, 88
Power Test, 48–49
Pratecs Technologies Inc., 250–251,
254, 255
Promstroybank, 230
prostitution, 238, 242, 253n
Prudential Securities, 135
Puzyretsky, Emile, 18, 24–25, 97, 99

Rabin, Yitzhak, 58, 282
Rabinovich, Vadim, 268–269, 277
Racer, Sam, 46–47, 64–65
Ragsdale, Tina, 77–78

Raichel, Maria. *See* Fainberg, Maria
   Raichel
Raichel, Naum (*Psyk*), 146
Raichel, Semion (*Psyk*), 146–147
Rainbow Amusements, 35
Rasputin (Brooklyn nightclub), 30, 70,
   71, 79, 91, 95, 99, 120, 138, 267
Red Brigades, 57, 146
Red *Mafiya*, xiii, 213, 237–261, 263,
   266
Rehbock, Richard, 92–94
Remnick, David, 7
Reno, Janet, 88
Republic National Bank, 207, 219,
   220–230, 232
Reznikov, Vladimir, 54–55, 83,
   149
Rich, Marc, 32, 51, 58
Rivera, Charlie, 35, 36, 37
R. J. Reynolds Tobacco Co., 190
Roberts, Clare, 216
Rocky (Porky's day manager), 141, 142
Rodio, James, 49
Rohr, Klaus C., 88
Roizes, Grecia (the Cannibal), 147,
   160–162, 168
Rose, Charles, 64, 65
Rose, Pete, 200
Rosenberg, Philip, 247
Rowe, Jerry, 218, 219
Royal Bank of Scotland, 251, 252
Royal Canadian Mounted Police, 111,
   127, 128, 133, 159, 187–188, 190,
   218
Rushailo, V. B., 191n
Russia, 6–10, 249, 282–283
   anti-*Mafiya* efforts, 86–88, 94–95
   banking system, 208–212. *See also*
      Russian Central Bank
   corruption, 7, 8–9, 44, 126, 263–267
   journalist killings, xvi–xvii, 188n
   looting of government, 111–112,
      150, 209, 264
   organized crime influence, xix, 7–9,
      112–117, 120, 124, 133–134, 156
   police corruption, 113–114, 246
   underground economy, 7–8, 43–44
   See also KGB; *Mafiya*; *vor v zakonye*
Russian and Turkish Baths (N.Y.C.), 38
Russian Association of Bankers, 211
Russian Central Bank, 208, 211, 231,
   232–233, 265–266
Russian *Mafiya*. *See Mafiya* (Russian)
Russian Ministry of Internal Affairs,
   123n, 159
Russian Organized Crime Squad, xi,
   xvii, 88–89, 131–132
Russian Presidential Security Service,
   266
Russian World Art Gallery (N.Y.C.), 183

S&S Hot Bagel Shop (N.Y.C.), 101
Sachs, Jeffrey, 208
Sadko (N.Y. restaurant), 80
Sadykov, Roustam, 135
Safra, Edmond, 223–227, 230n
St. Petersburg (Colorado restaurant),
   189–190
San Francisco (Calif.), xix
Santora, Frank, 148
Sasha (Adeev's enforcer), 204, 205
Sasha (extortionist), 178
Schumer, Charles, 129, 271
Sciortino, Frankie (the Bug), 54, 92–94
Scotty, Gavin, 184–185
Scowcroft, Brent, 265, 282–283
Secret Service, U.S., 61, 62–63
Seidle, William (*Stariyk*), 150–151,
   153, 156
Selivanov, Vladislav, 264
Semionov, Anatoly, 125
Shahal, Moshe, 278, 281, 282
Shakarchi, Mahomoud (father),
   226–227
Shakarchi, Mohammed (son), 226
Shakarchi Trading, 226–227
Shapiro, Jay, 138–139
Sharansky, Natan, 279–281
Shenker, Morris, 32–33
Shevchencko, Natalia, 62, 66
Shin Bet, 282
Shuster, David (Napoleon), 34, 36,
   87–88, 90–91, 92, 94
Siegel, Bugsy, 38
Sierra Leone, xviii, 57–58, 59, 63–64,
   122
Sigalov, Joseph (Mr. Tomato), 127–128
Simis, Konstantin, 8
Skolnick, Alexander (Cabbagehead), 17
Slavic Inc., 181–183
Slepinin, Alexander (the Colonel),
   103–104, 149
Sliva, Vyacheslav, 128, 133, 186–188,
   190–191
Slotnick, Barry, 62, 64, 65, 91, 137,
   138, 182
Smith, Mike, 177
Smolensky, Alexander, 230
Social Security fraud, 286
Solntsevskaya crime family, 124, 126,
   128, 242–245, 251, 252, 272
Solzhenitsyn, Alexander, 139
Sommer, Bobby, 93–94
Sotheby's, 244
Soviet Jewish émigrés, xiv, 12–15, 23,
   45, 241, 276–277, 280
Spain, 261
sports, *Mafiya* control of, 174–175. *See
   also* hockey
Stahl, Robert, 93–94
Stalin, Joseph, 6, 10

Stasiuk, Gregory, 80, 99–100, 102, 132, 133
State Department, U.S., xx, 130, 166, 196, 217, 220, 256, 259, 268–270, 277, 280
Steinbrenner, George, 200
Stolichny Bank, 230
"Streetsweeper" incident (1993), 106–108, 120
Summit International, 134–135, 138
Sunday Times (London newspaper), xiii
Svo, Rafik. *See* Bagdasaryan, Rafik
Switzerland, 210, 225, 227, 271–276
Sych, Valentin, 200–201

Taj Mahal (N.J. casino), 132–133
Terminello, Louis, 167
Testa, Joe, 55
Texaco, 48
Thailand, 57, 122
Timofeyev, Sergei (Sylvester), 104, 125–126
Toronto Stock Exchange, 254, 258
Trade Development Bank, 224, 225
Treasury Department, U.S., 208, 210, 221, 228, 232
Trentacosta, Anthony, 93
Trump Organization, 132n
TSE 300 Index (stock index), 254, 256
Turkey, 225
Tverdovsky, Alexandra, 176
Tverdovsky, Oleg, 173–179
Twelve-LA (film company), 121
Twenty First Century Association, 115, 130, 194–195

Ubiriya, Vahtang, 269
U Holubu (Prague restaurant), 252–253
UJA-Federation, 129
Ukleba, Shlava, 106
Ukraine, 128, 245, 249, 269
uranium, 156n
Urov, Boris, xx
Uruguay, 216
U.S. Attorney's Office, 255, 256, 258

Valachi, Joseph, 72
Valiquette, Joe, 84
Vancouver Canucks, 193, 194
Vax, Michael, 54
Village Voice (newspaper), xiii, 17, 240
Vinnitsky, Mishka. *See* Yaponchick
Vinny (store clerk), 148
Vitale, Anne T., 222

Volkov, Alexander, 135–136, 138
Voloshin, Vladimir, 135–136, 138
Volovnik, Yakov (Billy Bombs), 137, 138
von Raab, William, 223, 225
vor v zakonye (thieves-in-law), 192, 193, 198, 277
  Bratsky Krug, 117, 123
  in Russia, 9–10, 23, 110, 111, 113, 117, 134

Wall Street Journal, 215
Wanner, Vladislav, 125
Washington Post, 267
Washington Times, 183n
weapons trafficking, xviii, 116, 195, 283
  Mogilevich's activities, 243, 244–245
  Tarzan (Fainberg) and, xii, 155–159, 163–164, 166–168
Weinberg, Lilly, 129
Weinberg, Valery, 129–130
Weinberger, Bernard, 32
Wexler, Leonard, 49, 65
Willard Hotel (Washington, D.C.), 217
Wilson, Murray, 28–29, 32–33
Winer, Jonathan, 210, 211, 216, 217, 232, 277, 280, 281
Wirtschafts Woche (Austrian magazine), 230
WNET (television station), 215–216
World Bank, 233

Yakuza (Japan), 242
Yaponchick (Russian bandit), 109
Yasevich, Alexander, 162–163, 166
YBM Magnex International, 249–251, 253–259, 269–270, 284
Yegorov, Mikhail Konstantinovich, 86–87
Yeltsin, Boris, xix, 114, 116, 194, 213, 214, 265, 266
Yugorsky Bank, 211
Yukos Oil, 214

Zapivakmine, Oleg, 106, 107–108
Zarkova, Anna, xvi–xvii
ZDF (German television network), 246
Zhitnik, Alexei, 177–178
Zhukov, Marshal, 213
Ziegler, Jean, 271–272, 276
Zilber, Vladimir and Alex, 70–73, 90–91, 99, 120, 267